PENGUIN BOOKS

A TERRIBLE LOVE OF WAR

James Hillman has written more than twenty books, including *The Force of Character*, *Re-Visioning Psychology* (nominated for a Pulitzer Prize in 1975), and *The Soul's Code*, which debuted at #1 on the *New York Times* bestseller list in 1996. He studied with Carl Jung in the 1950s and served as director of studies at the Jung Institute in Zurich. Hillman is an internationally renowned lecturer, teacher, and psychologist and has taught at Yale, Syracuse, and the University of Chicago. He lives in Thompson, Connecticut.

A
TERRIBLE
LOVE
OF WAR

JAMES HILLMAN

PENGUIN BOOKS

PENGUIN BOOKS

Published by the Penguin Group

Penguin Group (USA) Inc., 375 Hudson Street,
New York, New York 10014, U.S.A.
Penguin Group (Canada), 10 Alcorn Avenue, Toronto,
Ontario, Canada M4V 3B2 (a division of Pearson Penguin Canada Inc.)
Penguin Books Ltd, 80 Strand, London WC2R 0RL, England
Penguin Ireland, 25 St Stephen's Green, Dublin 2, Ireland (a division of Penguin Books Ltd)
Penguin Group (Australia), 250 Camberwell Road, Camberwell,
Victoria 3124, Australia (a division of Pearson Australia Group Pty Ltd)
Penguin Books India Pvt Ltd, 11 Community Centre, Panchsheel Park,
New Delhi - 110 017, India
Penguin Group (NZ) Cnr Airborne and Rosedale Roads, Albany,
Auckland 1310, New Zealand (a division of Pearson New Zealand Ltd)
Penguin Books (South Africa) (Pty) Ltd, 24 Sturdee Avenue, Rosebank,
Johannesburg 2196, South Africa

Penguin Books Ltd, Registered Offices: 80 Strand, London WC2R 0RL, England

First published in the United States of America by The Penguin Press,
a member of Penguin Group (USA) Inc. 2004
Published in Penguin Books 2005

1 3 5 7 9 10 8 6 4 2

Pages 225–226 constitue an extension of this copyright page.

THE LIBRARY OF CONGRESS HAS CATALOGED THE HARDCOVER EDITION AS FOLLOWS:
Hillman, James.
A terrible love of war / James Hillman.
p. cm.
Includes bibliographical references and index.
ISBN 0-59420-011-4 (hc.)
ISBN 0 14 30.3492 8 (pbk.)
1. War. 2. War—Psychological aspects. I. Title.
U21.2.H5435 2004
303.6'6—dc22   2003069049

Printed in the United States of America
Set in Bembo
Designed by Amanda Dewey

"The Lord is a man of war, The Lord is His name."

—EXODUS 15: 3

CONTENTS

A
TERRIBLE
LOVE
OF WAR

Chapter One:

WAR IS NORMAL

ONE SENTENCE in one scene from one film, *Patton*, sums up what this book tries to understand. The general walks the field after a battle. Churned earth, burnt tanks, dead men. He takes up a dying officer, kisses him, surveys the havoc, and says: "I love it. God help me I do love it so. I love it more than my life."

We can never prevent war or speak sensibly of peace and disarmament unless we enter this love of war. Unless we move our imaginations into the martial state of soul, we cannot comprehend its pull. This means "going to war," and this book aims to induct our minds into military service. We are not going to war "in the name of peace" as deceitful rhetoric so often declares, but rather for war's own sake: to understand the madness of its love.

Our civilian disdain and pacifist horror—all the legitimate and deep-felt aversion to everything to do with the military and the warrior—must be set aside. This because the first principle of psychological method holds that any phenomenon to be understood must be sympathetically imagined. No syndrome can be truly dislodged from its cursed condition unless we first move imagination into its heart.

War is first of all a psychological task, perhaps first of all psychological tasks because it threatens your life and mine directly, and the existence of all living beings. The bell tolls for thee, and all. Nothing can escape thermonuclear rage, and if the burning and its aftermath are unimaginable, their cause, war, is not.

War is also a psychological task because philosophy and theology, the fields supposed to do the heavy thinking for our species, have neglected war's overriding importance. "War is the father of all," said Heraclitus at the beginnings of Western thought, which Emmanuel Levinas restates in recent Western thought as "being reveals itself as war."[1] If it is a primordial component of being, then war fathers the very structure of existence and our thinking about it: our ideas of the universe, of religion, of ethics; war determines the thought patterns of Aristotle's logic of opposites, Kant's antinomies, Darwin's natural selection, Marx's struggle of classes, and even Freud's repression of the id by the ego and superego. We think in warlike terms, feel ourselves at war with ourselves, and unknowingly believe predation, territorial defense, conquest, and the interminable battle of opposing forces are the ground rules of existence.

Yet, for all this, has ever a major Western philosopher—with the great exception of Thomas Hobbes, whose *Leviathan* was published three and a half centuries ago—delivered a full-scale assault on the topic, or given it the primary importance war deserves in the hierarchy of themes? Immanuel Kant came to it late (1795) with a brief essay written when he was past seventy and after he had published his main works. He states the theme of this chapter in a few words much like Hobbes: "The state of peace among men living side by side is not the natural state; the natural state is one of war." Though war is the primary human condition, his focus is upon "perpetual peace" which is the title of his essay. About peace philosophers and theologians have much to say, and we shall take up peace in our stride.

Fallen from the higher mind's central contemplation, war tends to be examined piecemeal by specialists, or set aside as "history" where it then becomes a subchapter called "military history" in the hands of scholars and reporters dedicated to the record of facts. Or its study is placed outside the mainstream, isolated in policy institutions (often at war themselves with rival institutions). The magic of their thinking transmutes killing into "taking out," bloodshed into "body counts," and the chaos of battle into "scenarios," "game theory," "cost benefits," as weapons become "toys" and bombs "smart." Especially needed is not more specialist inquiry into past wars and future wars, but rather an archetypal psychology—the myths, philosophy, and theology of war's deepest mind. That is the purpose of this book.

There are, of course, many excellent studies of aggression, predation, genetic competition, and violence; works on pack, mob, and crowd behavior; on conflict resolution; on class struggle, revolution, and tyranny; on genocide and war crimes; on sacrifice, warrior cults, opposing tribal moieties; on geopolitical strategies, the technology of weaponry, and texts detailing the practice and theory of waging wars in general and the analysis by fine minds of particular wars; and lastly, always lastly, on the terrible effects of war on its remnants.

Military historians, war reporters long in the field, and major commanders in their memoirs of wars from whom I have learned and respectfully cite in the pages that follow have offered their heartfelt knowledge. Individual intellectuals and excellent modern writers, among them Freud, Einstein, Simone Weil, Virginia Woolf, Hannah Arendt, Robert J. Lifton, Susan Griffin, Jonathan Schell, Barbara Tuchman, and Paul Fussell, have brought their intelligence to the nature of war, as have great artists from Goya, say, to Brecht. Nonetheless, Ropp's wide-ranging survey of the idea of war concludes: "The voluminous works of contemporary military intellectuals contain no new ideas of the origins of war. . . . In this situation a 'satisfactory' scientific view of war is as remote as ever."[2] From another more psychological perspective, Susan Sontag concludes similarly: "We truly can't imagine what it was like. We can't imagine how dreadful, how terrifying war is—and how normal it becomes. Can't understand, can't imagine. That's what every soldier, and every journalist and aid worker and independent observer who has put in time under fire and had the luck to elude the death that struck down others nearby, stubbornly feels. And they are right."[3] But, here, she is wrong.

"Can't understand, can't imagine" is unacceptable. It gets us off the hook, admitting defeat before we have even begun. Lifton has said the task in our times is to "imagine the real."[4] Robert McNamara, secretary of defense during much of the Vietnam War, looking back, writes: "we can now understand these catastrophes for what they were: essentially the products of a failure of imagination." Surprise and its consequents, panic and terror, are due to "the poverty of expectations—the failure of imagination," according to another secretary of defense, Donald Rumsfeld.[5] When comparing the surprise at Pearl Harbor with that of the Twin Towers, the director of the National Security Agency, Michael Hayden, said, "perhaps it was more a failure of imagination this time than last."[6]

Failure of imagination is another way of describing "persistence in error," which Barbara Tuchman says leads nations and their leaders down the road to disaster on "the march of folly,"[7] as she calls

War has become so normal we fail to see it for what it is.

her study of wars from Troy to Vietnam. The origin of these disasters lies in the unimaginative mind-set of "political and bureaucratic life that subdues the functioning intellect in favor of "working the levers."[8] Working the levers of duty, following the hierarchy of command without imagining anything beyond the narrowness of facts reduced to yet narrower numbers, precisely describes Franz Stangl, who ran the Treblinka death camp,[9] and also describes what Hannah Arendt defines as evil, drawing her paradigmatic example from the failure of intellect and imagination in Adolf Eichmann.

If we want war's horror to be abated so that life may go on, it is necessary to understand and imagine. We humans are the species privileged in regard to understanding. Only we have the faculty and the scope for comprehending the planet's quandaries. Perhaps that is what we are here for: to bring appreciative understanding to the phenomena that have no need to understand themselves. It may even be a moral obligation to try to comprehend war. That famous phrase of William James, "the moral equivalent of war," with which he meant the mobilization of moral effort, today means the effort of imagination proposed by Lifton and ducked by Sontag.

The failure to understand may be because our imaginations are impaired and our modes of comprehension need a paradigm shift. If the ponderous object war does not yield to our tool, then we have to put down that tool and search for another. The frustration may not lie simply in the obduracy of war—that it is essentially un-understandable, unimaginable. Is it war's fault that we have not grasped its meanings? We have to investigate the faultiness of our tool: why can't our method of understanding understand war? Answer: according to Einstein, problems cannot be solved at the same level of thinking that created them.

You would expect that the war-wise, the masters of war, like Sun Tzu, Mao Tse-tung, Machiavelli, and Clausewitz, would have come to conclusions about war beyond advice for its conduct. For

[Heart of Darkness) Carl Gustav Jung

warrior page 2 by Rose Books .com Pref Conrad/Heart of D

them, however, it is a matter of practical science. "The elements of the art of war are first, measurement of space; second, estimation of quantities; third, calculations; fourth, comparisons; and fifth, chances of victory."[10] Long before there were glimmerings of modern scientific method, that mind-set was already applied to war. The empirical mind-set is timeless, archetypal. It starts from the given—war is here, is now, so what's to do? Speculations about its underlying reason, and why or what it is in the first place, distract from the huge task of how to bring war to victory. "No theorist, and no commander," writes Clausewitz, "should bother himself with psychological and philosophical sophistries."[11] Even though the rational science of war admits the obvious, that in "military affairs reality is surprisingly elusive,"[12] it omits from its calculations the elusive—and often determining—factors such as fighting spirit, weather, personal proclivities of the generals, political pressures, health of participants, poor intelligence, technological breakdowns, misinterpreted orders, residues in memory of similar events. War is the playground of the incalculable. "As flies to wanton boys, are we to the Gods, / They kill us for their sport" (*Lear* 4.1.39). A key to understanding war is given by the normality of its surprisingly elusive unreason.

War demands a leap of imagination as extraordinary and fantastic as the phenomenon itself. Our usual categories are not large enough, reducing war's meaning to explaining its causes.

Tolstoy mocked the idea of discovering the causes of war. In his postscript to *War and Peace,* widely considered the most imaginative and fullest study of war ever attempted, he concludes: "Why did millions of people begin to kill one another? Who told them to do it? It would seem that it was clear to each of them that this could not benefit any of them, but would be worse for them all. Why did they do it? Endless retrospective conjectures can be made, and are made, of the causes of this senseless event, but the immense number of these explanations, and their concurrence in one purpose, only proves that the causes were innumerable and that not one of them deserves to be called the cause."[13] For Tolstoy war was governed by something like a collective force beyond individual human will.

The task, then, is to imagine the nature of this collective force. War's terrifying prospect brings us to a crucial moment in the history of the mind, a moment when imagination becomes the method of choice, and the sympathetic psychologizing learned in a century of consulting rooms takes precedence over the outdated privileging of scientific objectivity.

As a psychologist I learned long ago that I could not explain my patients' behavior, nor anyone's, including my own. There were reasons enough: traumas, shames and miseries, defects in character, birth order within the family, physiology—endless causes that I imagined were explanations. But these possible causes gave little understanding that seemed to depend on something else, reasons of another sort. Later on, I learned that this division that baffled me in practice—explaining and the method of science on the one hand and, on the other, understanding and the approach of psychology—had already been made clear by German thinkers from Nietzsche and Dilthey through Husserl, Heidegger, Jaspers, and Gadamer. Ancestor to them all was the Neopolitan genius, Giambattista Vico, who invented a "new science" (the title of his book of 1725) in revolt against unsatisfactory explanations of human affairs that rested on Newton's and Descartes' kind of thinking.

Vico thinks like a depth psychologist. Like Freud, he seeks to get below conventional constructs into hidden layers and distant happenings. Causal reasoning comes late on the stage, says Vico. The basic layer of the mind is poetic, mythic, expressed by *univer-*

sali fantastici, which I translate as archetypal patterns of imagination. Thematics are his interest, whether in law or in language or in literature—the recurring themes, the everlasting, ubiquitous, emotional, unavoidable patterns and forces that play through any human life and human society, the forces we must bow to and are best generalized as archetypal. To grasp the underlying pressures that move human affairs we have to dig deep, performing an archeology in the mind to lay bare the mythic themes that abide through time, timelessly. War is one of these timeless forces.

The instrument of this dig is penetration: continuing to move forward with insight to gain understanding. "Understanding is never a completed static state of mind," writes the profound philosopher Alfred North Whitehead. "It always bears the character of the process of penetration . . . when we realize ourselves as engaged in a process of penetration, we have a fuller self-knowledge." He continues: "If civilization is to survive, the expansion of understanding is a prime necessity."[14] And how does understanding grow? "The sense of penetration . . . has to do with the growth of understanding."[15]

War asks for this kind of penetration, else its horrors remain unintelligible and abnormal. We have to go to deep thinkers with penetrating minds, and these may not be the experts on war with wide experience or those who breed their theories in think tanks. The fact that philosophers have not put war in the center of their works may be less a sin than a blessing, since what philosophy offers best to this inquiry is less a completed theory than the invitation to enjoy hard thinking and free imagining. The ways philosophers' minds work, their ways of thinking are more valuable to the student than the conclusions of their thought.

Archetypal patterns of imagination, the *universali fantastici,* embrace both rational and irrational events, both normal and abnormal. These distinctions fade as we penetrate into the great universals of experience. Worship; sexual love; violence; death, disposal, and mourning; initiation; the hearth; ancestors and descendents; the making of art—and war, are timeless themes of human existence given meaning by myths. Or, to put it otherwise: myths are the norms of the unreasonable. That recognition is the greatest of all achievements of the Greek mind, singling out that culture from all others. The Greeks perfected tragedy, which shows directly the mythic governance of human affairs within states, within families, within individuals. Only the Greeks could articulate tragedy to this pitch and therefore their imagination is most relevant for the tragedy with which we are here engaged: war.

This means that to understand war we have to get at its myths, recognize that war is a mythical happening, that those in the midst of it are removed to a mythical state of being, that their return from it seems rationally inexplicable, and that the love of war tells of a love of the gods, the gods of war; and that no other account—political, historical, sociological, psychoanalytical—can penetrate (which is why war remains "un-imaginable" and "un-understood") to the depths of inhuman cruelty, horror, and tragedy and to the heights of mystical transhuman sublimity. Most other accounts treat war without myth, without the gods, as if they were dead and gone. Yet where else in human experience, except in the throes of ardor—that strange coupling of love with war—do we find ourselves transported to a mythical condition and the gods most real?

Before wars begin until their last skirmish, a heavy, fateful feeling of necessity overhangs war; no way out. This is the effect of myth. Human thought and action is subject to sudden interventions of fortune and accident—the stray bullet, the lost order; "for the want of a nail, the shoe was lost . . ." This unpredictability is attested to throughout history. Therefore, a rational science of war can only go so far, only to the edge of understanding. At that point a leap of imagination is called for, a leap into myth.

The explanations given by scientific thinking are indeed required for the conduct of war. It can calculate and explain the causes of artillery misses and logistic failures, and it certainly can build precisely efficient weapons. But how can it take us into battle or toward grasping war? We cannot understand the Civil War by pointing to its immediate cause—the firing on Fort Sumter in South Carolina in 1861—nor by its proximate cause—the election of Lincoln in the autumn of 1860—nor by a list of underlying causes, i.e., the passions that riled the union: secession, abolition, the economics of cotton, the expansion westward, power contest in the Senate . . . ad infinitum. Nor will a compilation of the factors of that war's complexity yield what we seek. Even the total sum of every explanation you can muster will not provide meaning to the horrific, drawn-out, repetitive butchery of battle after battle of that four-year-long war. Same for Vietnam, for the Napoleonic wars. The missing link in the chain of causes is the one that ties them to understanding. Patton's emotional eruption—"I love it. God help me I do love it so"—leads us closer than an entire network of explanations.

Now we are in a better position to agree with Ropp's conclusion (quoted above) that a "'satisfactory' scientific view of war is as remote as ever." It will remain remote forever because the meaning of war is beyond the assemblage of its data and causal explanation. This dour conclusion promotes an unfortunate belief: because war cannot be explained, it cannot be understood.

I expect this book to pull us out of this predicament, that something so powerful and so usual cannot find adequate measure. A psychology that is philosophical, a philosophy that is psychological, ought to be able to fathom its darkness. War begs for meaning, and amazingly also gives meaning, a meaning found in the midst of its chaos. Men who survive battle come back and say it was the most meaningful time of their lives, transcendent to all other meanings. Major books have collected these accounts and are dedicated to this theme. Despite the wasting confusion, accidental senselessness, and the numbing dread, meaning appears among those engaged, meaning without explanation, without full understanding, yet lasting a lifetime. After World War II a Frenchwoman said to J. Glenn Gray, "You know that I do not love war or want it to return. But at least it made me feel alive, as I have not felt alive before or since."[16]

The Personal Part

How can I assume the role of Analyst of War? How do I dare point to the omissions of others and set myself up as an authority deserving your attention? I never "fought . . . knee deep in the salt marsh, heaving a cutlass," as T. S. Eliot in "Gerontion" says of an old man reflecting on his life. My "war experience" was all stateside in a naval hospital, pharmacist mate 2nd class, a corpsman assigned initially to a ward of the war-deafened and to night duty with amputees, and then for over a year as a specialist assistant to the war-blinded. I was just eighteen, and twenty when discharged. What I knew of battle was only its remnants. Remnants too in what was then called "war-torn Europe" where, as a radio newswriter (1946), the environment was scavengers, rubble, and displaced persons.

Altogether different from the war maps I loved to study—the Solomon Islands, Burma, the Ukraine—and the campaign strategies I overheard when I was a copyboy in the newsroom of WTOP in Washington during the perilous year, 1943. The closest I got to the action was picking up press releases over at the Pentagon and standing in the back of the room when dashing war correspondent Eric Sevareid came in and told about events miles and miles away.

The big wars (Korea, Vietnam) that followed "my" war came to me, then living far away from America, not as wars but as news, much like the recent wars in former Yugoslavia, Rwanda, and Afghanistan are for Americans, oceans apart. Wars for discussion; the engagement of strangers.

Back to sophomore English, Room 214. The Shakespeare play for that year was *Julius Caesar*. The only piece I chose and learned by heart was:

> *Domestic fury and fierce civil strife*
> *Shall cumber all the parts of Italy;*
> *Blood and destruction shall be so in use*
> *And dreadful objects so familiar,*
> *That mothers shall but smile when they behold*
> *Their infants quarter'd with the hands of war;*
> *All pity choked with custom of fell deeds:*
> *And Caesar's spirit, ranging for revenge,*
> *With Ate by his side come hot from hell,*
> *Shall in these confines with a monarch's voice*
> *Cry 'Havoc!' and let slip the dogs of war. . . .*
>
> (3.1.263ff.)

As a small boy I had played with lead soldiers whose heads could come off, and later I built my fleet of a hundred self-designed warships of balsa wood for a complicated war game spread out on the floor. (I owned a precious copy of *Jane's Fighting Ships.*) In the streets we played with water pistols and cap guns. Cops and Robbers, not Cowboys and

Indians: this was New Jersey. I remember too my father's stereopticon of World War I, images on glass which we sneaked to look at because he never showed it: 3-D images of battlefields in Belgium—muddy trenches, blown trees, gaunt men under round helmets.

I can even recall the military parades on the Boardwalk on Memorial Day and Armistice Day in the early 1930s. First came the veterans of the Civil War and the Spanish-American War. Some still walking. And terrifying men with blue-gray faces, from gassing and shrapnel I was told. Remnants of wars long ago and far away.

As a boy of eleven "heroic adventure" meant Richard Halliburton and Amelia Earhart, deep-sea divers and arctic explorers on the Steel Pier. I had no military idols. I didn't even own a BB gun.

By 1944 when I was drafted into the Navy, my high school buddies had long been in uniform. One was already drowned, washed off the deck of a destroyer. My brother-in-law was a captain in the Quartermaster Corps running a truck company in the Red-Ball Express supplying Patton's army; my father had come into Normandy with the Canadians; my brother was flying a P-47. Me? I was learning bandaging. But something was working on me, in me. I wrote sob-sister war poems.

Whatever it was struck directly while I was driving past an old battlefield of 1914–18 France. Suddenly I found myself choked up—just looking through a car window. For whom, for what? War as an inexplicable emotion. Which battle? Who died here? I had no idea, but I did recall Sandburg's "Grass":

Pile the bodies high at Austerlitz and Waterloo.
Shovel them under and let me work—
       I am the grass; I cover all.

       . . . .

Two years, ten years, and the passengers ask the conductor:
       What place is this?
       Where are we now?

       I am the grass.
       Let me work.

The grass never grew on my memories of amputees. I could not sit down in a Paris Metro seat marked "reserved for the mutilated of war." My generation remembers men with no legs sitting on little rolling platforms, selling pencils and shoestrings(!). As part of my job in the naval hospital I took Talking Books (recorded readings for the blind) to other wards. I used to visit a Marine my age who had lost all four. I look at my hands now as I write this.

When I went with a friend on a month's walk-around-train-around Italy in the spring of 1947, I pushed to go beyond Siracusa to the beach of Gela, imagining Patton's troops beginning their invasion of Europe only four years before.

Finally, the Civil War. Our war, our "Iliad"—as remote, heroic, and unfathomable as the world of Homer. In my later years I have been going to battlefields—Shiloh, Antietam, Vicksburg, Cold Harbor, Petersburg, Chickamauga, Appomattox—talking and walking with friends. A mood of puzzlement, reverie, and a kind of sacred sadness. For what?

Maybe, for writing this book.

Writing books for me is anyway much like a military campaign. I confess to fighting my way through with military metaphors. There is a strategy, an overall concept, and there are tactics all along the way. When stuck, don't dig in; keep moving forward. Don't obsess trying to reduce a strongpoint by sheer force or laying siege. Isolate it and in time it will fall by itself. No pitched battles with the interior voices of saboteurs, critics, adversaries. A light skirmish, a shower of arrows, and disappear into the next paragraph. Camouflage your own vulnerability, your lack of reserves with showy parades and bugles—remember everyone else is equally vulnerable. Pillage the storehouses of thought, refurbish old material and use it to reinforce your lines. Abandon ground you can't exploit, but when you've got an issue on the run, take all the territory you can.

Writing on war brings war closer, brings death closer. Will I see this through to its end; could I be stopped in my tracks? Let us imagine this to be a propitiation, an offering to the gods who govern these things.

These occasional confessions and distant images are my pedigree. Your author's authority rests only on this thin red line of calling. That calling, astrologers would claim, was already written in the heavens: Pluto ascending, Sun and Moon conjunct in Aries; Mercury there, too. Tradition would say I was a "child of Mars." Strange indeed that what I am assuming to be my last book should land on the shores of this theme; again, as so often with my themes, this does not derive from personal experience—unless "personal experience" includes the ferments of the soul and not only biographical actualities. We are usually taught to write what we really know, but are we not drawn more into the depths by what we don't quite know? An old adage says: "Approach the unknown by way of unknowing." I am not an empiricist, so my passion is not encumbered with expertise. I like Sartre's philosophical dictum: "He who begins with facts will never arrive at essences." My having been witness only to war's remnants and saved from war's action, has perhaps saved this theme for my late life. Whatever it was that earlier gave me pause now gives me cause.

The step into the mind of war is a change of pace. Abrupt. Disturbing. The civil world and its civilities left behind. It is as if we are under orders to get on with it swiftly. The very style of writing accommodates to its subject, submitting to what the Renaissance writers knew as the "rhetoric of speed" whose patron was Mars, god of war. His metal is iron which likes fire, and rusts when set aside in reflection; iron makes a poor mirror.

Psychologists are not at home in this style. We are armchair generals; we like to watch. We listen for echoes and prefer to move sideways. Our passion is for the past, how things got this way, rather than hoping for a decisive victory. Besides, we prefer the wounded to the victors. A psychology book whose subject under analysis is war will have to develop different tactics for winning over its readers, who will most likely defend against its offensive tone and its assaults on entrenched thought. Readers may find themselves joining an underground resistance, looking for weak spots and exposed positions. It will seem as if the book is written less to cajole the reader than to knock him, or her, out flat. But war is not a normal condition, so why expect a normal study? Shouldn't the abnormalities of war sound in the voice speaking about it?

Halt! Is war abnormal? I find it normal in that it is with us every day and never seems to go away. After World War II subsided and the big conflicts that followed it (India, Korea, Algeria, Biafra, Vietnam, Israel/Egypt), war went right on. Since 1975 the globe has been engaged in wars in Haiti, Grenada, the Falklands, Peru, Panama, Colombia, Nicaragua, El Salvador, Guatemala; in Lebanon, Palestine, Israel, Iran, Iraq, Kuwait; in Uganda, Rwanda, Mozambique, Angola, Sierra Leone, Liberia, Congo, Eritrea, Chad, Mauritania, Somalia, Algeria (again), Sudan; in Afghanistan, Myanmar, India/Pakistan, Kashmir, Sri Lanka, the Philippines, Cambodia, East Timor, Sumatra, Irian; in Bosnia, Croatia, Kosovo, Ireland, Chechnya, Georgia, Romania, Basque/Spain . . . You may know of others; still others only the participants know. Some on this list are still going on as I write, while new ones break out as you read. Some of them are sudden eruptions like the Falklands, and the sheep graze again. Others in places like Algeria and the Sudan and Palestine belong to the normal round, utterly normative for defining daily life.

This normal round of warfare has been going on as far back as memory stretches. During the five thousand six hundred years of written history, fourteen thousand six hundred wars have been recorded. Two or three wars each year of human history. Edward Creasy's *Fifteen Decisive Battles* (1851) and Victor Davis Hanson's *Carnage and Culture* have taught us that the turning points of Western civilization occur in battles and their "killing sprees": Salamis and Carthage, Tours and Lepanto, Constantinople, Waterloo, Midway, Stalingrad. Which you choose as the top fifteen depends on your own criteria, but the point is carried—the ultimate determination of historical fate depends on battle whose outcome, we have also been taught, depends upon an invisible genius, a leader, a hero, who, at a critical moment, or in prior indefatigable preparation, "saves the day." In him a transcendent spirit is manifested. The battle and its personified epitome, this victor, this genius, become salvational representations in our secular history. Laurels for halo. The statues in our parks, the names of our grand avenues, and the holidays we celebrate—and not only in Western societies—commemorate the salvational aspect of battle.

Neglected in Creasy and Hanson are the thousands of indecisive ones, fought with equal valor, yet which ended inconclusively or yielded no victory for the ultimate victor of the war. Centuries of nameless bodies in unheralded fields. Unsung heroes; died in vain; lost cause. The ferocity of battle may have little to do with its outcome and the outcome little to do with the outcome of the war. Italy, a "victor" of World War I, suffered more than half a million deaths in the fierce Isonzo campaign whose fruit was only a disastrous defeat. At Verdun a million French and German casualties accomplished nothing for either side. "The bones of perhaps 170,000 French soldiers lie in the massive ossuary of Douaumont above Verdun."[17] Speaking of bones, more than a million bushels of men and horses were harvested from the battlefields of Napoleon's wars (Austerlitz, Leipzig, Waterloo, and others), shipped to England, ground into bone meal by normal workers at normal jobs.[18]

EXCURSION:

"Normal"

What is "normal"? What are the effects of this word, what does it imply? Let's first look at its beginnings. "Norm" and "normal" derive from the Latin word *norma,* meaning a carpenter's square. *Norma* is a technical instrumental term for a right angle; it belongs first to applied geometry. *Normalis* in Latin means "made according to the

square"; *normaliter,* "in a straight line, directly." In the sixteenth and seventeenth centuries "normal" meant rectangu-
lar, standing at a right angle; then, in the eighteen hundreds
usage widened and flattened the strictness of its meaning:
normal as regular (1828); normal school for teacher training
(1834); normal as average in physics (1859); normalize
(1865); and normal as usual (1890).

The troubled feeling that arises when we hear "war is
normal" comes from troubles in the way the word is used.
"Normal" can be understood in two ways, which tend to
fuse so that we tend to believe what is average (normal) is
also standard and right, i.e., the right standard. The average
sense of "normal" is statistical, referring to occurrences that
are usual, common, frequent, regular. This sense of the word
can be depicted by means of a graph, for instance, the middle section of a Gaussian curve where it swells. Hence, normal as middle, mean, centered; and abnormal as marginal,
eccentric, at the edge. Abnormal then relies on quantitative
or mathematical descriptions, as unusual, infrequent, exceptional, deviate, rare, odd, anomalous.

The second use of "normal" does not imply average and
ordinary, but rather ideal. This second meaning still relies
on the root—square, straight, upright; but these technical
descriptive terms now become normalized into metaphors.
Norms now mean standards. A preestablished image prescribes the norm, the model, the rule. Whatever is closest to it
is the most normal, even when that singular example is statis-
tically rare, if not an impossibility in fact. The norms of conduct should be straight and upright—no lying, no cheating,
no killing. The norms of bodily beauty should show no gross

distortions or blemishes. If "normalize" brings one down to the average, "normative" lifts one toward an ideal.

The ideal standard against which you may measure your conformity or deviation may be set by theology (*imitatio Christi*); by law (the citizen, the comrade); by medicine (weight/height/age/gender ratio); by philosophy (Stoic man, Kantian man, Nietzschean man); by education (test scores, intelligence quotient); by the cultural canons of a society. Normal in the first sense simply describes the way most things are; normal in the second sense prescribes things as they might be best.

When the two meanings merge, then average becomes the standard. In fact, the very word "standard" shows this merging. Today it tends to mean usual, ordinary, regular rather than ideal. Or, worse, the ideal becomes conformity with the average rather than an image of perfection.

When the two meanings merge in regard to war, then descriptions of battle become prescriptions for battle. "Should" devolves to "what most people do." If war is hell, as Sherman said, then war ought to be hell; ideally, war will be hellish, which Sherman demonstrated according to residents of Georgia. Since butchery happens, it ought to happen, and a medal shall be bestowed upon the one who approximates the ideal norm by killing the most. Pentagon planners laying out thermonuclear scenarios are following the logic of normalcy, in which the greatest horror fuses with the greatest good. "The state of war suspends morality . . . renders morality derisory," writes Levinas.[19] This is a terrible thought, as terrible as war.

The way beyond this devastating dilemma is to break

apart the fusion, so as to contain the term "normal" and the statement "war is normal" within the limits of its own paradigm. In war, at war, while engaged, immersed, under its sway. The norms war generates within itself are not normative beyond itself. This omnivorous appetite to encroach and consume other norms of other gods, suspending their norms, is war's gravest danger. Because war is total on the battlefield (McClellan did not grasp this, keeping back his reserves at Antietam; nor did Meade, who was too spent to follow up on Gettysburg), war must be all-out, totalitarian, monomanic in its single-minded pursuit, and ruthlessly monotheistic in its demand for negating all other norms. That war is now considered total war, world war, global, and with no foreseeable end in time or limit in target, equal in concept to the totalizing power of its instruments, reveals that war is monotheistic in essence. The response to the megalomania of its normalcy requires maintaining the countervailing powers of all the other gods and their norms. This connection between monotheistic thinking, religion, and war we shall explore in chapter 4.

To declare war "normal" does not eliminate the pathologies of behavior, the enormities of devastation, the unbearable pain suffered in bodies and souls. Nor does the idea that war is normal justify it. Brutalities such as slavery, cruel punishment, abuse of young children, corporal mutilation remain reprehensible, yet find acceptance in the body politic and may even be incorporated into its laws. Though "war is normal" shocks our morality and wounds our idealism, it stands solidly as a statement of fact.

"War" is becoming more normalized every day. Trade war, gender war, Net war, information war. But war against cancer, war against crime, against drugs, poverty, and other ills of society have nothing to with the actualities of war. These civil wars, wars within civilian society, mobilize resources in the name of a heroic victory over an insidious enemy. These wars are noble, good guys against bad and no one gets hurt. This way of normalizing war has white-washed the word and brainwashed us, so that we forget its terrible images. Then, whenever the possibility of actual war approaches with its reality of violent death-dealing combat, the idea of war has been normalized into nothing more than putting more cops on the street, more rats in the lab, and tax rebates for urban renewal.

I base the statement "war is normal" on two factors we have already seen: its *constancy* throughout history and its *ubiquity* over the globe. These two factors require another more basic: *acceptability*. Wars could not happen unless there were those willing to help them happen. Conscripts, slaves, indentured soldiers, unwilling draftees to the contrary, there are always masses ready to answer the call to arms, to join up, get in the fight. There are always leaders rushing to take the plunge. Every nation has its hawks. Moreover, resisters, dissenters, pacifists, objectors, and deserters rarely are able to bring war to a halt. The saying, "Someday they'll give a war and no one will come," remains a fond wish. War drives everything else off the front page.

If war is normal, is this because it is lodged in human nature or because it is inherent to societies? Is war basically an expression of human aggression and self-preservation or an extension of pack behavior—the hunting pack, the raiding pack, all the way up to a coalition of millions in a distant land?

The New Testament opts for the first: "Whence come wars—come they not hence, even of your pleasures that war is in your members. Ye lust and have not: ye kill and covet and cannot obtain:

ye fight and war; ye have not because ye ask not" (James 4:1–2). Wars begin in the lowliness of our all-too-human material desires. Plato concurs: "The body fills us with loves and desires and fears and all sorts of fancies and a great deal of nonsense, with the result that we literally never get an opportunity to think at all about anything. Wars and revolutions and battles are due simply and solely to the body and its desires. All wars are undertaken for the acquisition of wealth, and the reason we have to acquire wealth is the body."[20]

That was earlier Plato; later he found another source of war: "All states by their very nature, are always engaged in an informal war against all other states."[21]

But Kant, like Hobbes before him, takes it back from society, finding war to be an uncaused component of human nature for which no explanation need be sought. "War," he writes, "requires no motivation, but appears to be ingrained in human nature and is even valued as something noble."[22] Agreed, opines Steven LeBlanc's book *Constant Battles*. Warfare is ingrained from earliest times, back to chimpanzees. Not so, argues R. B. Ferguson: archeology supports his view that warfare is a development of only the past ten thousand years.

Ingrained or acquired? Individual person's aggressive instinct or social group's aggrandizing claims? The various contesting assertions about the origins of war can be reduced to two basic positions. On the one side, theories of psychoanalysis that take human nature back to early loss of love objects and to the birth trauma; theories of animal biology (inborn release mechanisms of fight-or-flight; theories of determining genes pushing to get what they want). On the other side, war is a product of the internal structure of groups, their belief systems, their territorial claims, their exogamous fertility requirements, and the collective psyche of the crowd as such.

In both cases, whether human drive or societal necessity, war requires an imagined enemy. "Warre," writes Hobbes, is that condition "where every man is Enemy to every other man," and Clausewitz insists that "the enemy must always be kept in mind." The idea of otherness or alterity that currently dominates thinking about gender and race and ecology is too abstract to unleash the dogs of war. Can you imagine a war without first imagining an enemy? Whether the focus be upon prey, sacrificial victim, evil spirit, or object of desire, enmity mobilizes the energy. The figure of the enemy nourishes the passions of fear, hatred, rage, revenge, destruction, and lust, providing the supercharged strength that makes the battlefield possible.

War certainly does rely upon the individual's repressions and/or aggressions, pleasure in demolition, appetite for the extraordinary and spectacular, mania of autonomy. War harnesses these individual urges and procures their compliance without which there could be no wars; but war is not individual psychology writ large. Individuals certainly fight ruthlessly and kill; families feud and harbor revenge, but this is not war. "Soldiers are not killers."[23] Even well-trained and well-led infantrymen have a strong "unrealized resistance toward killing"[24] which tactically impedes the strategy of every engagement. Only a *polis* (city, state, society) can war: "The only source of war is politics," said Clausewitz.[25] "Politics is the womb in which war develops."[26] For war to emerge from this womb, for the individual to muster aggressions and appetites, there must be an enemy. The enemy is the midwife of war.

The enemy provides the constellating image in the individual and is necessary to the state in order to collect individuals into a cohesive warring body. René Girard's *Violence and the Sacred* elaborates this single point extensively: the emotional foundation of a unified society derives from "violent unanimity," the collective destruction of a sacrificial victim, scapegoat, or enemy upon whom all together, without exception or dissent, turn on and eliminate. Thereby, the inherent conflicts within a community that can lead to internal

violence become exteriorized and ritualized onto an
an enemy has been found or invented, named, and e
"unanimous violence" without dissent, i.e., patriotism ~~~ ~~~ ,
emptive strikes of preventative war, become opportune consequents.

The state becomes the only guarantor of self-preservation. If
war begins in the state, the state begins in enmity. Thirteen colonies;
a variety of geographies, religions, languages, laws, economies, but
a common enemy. For all the utopian nobility of the Declaration
of Independence, the text actually presents a long list of grievances
against the enemy of them all, the king.

Mind you now: there may not actually be an enemy! All along
we are speaking of the *idea* of an enemy, a phantom enemy. It is not
the enemy that is essential to war and that forces wars upon us, but
the imagination. Imagination is the driving force, especially when
imagination has been preconditioned by the media, education, and
religion, and fed with aggressive boosterism and pathetic pieties by
the state's need for enemies. The imagined phantom swells and
clouds the horizon, we cannot see beyond enmity. The archetypal
idea gains a face. Once the enemy is imagined, one is already in a
state of war. Once the enemy has been named, war has already
been declared and the actual declaration becomes inconsequential,
only legalistic. The invasion of Iraq began before the invasion of
Iraq; it had already begun when that nation was named among the
axis of evil.

Enmity forms its images in many shapes—the nameless women
to be raped, the fortress to be razed, the rich houses to be pillaged
and plundered, the monstrous predator, ogre, or evil empire to be
eliminated. An element of fantasy creates the rationality of war.
Like the heart, war has its reasons that reason does not comprehend. These exfoliate and harden into paranoid perceptions that
invent "the enemy," distorting intelligence with rumor and speculation and providing justifications for the violent procedures of war

and harsh measures of depersonalization at home in the name of security.

Tracking down the body of a young Vietcong freshly killed in a firefight, Philip Caputo writes: "There was nothing on him, no photographs, no letters or identification . . . it was fine with me. I wanted this boy to remain anonymous; I wanted to think of him, not as a dead human being, with a name, age, and family, but as a dead enemy."[27]

A dead enemy, however, leaves an existential gap; no one there to fight. Because the enemy is so essential to war, if one party gives in to defeat, the victor also loses his raison d'être. He has nothing more to do, no justification for his existence. Therefore, rites of triumph to ease the despair of the victors whose exaltation does not last. Celebrations, parades, dancing, awarding ribbons and medals, or a rampage against civilians and collaborators to keep an enemy present. As the war against Nazi Germany drew to a close, Patton grew gloomy; he expected "a tremendous letdown,"[28] but soon found a new enemy in Communist Russia: "savages," "Mongols" . . . In short, the aims of war are none other than its own continuation, for which an enemy is required.

With the defeat of the Confederates in 1865, who could next serve as enemy for Union troops and their generals? General Sherman urged Grant to exterminate the Sioux, including the children, and General Sheridan famously declared "the only good Indian is a dead Indian." General Custer, hero of the Shenandoah compaigns, was already out West in 1866 and smashing the Cheyenne in 1868. Like war, the fantasy of the enemy has no limit, so that a dead Indian meant also a dead buffalo. Some six hundred eighty thousand were shot down—one man could take a hundred a day—between 1871 and 1874, and nearly eleven million pounds of buffalo bone were shipped from the killing fields, according to Roe's analyses of the records.

If the enemy is evil, then any means used to oppose evil are ipso facto good. If the enemy is a predator (consider the monster films, the dinosaur films, the gangster films), then kill any which way you can. If the enemy is an obstacle standing in the way of your self-preservation, self-establishment, or self-aggrandizement, then knock it down and blow it apart. Carthage must be destroyed; Tokyo fire-bombed. Alexander ordered the leveling of every single structure in Persepolis; Christians defaced all the statues of the Egyptian gods they could get their hands on. Protestant Christians in England even destroyed Catholic images of Mary and Jesus. The Taliban blew up the giant Buddhist images carved in the rock of Bamian. Israelis bulldozed West Bank houses and gardens.

These are not exceptional, deviate instances. So why does Sontag say, "We can't imagine how normal [war] becomes"? All that happens in it, during it, after it, is always the same, regular, to be expected, predictable in general, conforming to its own standards, meeting its norms. S.O.P. The imagination can be gradually inducted into the battlefield and can follow that creeping desensitization of civilian, outsider mentality ("journalist, and aid worker and independent observer"), that process from the intolerable through the barely endurable to the merely normal.

How can the living cells in any person at the extreme of exhaustion amid dying friends and mangled dead, howitzer shells whooshing past like freight trains, accommodate to this "normality"? How can any person thrice wounded climb back on his horse and continue the charge straight "into the cannon's mouth"? The human psyche's capacity to normalize the most adverse conditions, adapt to them, find them usual (people in extreme climates rarely move to another geography; very few captives resist their imprisoners) has kept the species globally spread, diverse, and alive through millennia. Normalization may allow survival—and, normalization may also be one of the dumbest of human faults. How does it differ from denial, willful unconsciousness, ignorance, psychic numbing? Doesn't accepting all also lead to pardoning all? The shadow side of tolerance is the loss of the sense of the intolerable. To normalize may mean to take the side, not of survival, but of death.

War achieves an accommodation with death. After a series of missions through dense antiaircraft fire, bomber crews begin to believe they will not make the last few mandatory runs before rotation; veterans on patrol cling to superstitious routines to fend off the expectation that the next bullet will find them. Prolonged combat turns the soul into an *automatisme anesthésiant*;[29] a German writes of having "lost feeling for a lot of things"; an Englishman compares the state with going under an anesthetic, with autohypnosis.[30] Yet the senses may remain vigilant, especially a hyperacuity of the sense of smell. (Both Vietcong and Americans detected the hidden presence of each other by characteristic odors.) "In the abysmal dark of Hades the soul knows/is known by scent."[31] Not the senses, but the psyche seems to have vacated the person and entered the mythical underworld populated by shades and phantoms. Combatants speak of "seeing things," firing away into illusions. The person whose identity is given by life and its expectancies (sometimes called "hope") has been abandoned by these expectations.

The psyche is no longer the same. "I am all right—just the same as ever," writes a British soldier to his wife in 1916, "but no—that can never be. . . . No man can experience such things and come out the same."[32] War's "violence does not consist so much in injuring and annihilating persons as in interrupting their continuity . . . making them betray not only commitments but their own substance. . . . War . . . destroys the identity of the same," writes Levinas.[33] The psyche cannot be the same as before because it has become a partner with the soul of the dying, companion of the dead, "half in love with easeful death." Normal means becoming one with the norm, dead among the dead. "If these pages are thick with death," says Susan Griffin, "think of the battlefield. Corpses in different stages of decay, the slowly dying, moments of death exist around you everywhere. Who are you? You are among the living, but can you be certain?"[34]

EXCURSION:

Peace

If these pages, too, are thick with death it is because the written page is where memory is brought back from the burial ground and kept alive. Because the dead are speechless and the veterans don't talk, because "the earthy and cold hand of death/Lies on my tongue" (*1 Hen. IV* 5.4.84), the written page becomes a memento mori. As far back as Thucydides, Herodotus, and the books of Joshua, Kings, and Samuel, writing transmutes war into chronicles, memoirs, novels, poems, films. Paul Fussell's superb research lays out in detail how the death of 1914–18 remains alive in the written imagination. Writers, especially writers of war, do not create; they re-create, and reading is both a recreation and the re-creation of what has slipped away from present grasp and into the soul's recesses, avoided, forgotten.

The name of this void of forgetfulness is peace, whose short first definition is: "the absence of war." More fully, the *Oxford English Dictionary* describes peace: "Freedom from, or cessation of, war or hostilities; a state of a nation or community in which it is not at war with another." Further, peace means: "Freedom from disturbance or perturbation, especially as a condition of an individual; quiet, tranquility."

When Neville Chamberlain and his umbrella returned from Munich in 1938 after utterly failing to grasp the nature of Hitler, he told the British people he had achieved peace in our time and that now everyone should "go home and get a nice quiet sleep."[35]

These pages are thick with death in order to disturb the peace.

The worst of war is that it ends in peace, that is, it absents itself from remembrance, a syndrome Chris Hedges calls "collective or blanket amnesia,"[36] beyond understanding, beyond imagining. "Peace is visible already," writes Marguerite Duras. "It's like a great darkness falling, it's the beginning of forgetting."[37]

I will not march for peace, nor will I pray for it, because it falsifies all it touches. It is a cover-up, a curse. Peace is simply a bad word. "Peace," said Plato, "is really only a name."[38] Even if states should "cease from fighting," wrote Hobbes, "It is not to be called peace; but rather a breathing time."[39] Truce, yes; cease-fire, yes; surrender, victory, mediation, brinkmanship, standoff—these words have content, but peace is darkness falling.

When peace follows war, the villages and towns erect memorials with tributes to the honor of the fallen, sculptures of victory, angels of compassion, and local names cut in granite. We pass by these strange structures like obstacles to traffic. Even the immediate presence of war's aftermath, the rubble of London, the rubble of Frankfurt, the desolation through Russia, the Ukraine, become unremarkable to its citizens in the anesthesia of peace. The survivors themselves enter a state of unperturbed quiescence; they don't want to talk about it.

The dictionary's definition, an exemplary of denial, fails the word, peace. Written by scholars in tranquillity, the definition fixates and perpetuates the denial. If peace is merely an absence of, a freedom from, it is both an emptiness and a repression. A psychologist must ask how is the emptiness filled, since nature abhors a vacuum; and how does the repressed return, since it must?

The emptiness left by repressing war from the definition of peace bloats it with idealizations—another classic defense mechanism. Fantasies of rest, of calm security, life as "normal," eternal peace, heavenly peace, the peace of love that transcends understanding; peace as ease (*shalvah* in the Hebrew Bible) and completeness (*shalom*). The peace of naiveté, of ignorance disguised as innocence. Longings for peace become both simplistic and utopian with programs for universal love, disarmament, and an Aquarian federation of nations, or retrograde to the status quo ante of Norman Rockwell's apple pie. These are the options of psychic numbing that "peace" offers and which must have so offended Jesus that he declared for a sword.[40]

To dispel such quieting illusions, writers along with those hounded by Mars roil the calm. The pages are thick with death because writers do not hold their peace, keep silent, play dumb. Books of war give voice to the tongue of the dead anesthetized by that major syndrome of the public psyche: "peace."

The specific syndrome suffered by American veterans— post-traumatic stress disorder—occurs within the wider syndrome: the endemic numbing of the American homeland and its addiction to security. The present surroundings of the veteran in "peacetime" can have as strong, if subtle, traumatic effect and can cause as much stress as past stress and trauma. PTSD breaks out in peacetime because peace as defined does not allow upsetting remembrances of war's continuing presence. War is never over, even when the fat lady sings on victory day. It is an indelible condition in the soul, given with the cosmos. The behavior of veterans— their domestic fury, suicides, silences, and despairs—years after a war is "over" refutes the dictionary and confirms war's archetypal presence. Peace for veterans is not an "absence of war" but its living ghost in the bedroom, at the lunch counter, on the highway. The trauma is not "post" but acutely present, and the "syndrome" is not in the veteran but in the dictionary, in the amnesiac's idea of peace that colludes with an unlivable life.

PTSD carriers of the remnants of war in their souls infect the peaceable kingdom. They are like initiates among innocents. The pain and fear, and knowledge, absorbed in their bodies and souls constitute an initiation—but only halfway. It is an initiation *interruptus* still asking for the wise instruction that is imparted by initiations. Why war; why that war; what is war? How can what I now know in my bones about treachery and hypocrisy, about loving compassion and courage, and killing, reenter society and serve my people? If peace means no war and I am soaked in war's blood, what am I doing here? Again that failure of imagination and philosophic understanding. The potential of the veteran is phased out with the war in which he matures; I have been mothballed by peace. Peacetime has no time for my awareness. There is no response in the least way adequate to the ordeal from the civilization I have been sent by and returned to.

The return from the killing fields is more than a debriefing; it is a slow ascent from hell. "Their eyes looked as if they had been to hell and back."[41] The veteran needs a *rite de sortie* that belongs to every initiation as its normal conclusion, making possible an intact return. This procedure of detoxification, that gives meaning to the absurd and imagination to oppressive facts, should take as long and be as thorough as the *rite d'entrée* of boot-camp basic training.

Society has still to recognize the value offered to it by the disturbed vet. Initiates often serve as leaders of traditional societies. They have been to the edge, stood among the ancestors in the underworld. In our societies, combat veterans are marginalized. "Of those unemployed between the ages of thirty and thirty-four in Britain at the end of the [nineteen] twenties, 80 percent were ex-servicemen."[42] U.S. veterans tend to become misfits, outcasts, drifting backwards into belligerency, or they find themselves in a pressure group of old boys lobbying for rewards in compensation for the recognition failed them. We pay them off with veterans' benefits instead of reaping the benefits they could bring.

Ambrose's careful follow-up of what became of the survivors of the company whose story he tells in *Band of Brothers* shows that ideal potential in men who were exceptionally led and exceptionally close, i.e., initiates. "A number of men went into some form of building, construction, or making things."[43] An even larger number began to teach, and one of them asks: "Is it accidental that so many ex-paratroopers from E company became *teachers?*"[44]

Even though our disturbed veterans may only be incomplete initiates, their presence all through the nation could serve to inoculate the body politic against the worst disease brought by the god of war: the headlong rush into action by the uninitiated. Is that why many older generals and veteran citizens speak out and hold the line against the march of folly?

"Veteran" from *vetus,* old, ripe, worn, belonging to the past. Time alone does not make veterans. A twenty-year-old German student writes: "all about us death hissed and howled. Such a night is enough to make an old man of one."[45] Combat is instant aging. The veteran has survived an initiation; the fact of that survival, that chance or miracle, forces upon one the deepest questioning and the veteran's burden of carrying the dead into life. Of course a veteran is ripe and worn and burnished by the past.

The one virtue of the dictionary's definition of peace is its implied normalization of war. War is the larger idea, the normative term giving peace its meaning. Definitions using negation or privation are psychologically unsophisticated. The excluded notion immediately comes to mind and, in fact, the word "peace" can be understood only after you have grasped the "war."

War is also implied in another common meaning of peace: peace as victory. The fusion of peace with military victory shows plainly enough in the prayers for peace which tacitly ask for winning the war. Do people ever pray for surrender? Unconditional surrender would bring immediate peace. Do they ever light candles and march in supplication of defeat?

The Romans understood this inner connection between peace and victory. Pax, the goddess of peace, was usually configured with a cornucopia of riches and plenty, an idealization that recurred in recent fantasies of a "peace dividend" to fill our coffers now that the Cold War was won. Also accompanying Pax were a caduceus (twin serpents winding around a staff indicating the healing arts) and an olive branch. Soon enough (around the turn of the era, 40 BC), she became Pax-Victoria and the olive branch merged with laurel leaves, the crown of victors.

Victory requires victims; someone had to lose, be beaten, conquered. The Greek cult of Eirene, the personification of peace, required huge bloody sacrifices: seventy to eighty oxen were slain at a time.[46] The most elaborate Roman temple to Pax was built in Vespasian's reign and celebrated victory over the Jews, while the earlier altar and cult established around 9 BC upon the emperor's return from campaigns in Spain and Gaul was set up outside the city on the Field of Mars. Again: peace is grounded in the territory of war.

The upshot of this excursion into peace is simple enough: it is more true to life to consider war more normal than peace. Not only does "peace" too quickly translate into "security," and a security purchased at the price of liberty. Something more sinister also is justified by peace which de Tocqueville superbly describes as a "new kind of servitude" where a "supreme power covers the surface of society with a network of small, complicated rules, minute and uniform, through which the most original minds and the most energetic characters cannot penetrate to rise above the crowd. The will of man is not shattered but softened, bent and guided; men are

d by it to act, but they are constantly restrained from
power does not destroy, but it prevents existence; it
does not tyrannize, but it compresses, enervates, extinguishes and
stupefies a people, till each nation is reduced to be nothing better
than a flock of timid and industrial animals, of which government
is the shepherd."[47]

War must stay on our minds, its weight press us into thinking
and imagining. Machiavelli is right: "A prince . . . should have no
other aim or thought, nor take up any other things for his study, but
war; [he] ought . . . never to let his thoughts stray from the exercise
of war; and in peace he ought to practise it more than in war."[48]
Otherwise, "psychic numbing," the term Lifton conceived for the
paralysis of the mind and blunted feelings in everyday life.[49] Peace
in our contemporary society is characterized both by the tranquillity of soporific and sophomoric teddy-bearism and by the frantic
overload of stimuli. This ever-shifting involvement from one set of
stimuli and engagements to the next Lifton calls Protean after the
Greek sea-god who defended himself by taking on a different form
from moment to moment, never still long enough to be appre-
hended. The Protean defense mechanism is like surfing, like multiple
tasking, like attention deficit, hyperactivity. The prince, as generous
metaphor for responsible citizen and concerned member of the polis, will keep a focused mind, a mind undistracted by the multiple
diversions of peace, and a psyche neither numbed nor in denial. And
he will maintain this clarity not merely by meditating or praying to
benefit his own "mental health," but for the common good and the
defense of the community. Hence, the prince "ought never let his
thoughts stray from . . . war."

At best, the assumption that war is normal does not enervate
and stupefy a people. At worst, it promotes Hobbes's anarchy, placing the people "in continuall feare, and danger of violent death;
And the life of man, solitary, poore, nasty, brutish, and short."[50]

Everyone the enemy of everyone. But—only if Hobbes is taken literally. He may also be understood psychologically so that the anarchic state of "Warre" awakens the citizen from the psychic numbing fostered by peace.

Then "solitary" does not mean the lonely isolation of heroic individualism in competition with all others. Rather, "solitary" would mean the single focus of the soul which is one's invisible and indivisible companion. We are solitaries each with our own dying, and from this comes our values of courage and dignity and honor, those qualities of character that sometimes appear only under the ruthless conditions of battle. Solitary, as Camus wrote in a late ironic work, may be indistinguishable from solidarity—steadfastness, side by side with one's soul.

The other four terms in Hobbes's famous dictum describing war also reshape their meanings. "Brutish" affirms the strength of our animal natures; "poore" restricts our human hubris. We simply do not have the means for the rampant exaggeration that pushes too far and asks too much, humbly recognizing as did Lear on the heath and the soldier in the trench that "man is no more but such a poor, bare, forked animal" (3.4.113). "Nasty" invites inspections of oneself and every other as the enemy, to plumb for shadows of ugliness, to sharpen street smarts, to perceive below the smiles and shibboleths that maintain the peaceful sheepish flock, worshipping the lamb of innocence. "Nasty" is the tiger who educates the lamb.

And finally "short": war does not permit the childishness that looks forward to a long life wrapped in the security of expectancy statistics. "Short" states that there is no security in the human condition; "short" exposes all of us to the arbitrary carelessness of the gods, without insurance; and that the length of life expectancy is not the measure of life. Life is better measured by the intensity and greatness of our expectations, because life is "short."

When these stark truths are steadily before us what comes to our hearts and habits is not more brutish nastiness only, but frequent instances of civility, decency, fairness, and kindness, because the soul recognizes these virtues to be supremely important when limned against the normalcy of "Warre." This surprising fact, though seldom and imperfect, has been witnessed in reports from concentration camps, combat soldiers, prisoners of war, and others under extremes of duress where the conditions of the day were solitary, poor, nasty, brutish, and short.

These civilized virtues arise as from the underworld of death rather than as preached moralities to be imposed from above. Kant finds war serving a purpose in advancing history toward civilization, and he uses words such as courage and nobility. Freud writes (in the midst of the Great War, 1915), "It might be said that we owe the fairest flowers of our love-life to the reaction against the hostile impulse which we divine in our breasts."[51] He goes on to say: "war is not to be abolished; so long as the conditions of existence among nations are so varied, and the repulsions between peoples so intense, there will be, must be, wars." The question then arises: "Is it not we who must give in, who must adapt ourselves . . . would it not be better to give death the place in actuality and in our thoughts which properly belongs to it?"

When Kant and Freud in distinctly different times and modes of thought consider that civilization gains its progressive impetus from its base in the naturalness of death and the normality of war, they are confirming Heraclitus: yes, war is the generative principle—war fathers awakening, which was, I believe, Heraclitus's, the psychologist's, main and urgent message.

Heraclitus receives further confirmation from Michel Foucault, who, like Levinas, continues the great French tradition of penetrating thought. His "hypothesis of war" reverses Clausewitz's dictum (war is the continuation of politics by other means), by saying politics is war continued by other means—and not only politics, but "law and order" as well. Law in Western states derives as much from Germanic custom where trials were settled by force, yielding decisive winners and losers, so that "law was a regulated way of making war."[52] Juridical inquiry into the facts of a case to ascertain impartial truth arrives later on the historical scene as a reemergence of Greek and Roman practices. Old law, Germanic law,[53] provides a model for Foucault's sweeping hypothesis that raises war to the foundation of social order: "the history that bears and determines us has the form of war rather than that of a language—relations of power, not relations of meaning."[54] Legal arguments and political debates use language to disguise warring conflict, "avoiding its violent, bloody and lethal character by reducing it to the calm Platonic form of language and dialogue."[55] In the beginning was, not the Word, but War. "The state is born in violence," concurs Philip Bobbitt; "only when it has achieved a legitimate monopoly on violence can it promulgate law."[56]

A nagging question still persists. Could the state of war become normal were it not in tune with something in the human soul, a force, a factor other than aggression and self-preservation, other than group bonding? It is as if a recognition occurs: "so this is it." This is Hell; the Kingdom of Death; the ultimate truth below all else. This is terror, this is a love more than my life, this is panic and madness. I know war already before I have gone to it. The psyche normalizes because it is archetypally in tune a priori, prior to the event; the event, like love in a flash, like the response to beauty, like taking the newborn to the breast, or when the temper boils at an instance of injustice. Perhaps we do come into the world knowing it all and that war is in us—not because of a fighting instinct, but in our soul's knowledge of the cosmos of which war is a foundation. The great realities are given; life displays and confirms them. If war is present to the archetypal imagination, we don't need wars to know them.

The old either/or between the individual and society, between instinct and culture, sets the mind on a goose chase only to come up with zeros. Aristotle resolved the question before it had ever begun with his famous sentence: *anthropos phúsei politikon zōon*—"man is by nature a political animal."[57] We are endowed with a political instinct; politics comes with our animal nature. The state is preformed in our individual souls like an appetite, like a passion. If war is "a continuation of politics by other means" (the dictum of Clausewitz), then war is a consequent of our political nature. We do not have to search for war's causes in an id erupting against a superego, in male castration anxieties, in splitting, paranoid projections, overcompensated inferiority feelings, nor load it onto testosterone. The unconscious grounds of war are more likely the neglect of grasping the full extent of our animal natures—that our animality is not sheerly nasty and brutish, but in tune harmoniously with war because we are each a *politikon zōon.*

If war fathers the cosmos (Heraclitus), if being reveals itself as war (Levinas), if the natural state is one of war (Kant), it must be the first of all norms, the standard by which all else be measured, permeating existence and therefore our existence as individuals and as societies. War then is permanent, not irruptive; necessary, not contingent; the tragedy that makes all others pale, and selfless love possible. Was it Yeats who said something like, "You only begin to live when you conceive life as a tragedy"? And Conrad: "Immerse yourself in the destructive element."

Kant recognized the necessity of war, but then enlightened this somber truth by finding war useful for historical progress. Machiavelli and Clausewitz aligned war's necessity to a function: the advancement of the state's political ambition. Marx showed the necessity to be the inevitable outcome of capitalism. I prefer to swallow the bare truth whole, uncoated with justifications: the ne-

cessity of war is laid down in the cosmos and affects ?
unbearable, the terrible, and the uncontrollable to wl
sures of normalcy and abnormality must adjust.

"Being reveals itself as war," reflects the monotheistic tradition
which nourished Levinas's thought. The statement represents in
philosophical language the nature of Jahweh of the Bible who was a
"warrior God,"[58] much as the earliest Christians were "soldiers of
Christ." Later ones, too: "Onward Christian soldiers, marching off to
war; with the Cross of Jesus, going on before." "Into it, in the name
of God," writes a German soldier from the trenches; "at any rate,"
writes another, "we have not lost our belief that God is leading us to
a good end—otherwise the sooner we are dead the better."[59]

If the biblical god who claims to be the foundation of all being
is a war god, then war presents the ultimate truth of the cosmos.
The three main monotheistic faiths, deriving their religions from
that particular god, will continually attempt to deny and escape
from their first premise by enunciating doctrines of peace and elab-
orating systems and laws to maintain peace. Their language of peace
is not mere hypocrisy; rather it recognizes that war founds and lives
in their religion, and that Patton's love of war states love of the god
of the Bible which he read every day.[60] For these monotheisms religion is war, since their faith in the being of the cosmos is exactly
as Levinas said: "being reveals itself as war."

Still, Levinas's statement is not exclusive; there is a tacit opening,
a way out. He does *not* say: being reveals itself *only* as war. In a polytheistic cosmos there are many revelations of being, many styles of
existence. War is but one god among many. Even when Heraclitus
declares strife to be father of all, there are also other fathers, and
mothers too. When we come at "being" differently, that is, from a
Greek or Roman or pagan perspective, then there are many gods and
goddesses. Then, too, that coincidence of individual bellicosity and

political militarism which together make war actual are revelations of a single source, the god of war—Mars, Ares, Indra, Thor—a divinity who rages, strikes death, stirs panic, driving individual humans mad and collective societies blind. This is the Inhuman to which we turn next.

Chapter Two:

WAR IS INHUMAN

EVEN THE EARTH SUFFERS. General Patton trained tank crews in the Mojave Desert of California in 1940. "Fifty years later the tracks are still visible . . . it may take more than 1000 years for some of this damaged area to recover completely." Who would imagine a desert could be this fragile! The desert—so ideally suited for massive mechanized battles: El Alamein, Sinai, Iraq. "Once the crucial top layer of desert soil is disturbed, dust storms and gullies form more readily, more sediment runs off into reservoirs, and less vegetation is available for animals to eat."[1]

Daisy-cutter bombs detonated just above the surface of Vietnam scythed terrain the size of football fields so that helicopters could land. When bombs didn't do the job, thirty-two-ton Rome

Plow bulldozers, sometimes operating twenty abreast, scraped away topsoil from an area the size of Rhode Island.[2] Bomb the earth and bulldoze it, then try chemicals. More than seventeen million gallons of Agent Orange were sprayed over five million acres of South Vietnam. A third of the country's upland forest was treated more than once; a half million acres of crops sprayed; a fifth of its mangrove forest destroyed. "It will take a century to heal."[3] Agent Orange was only one of the six defoliants used in the war in Vietnam. (Already in 1675–76 during "King Philip's War" colonists set fire to the scrub and dried swamps of Rhode Island to "smoke out" the Nipmucks and Narragansetts.)

Every now and then an unexploded artillery shell in a Flanders field, there since 1915, is struck by a plow; land mines infest Southeast Asian rice paddies; Pacific atolls, their coral reefs blasted to bits. Pine trees planted around Verdun grow "uncommonly slowly" and it "will take at least another hundred years . . . to have a normal forest again."[4] At the Bloody Angle (Spotsylvania, Virginia) an oak nearly two feet thick crashed to the ground. It had been cut down by the bullets fired by Federal troops during twenty-three hours of desperate combat. The land gives its names to the places of battle: Vimy Ridge, Missionary Ridge, Huertgen Forest, Little Round Top, Orchard Knob, the Peach Orchard, Apple Orchard, Wheatfield, Cornfield. The fertile soils of France and Belgium into which the trenches had been dug became slowly polluted by their human inhabitants. The English poet John Masefield in a letter to his wife writes: "It was not like any mud I've ever seen. It was a kind of stagnant river, too thick to flow, yet too wet to stand, and it had a kind of glisten and shine on it like reddish cheese, but it was not solid at all and you left no tracks in it, they all closed over, and you went in over your boots at every step and sometimes up to your calves."[5] "The stinking mud becomes more evilly yellow, the shell-holes fill up with green-white water, the roads and tracks are covered in inches of slime, the black dying trees ooze and sweat and the shells never cease . . . they plunge into the grave which is the land."[6]

Susan Griffin can imagine the land as a ravaged woman whose "great telluric body stretches the whole length of the trenches,"[7] drawing down into her the life of the men and animals struggling through the mud on their killing mission. Rats thrive, even in daylight, feeding on kitbags, boots, rotting corpses. These last reports come from only one war, 1914–18, and one narrow front in that war.

Add Vietnam: "The mud was waist-deep in places. It tugged at our boots, almost pulling them off when we lifted our feet to walk; and with each step the rotten-egg stench of escaping marsh gas rose into our nostrils. All of us were soon covered with leeches, black things as big as a man's thumb."[8] The earth's resistance to war, its inhabitants—rats and bugs and leeches—at war with the warriors. Add the siege of Vicksburg and the river rats, the siege of Leningrad when every tree, branch, and twig was chopped for fuel and hundreds of thousands died slowly of disease, starvation, and cold; the fly-blown bellies of dead horses in the hot sun of Antietam; the burial pits with hunks of bodies shoveled into the ground. Into rivers: tens of thousands of slaughtered bodies dumped into the Nanking River during December 1937. Celts buried warriors in bogs, and the booty captured in the heat of battle was not kept as trophies but thrown collectively in lake waters to propitiate the gods.[9] And still we have not mentioned the ruination of the land from "scorched earth" policies; the fires that roared through Hamburg, Dresden, London, Hiroshima, Nagasaki. How many pages do we need to establish human inhumanity to the earth itself?

The earth is where the dead live, and the soul of a people's history. Jon Lee Anderson talks with an Iraqi doctor, who says: "The sandstorm is coming back. . . . You can smell it. It smells like earth. . . . Whenever I smell this, it reminds me of dead people. Think about it. Think of Iraq's history. What is that history but thousands of years of wars and killings . . . right back to Sumerian and Babylonian times. Millions of people have died on this earth and become part of it. Their bodies are part of the land, the earth we are breathing."[10]

Below the events are the ancestors drawing new history into old patterns. Northern France as example, drawing down victims not merely from old buried land mines, but because the dead in the underworld of Hades thirst for blood.[11] The worst bloodshed in the western theater of the Civil War (September 1863) occurred at a place that had long before been named in Cherokee: *Chicka-mauga*—River of Death.

This is not the cyber-earth of a 3-D electronic simulation, nor the earth of the command center's sandbox over which the strategists plot the movements of thousands and thousands of men and women bringing their bodies into battle. The map room sunk in a bunker of *head*quarters sometimes thousands of miles from the action; the maps laid out in the Quonset hut, on the camp table, the pointer, the lecture, the orders, the field map in detailed topography . . . the great panorama of battle rolled into a tube, folded, and slipped into a field case without thunder or moans.

I would place the inhuman origins of war deep in the underground map room, close by the Halls of Hades. This is where sweating and thirsty men and women clambering uphill, or through barbed wire, among booby traps and land mines, under mortar explosions and unstoppable "friendly" bombing, mutate into itty-bitty pixels on a screen. The mind of war abstracts itself into signs and symbols, acronyms and units. Here is where the game begins, where ruthless instruments become toys, battles change into scenarios and theaters, and humans become nameless and faceless mutants.

how do we bury the dead

stacking up on the patio against
         our picture window? I can barely see
over the last body blown here by another cluster bomb—
every forty minutes, every twenty, every ten, every five,
every four every three every two
every one—
I can no longer see into the garden

what do we do with all these children
lying here outside our kitchen

until each of their deaths has been named a death
until each of us knows who it is we have killed
how young she is—four? eight? thirteen?
         twenty-two? did she often
hold her hands that way? was she about to ask a question?

her face once a freshly-turned field
where we would have lingered if we could
and let slip from our eyes seeds
born of our looking

but now

can we enunciate repeat enunciate repeat
kill, death, kill, death, kill, death
pausing after each as each deserves, repeating
in our sleep, under our breaths, out loud, on TV
till our words become sand stinging blood from our palms
raised to the rising wind

look now what is left of her face, the torn and barren ground—
hers, then his, too, and his, and hers again— repeat

hurry

sand to cover at least her slight
once radiant body

(MERMER BLAKESLEE)

War's inhumanity is captured best by poets and novelists, for their imaginations reach into the afflicted soul beyond the reporting of the facts. But the facts are bare and awful, inhumanity reduced to statistics, a transfiguration of cold death into cold numbers. "Look at the 1990's," says Chris Hedges: "2 million dead in Afghanistan; 1.5 million dead in the Sudan; some 800,000 butchered in ninety days in Rwanda; a half million dead in Angola; a quarter million dead in Bosnia; 200,000 dead in Guatemala; 150,000 dead in Liberia; a quarter of a million dead in Burundi; 75,000 dead in Algeria." His litany goes on through Chechnya, Sierra Leone, Northern Ireland, Kosovo, and the Persian Gulf War, where perhaps as many as 35,000 Iraqi citizens were killed. (The U.S. Defense Department estimated that one hundred thousand Iraqi troops retreating from Kuwait in 1991 had been killed in the notorious "turkey shoot.") "In the wars of the twentieth century not less than 62 million civilians have perished."[12] World War I delivered up six and a half million German casualties, more than three million British, four million French, and at least four and a half million Austro-Hungarians. Add to this the Russians, the Italians, Turks, Bulgarians, Australians, Americans. Who can hold in mind merely the wounded, twenty-one million of them?

During the siege of Petersburg, Virginia, the First Maine lost 635 men of their 900—in seven minutes. Six thousand lay dead or mortally wounded in one single day at Antietam; there, the First Texas Brigade suffered 82.5 percent casualties. Three thousand horses dead on the battlefield at Gettysburg. As the Civil War wound down in April 1865, the Union troops counted eleven thousand more casualties in the final days of the Appomattox campaign.

Beyond rattling off the death statistics, there is the lasting crippling aftermath condensed into each single casualty as a person. Studs Terkel reports the following account told him by a California woman of her time as a twenty-two-year-old army nurse on orthopedic and plastic surgery wards:

It was coming to the end of the war and now they needed plastic surgery. Blind young men. Eyes gone, legs gone. Parts of the face. Burns—you'd land with a fire bomb and be up in flames. It was a burn-and-blind center.

I spent a year and a half in the plastic-surgery dressing room. All day long you would change these dressings. When you were through with those who were mobile, who would come by wheel-chair or crutches, you would take this little cart loaded with canisters of wet saline bandages. Go up and down the wards to those fellas who couldn't get out of bed. It was almost like a surgical procedure. They didn't anesthetize the boys and it was terribly painful. We had to keep the skin wet with these moist saline packs. We would wind yards and yards of this wet pack around these people. That's what war really is.

I'll never forget my first day on duty.

I was so overwhelmed by the time I got to the third bed: this whole side of a face being gone. I wouldn't know how to focus on the eye that peeked through these bandages. Should I pretend I didn't notice it? Shall we talk about it?

Molly led me down to the next bed: The Nose, she called him. He had lost his nose. Later on, I got used to it, all this kidding about their condition. He would pretend to laugh. He would say, "Ah yes, I'm getting my nose." He didn't have any eyebrows, a complete white mass of scars. The pedicle was hanging off his neck. He had no ears—they had been burned off.

As soon as we got back to the nurse's station behind glass, I went to the bathroom and threw up.

I remember this one lieutenant. Just a mass of white bandages, with a little slit where I knew his eyes were. This one hand reaching out and saying, "Hi, Red." There were many, many, many more with stumps, you couldn't tell if there was a foot there or not, an eye, an arm.

V-J Day occurred while I was still at the hospital.

. . . The hospital closed and they sent the patients out to other places. Plastic surgery was going to go on for years on these people. I went down to Pasadena. This is '46. We took over the whole hotel, one of the big, nice old hotels right there on the gorge. All my friends were still there, undergoing surgery. Especially Bill. I would walk him in downtown Pasadena—I'll never forget this. Half his face completely gone, right?

Downtown Pasadena after the war was a very elite community. Nicely dressed women, absolutely staring, just standing there staring. He was aware of this terrible stare. People just looking right at you and wondering: What is this? I was going to cuss her out, but I moved him away. It's like the war hadn't come to Pasadena until we came there.

Oh, it had a big impact on the community. In the Pasadena paper came some letters to the editor: Why can't they be kept on their own grounds and off the streets? The furor, the awful indignation: the end of the war and we're still here.[13]

"War is cruelty, and you cannot refine it," said General Sherman.[14] Before the Japanese were driven from Manila (March 1945), the entire city and its inhabitants were "wasted," some sixty thousand Filipinos, including babies, young children, old women, and hospital patients.[15] Cruelty has no national borders. Grisly body parts cut from dead Japanese were American trophies. "*Life's* May 22, 1944 issue published, as its Picture of the Week, the photograph of an Arizona war worker, a well-dressed and well-groomed woman, writing her Navy boyfriend a thank-you note for the gift she was regarding appreciatively: a skull autographed by the lieutenant and thirteen of his friends."[16] On Peleliu one souvenir was a shriveled hand cut from a Japanese corpse. Some Americans collected gold teeth: "What you did is you took your K-bar [and] you extracted gold teeth by putting the rip of the blade on the tooth of the dead Japanese—I've seen guys do it to wounded ones—and hit the hilt."[17]

Deliberate cruelty is one of three characteristics that compose what John Keegan calls "the inhuman face of war."[18] *Coercion* and *impersonalization* are the other two. Coercion "keep[s] men in the killing zone. . . . [A]ll armies, whether of democracies or dictatorships, depend on the coercive principle . . . [and] it is a vital element in making battles work."[19] Coercion is a function of war's impersonalization, that is, not this particular man or woman, but "Charlie Company," a unit, so that impersonalization (such as we observe in the map room) is a function of thinking in numbers.

As we reconstruct tribal battles of prehistoric humankind or read of wars of heroic and chivalric times, numbers were far less relevant. The quantity of combatants and the amounts of weapons were far less significant than their quality: fighting spirit, well-made arrows, wily and ferocious leaders, huge strength of champions or ability with horse or sword. There may have been cruelty, and perhaps coercion in the clash of combat, but certainly not impersonalization. The thinking of modern warfare (until the advent of the lone teenage girl with a bomb under her blouse) operates in the "Reign of Quantity,"[20] demonstrating a materialistic ontology which reduces qualities to numbers—measurement, calculation, computation, simply "counting off," and dog tags with blood type and serial number. It is not merely the industrialization of warfare and the large population involved, but the ontology of numerical thinking, of science itself, that produces the impersonalization which creates a new kind of deliberate cruelty in the precisely calculated bombing of the unnamed by the unnamed.

Those who have endured artillery bombardment, ships' guns shelling the shore, air strikes, say nothing is worse than the concussive whistling and screaming from nowhere, aimed at no one, relentless and repeating. This is the military-industrial complex incarnated into the titanic war machine. Machines, Lewis Mumford shows, are logical, purposeful organizations such as built the pyramids in Egypt thousands of years before the steam engines. Only secondarily do machines require levers and pulleys and wheels; first is the systematic functioning of their cohesive parts. War turns humans into parts, spare parts.

Regarding the first of Keegan's factors, deliberate cruelty, we owe it to war's victims to recapitulate in memory paradigmatic incidents such as I am reporting in this chapter. This too is a way of honoring the dead. Before death, the deadening. "A [U.S.] veteran recalls a typical exchange between himself and other team members after deaths among them:"

> *"Fuck it. They're dead. No big fucking deal. Move on."*
> "_____'s dead."

"Fucking _____ fucked up. He's dead."

"He shouldn't have *fucked up.* He wouldn't be *fucking dead.*"

"Where, where's the compassion? Where's your sense of human— This is another fellow American."

Y'know? He didn't fuck up. He's dead. You know?

Why can't I feel? Y'know, why can't I grieve for him? That's where they put that hardening in you.[21]

The language in this exchange is not incidental. The martial concatenation of sex and anger, together with frustration and helplessness, terror and grief, explodes into furious yet apathetic violence especially vented onto women. Rape accompanies war and follows in its path, even though rapes are not recorded in the statistics. "Gang or individual rapes by soldiers—whether or not these end in the woman's murder—have never been counted" among civilian casualties. "Psychological injuries to the surviving rape victims are often lifelong."[22]

Rape can so dominate the imagination of a campaign that this particular atrocity among the many war produces seems to reveal the secret source of war's desire. Rape becomes a cover word for all of war's brutal conquests, a word for war itself. The Japanese invasion of China in the 1930s is largely recalled in the West as the "Rape of Nanking." In barely six weeks of occupation by Japanese troops, hundreds of thousands of Chinese died. Women of all ages were hounded out, herded, humiliated, and raped. A German businessman, who had been living in China for some thirty years and who did his best to intervene, kept diary notes and wrote reports:

"They would continue by raping the women and girls and killing anything and anyone. . . . There were girls under the age of 8 and women over the age of 70 who were raped and then, in the most brutal way possible, knocked down and beat up. We found corpses of women on beer glasses and others who had been lanced by bamboo shoots. I saw the victims with my own eyes—I talked to some of them right before their deaths and had their bodies brought to the morgue at the Kulo hospital so that I could be personally convinced that all of these reports had touched on the truth.[23]

When I say "the secret source of war's desire" I do not mean that source is sexual. Rape is more than sexual, beyond the sexual enactment which is symbolic of a more fundamental transgression. Rape is *pars pro toto* for war's transgression of human limits. Great warriors like Ajax, Alexander, and Napoleon attempt to break all previous laws, violate all boundaries, thereby affirming that all resistance submit to the totality of war's conquest. The victims of war are imagined as victims of rape: the "Rape of Belgium" by the "Huns" in World War I; the Catholic Church during the Spanish Civil War personified as nuns raped by Anarchists and Communists—though later inquiry could not show even one actual nun who suffered the crime.[24] The imagination conceives transgressions of every sort in unequal pairings: a mob of men with one girl; a father forced to rape his virgin daughter; natives by foreigners; whites by blacks; blacks by whites; old prison inmate and young punk; old woman and adolescent soldier; bourgeois and barbarian; beauty/beast; master/slave . . . These forced crossings of conventional boundaries state that the most intimate of human actions, the actual joining of bodies and the possible creation of a fruit in common so absolutely necessary for life to go on, is transgressed. The marauding rapist in the plundered town thereby finds his ultimate destiny as enemy of life, as warrior child of Mars, in the full potency of his inhuman calling. Therefore, too, the brutalization of women's bodies, even pregnant bodies, and especially the mutilation of their genitals, the symbolic focus of the continuity of life.

"When you resorted to force . . . you didn't know where you were going," said General Eisenhower. "If you got deeper and deeper, there was just no limit except . . . the limitations of force itself."[25] "Bodies of eight and a half million Quechua people exterminated in the first eighty years of the [Spanish] Conquest" of the high Andes.[26]

Nor are there limits to the inventive imagination of force. It occurs in fantasy, even wishful fantasy, after the firefight is over: "I've fired 203-grenade rounds into windows, through a door once. But the thing I wish I'd seen—I wish I could have seen a grenade go into someone's body and blow it up," says a Marine to Evan Wright accompanying a platoon in Iraq. Atrocities occur in the past and the present, in the third world, the first world, and the ancient world, and the imagination deployed in their execution neither mollifies nor coarsens with the "advances" of civilization. Nanking exhibits the army of a modern state defiling the people of another modern state. Other rapes have other perpetrators and other victims: for instance, Moroccan mercenaries officially allowed to rape Italian women in 1943; for instance, hundreds of thousands of Bengali women raped by Pakistani soldiers;[27] for instance, "The Serbian soldiers told the naked [Bosnian] girls to parade slowly in a circle. The men sat at the outside of the circle—smoking, drinking, calling out foul names. The witness estimates the 'parade' lasted about 15 minutes. Three soldiers took one girl—one to rape her while two others held her down . . . The witness said she fought and pulled his hair, but he bit her and hit . . . her hard with the butt of his gun on her cheek, causing extreme pain. Another rapist ran the blade of a knife across her breasts as if to slice the skin off . . . she was raped by eight more men before losing consciousness."[28]

Peter Maass points out that degradation and mutilation belong also to pornography, so that the viewing of war on TV and the graphic "eyewitness" reconstructions at trials share in the atrocity. The witness too enacts the phallic gaze, and the journalist "embedded" with the troops is paid by the entertainment industry. Complicity in war crimes has no clear boundaries; we all too much like to watch.

And there are no exceptions. Inhumanity is all too human. "Soldiers of the Canadian peace-keeping army in Somalia detained a sixteen-year-old boy for allegedly stealing food. . . . The boy was kicked, beaten senseless with truncheons, and the soles of his feet were burned with a cigar. Soldiers posed for trophy pictures, one of which showed a truncheon stuck into the boy's bleeding mouth. . . . After three hours the boy was dead. . . . At least half a dozen Canadian soldiers, including some officers, heard the beatings and the boy's screams—'Canada . . . Canada . . . Canada'—but did nothing. The boy's family later got one hundred camels as compensation."[29] In 1982, Great Britain battled Argentina over the Falkland Islands. "Afterward, a British soldier . . . accused fellow soldiers of executing Argentineans who surrendered at Mount Longden and cutting off their ears for war trophies. His commander later confirmed the account."[30]

Official memory is short. The evidence of atrocities desiccates in institutional archives, yet war's inhumanity does not fade with time. It lingers, haunts. Can the dead be fully buried? Anthony Loyd, a journalist in Chechnya "was trying to sleep, swinging in and out of half-consciousness. . . . Eventually I must have drifted off. . . . The dead child arrived in my room without warning, standing listlessly at the end of my bed . . . chopping me out of sleep with a single blow. He was silent and as I started upright he stared into my eyes with an unwavering gaze that seemed like an accusation. Two small severed heads lay on the blood-covered table behind him."[31]

Severed heads on stockade poles, on tree stumps, scalps, skulls delivered by the sackful, the cartload, by victorious troops to their chief. Kali with her necklace of heads dancing on the funeral pyre; Golgotha, place of skulls. The severed head as memento mori warning of what war can do, does do. Long after the deeds are done the gazing heads generate memories, and replications, visiting similar sins upon unborn generations much as the Bible says. Dreams bring back the dead. In the unconscious nothing changes, said Freud. The souls in Hades are doomed to repetition.

What holds true for memory in the individual psyche is true as well for the collective soul. Africa provides a vast example of multiple occasions. There wars are not of the sort that usually come to mind—great uniformed battalions, massed artillery, fleets of warships cannonading each other. Colonial wars of the nineteenth and twentieth centuries left much of that continent plagued with a style of inhumanity such as appalled the wider world in reports from Rwanda. But that genocide, that mass heartless butchery, had been institutionalized long before as a Belgian colonial tradition.

King Leopold of the Belgians, who once personally owned all of the Congo, reincarnates in Joseph Désiré Mobutu, one of our era's arch-potentates of long-term vicious rule. When Leopold passed his property on to the Belgian state in 1908, the records were burnt in furnaces in Brussels for eight days. "I will give them my Congo," Leopold said to his military aide, "but they have no right to know what I did there."[32] Mobutu, like Leopold, received the respectful homage of Western hypocrisy. He was greeted by Kennedy and by Reagan at the White House. George Bush Sr. said: "I was honored to invite President Mobutu to be the first African head of state to come to the United States for an official visit during my presidency."[33] The earlier alternative to the devastating rule of Mobutu had been an idealist, Patrice Lumumba, whose assassination was authorized by Allen Dulles of the CIA, and whose body ended up in the trunk of a CIA car and dumped into an unmarked grave. Even those who know history are doomed to repeat it because, though it may be easy to kill the living, it is hard to kill the dead.

EXCURSION:

Shell Shock

General Patton walked into a field hospital in Sicily to speak one by one and one-on-one to those men who had been wounded in battles he commanded, giving encouragement, praise, and decorations. One man appeared to have no wounds, no bandages. In reply to Patton's questioning the GI said, "I guess I can't take it." Patton exploded, slapped the man with his gloves, cursed him out, and exited the tent. On a second occasion going down the rows of cots, he came upon a man shivering. "It's my nerves," the man said, crying. "Your nerves hell," Patton shouted. "You are just a god-damn coward, you yellow son-of-a-bitch. . . . you are going back to the front to fight."[34] He pulled a pistol from his holster, and with his gloves he slapped this man too; then, on the way out of the station, turned and "hit the weeping soldier again." In his diary, Patton wrote: "one sometimes slaps a baby to bring it to."

These "slapping incidents" nearly cost Patton his command and almost ended his career in disgrace. They have been discussed, analyzed, condemned, explained almost from the moment the reports went through the American high command and out to the American public via the press. Was Patton right or wrong? Was this a sign of his own combat fatigue and an overcompensation for his fear of his own fears? Was he performing correctly by demonstrating best how to raise anger and the martial spirit? Remember Patton was an old general of the "old school": during the first two years of World War I (where Patton served) men exhibiting "symptoms we can now recognize as those of true psychiatric breakdown were shot for desertion."[35] The collapsed, terrorized soldier was trapped in a no-man's-land between bullets from the enemy and bullets from his own officers.

"I am convinced that, in justice to other men, soldiers who go to sleep on post, who go absent for an unreasonable time during combat, who shirk in battle, should be executed."[36] Summary execution for desertion, malingering, or even dereliction of duty has long been a standard mode for coercing troops to stay in combat. Until the twentieth century there were scant means for differentiating kinds and causes of collapse. Was the man showing shell shock, cowardice, mutiny, brain disorder, psychotic depression, substance toxicity, panic, hysterical conversion, malingering, or simply plain exhaustion? "Infantry troops can attack continuously for sixty hours. . . . Beyond sixty hours, it is rather a waste of time, as the men become too fatigued."[37]

Are the symptoms presenting genuine breakdown or is the disability "only" factitious—that is, simulated—owing to intricate complications of the soul? The large task of the war machine is hampered by overconcern with differential diagnosis. Its job is to maintain plenty of able-bodied men in line, and the line is only as strong as its weakest link. The threat of breakdown of just one man endangers all. The military must always be on guard against collapse or mutiny of the entire unit. In the mind of Mars, shirkers, skulkers, deserters, fakers can hide behind a psychiatric diagnosis. Summary execution then becomes a protective measure; the end justifies the means. "During the Civil War, over 300,000 Union and Confederate soldiers deserted the ranks."[38] We can imagine their reasons.

An analysis of Patton's behavior is not our issue. The incidents, however, do expose two aspects of war absolutely necessary for its understanding.

First, we witness an archetypal conflict, as if between two gods who cannot abide each other and must refuse each other's way of being. Mars commands the general; civilian society embraces the soldier, whose uninitiated psyche is still back home. The "abnormal" behavior displayed by the conscript and the volunteer soldier in the tent—then termed a psychoneurosis—affirmed that for him war was not normal, not human, and so his breakdown was all too human. Patton's abnormal behavior under that same tent showed he was still in the normal inhuman condition of battle, even when in the setting of an evacuation station dedicated to humane values. (The conflict of conscience within the souls of medical personnel when in uniform asks the same question: which of the gods am I bound by?)

Breakdown reveals the human under the calloused skin of the warrior. An unexpected appearance of the enemy as an ordinary human being can unnerve the citizen soldier, returning his psyche for an instant of hesitation to the status quo ante of his civilized emotions and civil values, taking him right out of war. Michael Walzer gives examples of sudden encounters with the naked enemy.[39] The image of the poor, bare, forked human inhibits squeezing the trigger. During the Spanish Civil War where George Orwell had gone to fight Fascists, as he says, he could not shoot at a man partly dressed running along holding up his trousers because "a man holding up his trousers isn't a 'Fascist,' he is visibly a fellow-creature, similar to yourself, and you don't feel like shooting him."[40] Nudity as such neither dignifies nor signifies the human, nor does it always inhibit martial action. The Celts roared into battle naked, the Norse sometimes too— but in these cases nudity followed the collective code. To be naked was to be dressed for battle, in uniform.

The human skin, the sense of touch, are in starkest contrast to the metal of the war-world, from helmet to shell casing to tank turret; unyielding, repelling hardness; impenetrable, reinforced, tungsten-sided toughness; ramrod straight, tightly wound, wired.

Something cracks under the strain, cracks up, breaks down, falls apart, stressed out. "Stress" begins in those very engines and materials of war. The word took on its contemporary human meaning of psychological overload, tension, and strain from engineering during the industrial explosion of the mid-nineteenth century. Stress became current together with industrialism's practice of work as exploitation, if not repression, of the soul and body obliged to keep pace with machines. The "stress" we humans feel has been imported from the torsion suffered by materials under duress, the metal fatigue of airplane wings, suspension cables, steel girders.[41]

The iron will of Mars can endure only so long: "Each moment of combat imposes a strain so great that men will break down in direct relation to the intensity and duration of their exposure . . . psychiatric casualties are as inevitable as gunshot and shrapnel wounds in warfare," states an American official report, *Combat Exhaustion*.[42] "A World War II study determined that after sixty days of continuous combat, 98 percent of all surviving soldiers will have become psychiatric casualties. . . . [A] common trait among the 2 percent able to endure . . . was a predisposition toward 'aggressive psychopathic personalities.'"[43] By not granting home leave from beginning to end, requiring men to stay with their units until killed or disabled,[44] was the Russian high command intentionally producing aggressive psychopaths? Which might also account for the wild terror of the Germans as the Red Army advanced.

"On Okinawa, American losses totaled 7,613 killed and missing . . . —and 26,211 psychiatric casualties."[45] Of all World War II U.S. medical evacuations from combat zones, one in four were psychiatric.[46] The Arab-Israeli war of 1973 lasted only a few weeks, yet almost one third of Israeli casualties were psychiatric;[47] the inhuman stress of war.

The very idea that human agony can be named a "stress syndrome" is inhuman, imagining a man as a machine part, a cog in a military wheel. To keep the war machine running, you kick the engine, boot up the computer, slap the soldier to get him back in line.

The eventually unbearable division between engine of war and human warrior commences already in the drills learned in basic training performed as ceremonies of separation. The hard-ass drill sergeant hollering at recruits is one way to imagine the beginnings of stress. Another way is this poem, "Naming of Parts," by Henry Reed.

NAMING OF PARTS

Today we have naming of parts. Yesterday,
We had daily cleaning. And tomorrow morning,
We shall have what to do after firing. But today,
Today we have naming of parts. Japonica
　　　Glistens like coral in all of the neighboring gardens,
And today we have naming of parts.

This is the lower sling swivel. And this
Is the upper sling swivel, whose use you will see,
　　　When you are given your slings. And this is the piling swivel,
　　　Which in your case you have not got. The branches
Hold in the gardens their silent, eloquent gestures,
　　　Which in our case we have not got.

This is the safety-catch, which is always released
　　　With an easy flick of the thumb. And please do not let me
　　　See anyone using his finger. You can do it quite easy
　　　If you have any strength in your thumb. The blossoms
Are fragile and motionless, never letting anyone see
　　　Any of them using their finger.

And this you can see is the bolt. The purpose of this
Is to open the breech, as you see. We can slide it
Rapidly backwards and forwards: we call this
    Easing the spring. And rapidly backwards and forwards
    The early bees are assaulting and fumbling the flowers:
    They call it easing the Spring.

They call it easing the Spring: it is perfectly easy
    If you have any strength in your thumb: like the bolt,
    And the breech, and the cocking-piece, and the point
        of balance,
Which in our case we have not got; and the almond-blossom
    Silent in all of the gardens and the bees going backwards and
        forwards
    For today we have naming of parts.

                                  (FROM *Lessons of the War*)

The slapping incidents in Sicily, like Reed's poem, open wide the gulf between human and inhuman. Now, a second issue is raised: what is this phenomenon called "shell shock" in the First World War, "combat fatigue" in the Second World War, now "stress" or PTSD (you will notice the decline in the power of the term from its original impact to an acronym for a medical report). Shell shock, as I am continuing to name this psychic distress, is so essential to combat and combat so necessary to war that we must work at its understanding. The figures of its victims alone are shocking: "35.8 percent of male Vietnam combat veterans met the full American Psychiatric Association diagnostic criteria for

PTSD at the time of the study in the late 1980's . . . almost twenty years after their war experience."[48] During the Civil War, medical and court-martial records, military reports, diaries and letters home describe what must have been similar psychological states with terms such as: played out, used up, worn out, rattled, dispirited, downhearted, sunstroke, anxious, nervous, demoralized, badly blown, darkness, gloom, and also frequently, the blues, blue days, blue and homesick.[49]

If we turn to the *Diagnostic and Statistical Manual,* Third Revision, used throughout the United States by the various branches of the health services (hospitals, insurance companies, Veterans Administration, prisons, medical and psychological practices, state agencies, etc.), we find that post-traumatic stress disorder officially refers to *"the experience of an event that is outside the range of usual human experience"* (my italics). The condition consists in four main descriptions which can be condensed here: I. Distressing repetition in any or all of a variety of ways of a past traumatic event, and which may have not been consciously traumatic at the time. II. Persistent detachment from or avoidance or denial or amnesia of past event. III. Persistent hypervigilance, irritability, susceptibility to reenactment in a variety of ways. IV. Duration of the above for at least one month.

I have set in italics the essential phrase in the diagnosis. It is the "linchpin" on which the whole syndrome depends, says Jonathan Shay in his brilliant study that compares the psychological behaviors of American combatants in Vietnam with Homer's descriptions of warriors in the *Iliad.* Shay shows inhuman gods still at work in the usual conditions of war.

Achilles was in Vietnam and the U.S. Marines were in Troy. The normalcy of war's madness does not change. All wars are the same war because war is always going on. As Clausewitz implied, peace is merely a superficial and temporary hiatus, an armistice, in the everlasting war. In its elemental nature, war is Freud's repetition compulsion enacted, Vico's *ricorso* confirmed, and it validates Thucydides' thesis that history demonstrates the general consistency of human nature: we can imagine what will happen by studying what has happened.

If shell shock belongs to battle even before there were shells, then it is folly—maybe worth inventing a new category for diagnosing the *Manual* itself—to refer a primary condition of war as "outside the range of human experience." Humans have been inside the range of war since recorded time. At the least, the *Diagnostic and Statistical Manual* shows that its notion of human experience is inadequate to the task of imagining war. Its description of the shell-shocked remnants of battle bypasses completely any attempt to understand the nature of what is outside the range, i.e., the very essence of war.

Susan Griffin brings a more sensitive imagination to shell shock. She reads the sudden paralysis and muteness, the trembling, the easing of the sphincters, and the widened pupils of the eyes blurred with tears to be the reappearance, after long repression by military indoctrination, of the feminine body of men. The repressed returns in the sympathetic and parasympathetic nervous systems. Softness of love for the blown-up buddies, sympathy for the whimpering hurt. The soldier in the combat zone is shadowed by a sympathetic "softer and sorrowing" self.[50] "Softness is all about; the softness of wounds, of deteriorating flesh, of the dead." And of the earth: "lying in the shallow dip in the ground, I made love to the earth," writes Philip Caputo, who dove for shelter under fire.[51] Earth as refuge, as bed, lap, woman.

Disdained by Patton: " 'Dig or die' is much overused and much misunderstood. Digging is primarily defensive. . . . Personally, I am opposed to digging . . . as the chance of getting killed while sleeping normally on the ground is quite remote, and the fatigue from digging innumerable slit trenches is avoided. . . . 'Hit the dirt' is another expression which has done much to increase our casualties."[52]

On page 880 of Tolstoy's *War and Peace,* we find this. Lying in a makeshift hospital tent, horribly wounded, "Prince Andrey wanted to cry. Either because he was dying without glory, or because he was sorry to part with life, or from memories of a childhood that could never return, or because he was in pain, or because others were suffering."[53] As many reasons for softness and sorrowing as Tolstoy gives to the many supposed causes of war, all we know for sure is that war's inhumanity never wholly eclipses human vulnerability.

Along with Susan Griffin I can imagine the weeping dissolution in the Sicilian tent as the inevitable return of the repressed, but not the repressed child, that abused, improperly parented infant on whose puny shoulders Lloyd de Mause places the burden of causing wars. The simplified explanation he offers for war's inhuman horror is so popular and accessible that there is clearly something wrong with it—yet right, in that it conforms so perfectly with the American psyche that has such trouble extricating itself from clinging needs of the child archetype. Americans love the idea of child-hood no matter how brutal or vacuous their actual child-hoods may have been.

Both the silly childishness (that the Bible condemns) and the innocence of childlikeness (that the Bible extols) are so appealing to American habits of mind and heart that all problems return there for their imagined source, and for their solution. Consequently, de Mause: the battering and cruelty of war are reenactments of vicious child-rearing practices. War simply repeats on a huge scale the repressed and hate-filled ugliness of childhood. We do unto others what was done unto us—twice and thrice over because so long stored. The simplistics of de Mause's idea addresses childish resentful minds which it satisfies. In short, he says, were child-rearing to change, wars would lose their motiva-tion and societal violence would go away, because (and this is the specific American catch in the formula) children treated rightly have no war in them, as if we are each born not in original sin, born without cosmic knowledge of the archetypal inclinations for the wrongs listed by the Ten Commandments and the Seven Deadly Sins, and the neces-sity of their suppression.

I imagine the "softness and sorrow" that melts the body to be the body's inner soul, not its inner child, the soul that knows death from the beginning as part of its innate knowl-edge; the body, death's instrument. I imagine that the re-pressed, returning through the body's shattered disarray, is the universal principle of Thanatos, an incursion of Lord Death into awareness as ultimate truth. The fear and trem-bling which assaults in shell shock, the muteness that mimics the unspeakable, displays the soul's recognition of being in the midst of Armageddon, the mythic final battle, of Ragnarök and the death of the gods themselves, the extinction, the wipeout, *nihil*. Nothing can save; nothing to go on for, nothing to die for. "Never, never, never, never, never" (*Lear* 5.3.308). The nerves cannot respond because the fatigue is of the spirit; the weeping, a premature grieving. Thanatos, the ultimate repressed, is honored by war and served by war; war, an apotropaic rite to keep death at bay by offering sacrificial victims, like the young hearts torn out in an Aztec ceremony so that death will not show its full force and obliterate all and everything. With disciplined and fierce dedication war serves one cosmic underlying certitude, that there is nothing, nothing at all, no salvation, nor help for pain— only death's strangely comforting companion appearing as softness: "Ah, love," writes Matthew Arnold at the end of one of the English language's most sweeping and stark metaphysical poems:

> . . . *let us be true*
> *To one another! For the world, which seems*
> *To lie before us like a land of dreams,*
> *So various, so beautiful, so new,*
> *Hath really neither joy, nor love, nor light,*
> *Nor certitude, nor peace, nor help for pain;*
> *And we are here as on a darkling plain*
> *Swept with confused alarms of struggle and flight,*
> *Where ignorant armies clash by night.*
>
> ("DOVER BEACH")

We can never close the book on the inhumanity of war. The limitlessness of its force, observed by Eisenhower (above), recapitulates one of Clausewitz's principles: "War is an act of force, and there is no logical limit to the application of that force."[54] Clausewitz wrote during the era of Napoleon. Two centuries later Qiao Liang and Wang Xiangsui carry his message further in their appropriately titled *Unrestricted Warfare*. War heeds no limits of time, of space, or of methods. Its inhuman potential, nevertheless, can be summarily grouped into three main kinds, each as normal to war as it is inhuman.

First, *disfiguring* the human frame, whether maiming the body, crippling the soul, or shattering the structures of human civilization—its laws with unilateral abrogations and calculated deceits, its treasuries of arts with fire and plunder, its habits of fairness with cold-blooded self-interest. Second, *deranged behaviors* such as the altered states of possession in combat, blind obsession of policy experts, leaders and generals, inspired foolhardy bravery, or the gradual addiction of journalist war-junkies[55] and mercenary soldiers of fortune. Third, war's inhuman *weaponry, accoutrements, and symbolic abstractions*. Whether stone-ax, knife-blade, or chlorine gas drifting on the wind, war's inhumanity refers in part to the hyperrationalism of its instruments. In map-room strategies and mathematical logistics, in the drill preparatory to battle and in battle formations (Spartan hoplites, Macedonian phalanx, Roman legion, British square), in chain of command, as well as in the role of the horse, uniform, metal, camouflage, battle cry, bugle, flag, escutcheon, as they transmute into the inhuman power of symbols.

To these three essentials, we need to add a fourth that reaches beyond the evident and into the heart of war's mysterious power: *uncontrollable autonomy*.

Wars break out, their dogs unleashed; the soldiers rampage, firestorms engulf cities. The fantasy of war spreads across continents, into star wars, cyberspace. The horizon recedes into the next field of operations: Napoleon onto Moscow, Alexander across the Indus, a new Crusade follows upon the last, MacArthur across the Yalu, Iraq after Afghanistan . . .

Since war's autonomy generates its own momentum, war has no cause other than itself! "Is war something which really does have 'a life of its own'?" asks Barbara Ehrenreich.[56] War's inhumanity tells war's truth: its origins lie outside the human sphere, beyond human control. "We have been misled," she argues, pinning war onto persons, politics, economics, gender; "it is the *autonomy* of war as an institution that we have to confront and explain."[57] Her explanation is remarkably imaginative: she conceives war on the model of a living organism, "a self-replicating pattern of behavior, possessed of a dynamism not unlike that of living things."[58] Suddenly, war emerges as a fictive figure, a robotic golem, a "brutal giant stalking his human prey," as in these lines from Thomas Sackville (1536–1608) and quoted by Michael Walzer:

> *Lastly stood War, in glittering arms y-clad,*
> *With visage grim, stern looks, and blackly hued;*
> *In his right hand a naked sword he had*
> *That to the hilts was all with blood embrued,*
> *And in his left (that kings and kingdoms rued)*
> > *Famine and fire he held, and therewithal*
> > *He razed towns, and threw down towers and all.*[59]

We are entering the territory of myth and approaching the war god himself. Ehrenreich hesitates at the threshold; her imagination searches through secular models for similar sorts of self-replicating living things. Perhaps, she says, war should be compared with self-

steering computer programs, "'new life forms' that have no material substance at all; they are . . . programs that have been designed
to reproduce themselves, and in some cases, even to undergo spon-
taneous 'mutations.'"[60]

Or perhaps this autonomy should be modeled upon epidemiol-
ogy: war as always latent in the human arena, emerging according
to circumstances, and then contagious as wildfire. Another comparison she offers is with the unreined ravenous appetite of free-
market capitalism that has "a dynamism of its own. . . . The market
comes to act like a force of nature."[61] Or, this self-replicating pattern of behavior has been transmitted generation after generation
through the ages since humankind was a prey to a savage predator
and then became a savvy predator hunting enemy prey. Here her
comparison derives from the cynical speculations of Richard
Dawkins's "meme," a cultural entity like a biological gene whose
interests are purely and simply its own perpetuation.[62] War's self-
serving and self-steering autonomy is literally self serving; any
larger purpose for it, any positive value we may attribute to it and
gain from it is altogether a human business. War is for itself, only.
Wars of freedom against tyranny, warrior codes of chivalry and
courageous self-sacrifice, wars that resolve political disputes and
foster assemblies of peoples and states in common causes—these
are human derivates, accidental results of war's basic inhumanity,
not war's own intentions, because war is in essence sui generis, autonomous, inhuman.

To say this does not place war beyond human reach. Imagination
invents ways of dealing with the inhuman powers of nature and of
fate. As technologies can tame the natural sphere, so cultural rituals
of sacrifice, art, and propitiation can mediate the inhuman spirits
that impel fate. However, a prior acknowledgment is necessary before we begin imagining modes of taming and mediation. First, we
have to imagine the full reality of the autonomous inhuman.

Inhuman

This word bears a closer look. "Inhuman" and "inhumanity" in ordinary usage mean cruel, callous, brutal, merciless. "Inhuman" is a normative term setting standards for what human beings should not do and should not be. Inhuman acts refer to those below the standards that distinguish human nature from "subhuman" species, i.e., animals (hence "inhuman"—beastly, brutal, savage, and the many animal epithets applied to disapproved human behavior). As well, "inhuman" refers to acts without the humane blessings of conventionally described civilization. "Inhuman" and "inhumanity" further imply that the norm for a human being is *homo sapiens*: rational, reflective, societal, and civil. Consequently, war can be declared inhuman—even though it is fought only by humans and not by animals (insects the exception), and fought barbarously not by barbarians but by civilized, rationalized societies. Inhuman as the acts of war may be, it is an organized human phenomenon, even when only a cattle raid or an incursion to capture neighboring women.

The passages quoted earlier from Hobbes and Kant, Levinas and Foucault, show that war's "inhumanity" actually reveals it to be basic to human nature. The Ten Commandments recognize that to be human entails callous, brutal behavior, else why the universal injunction against lying, cheating, coveting, stealing, and killing?

So, what is it to be human? What is the central quality of humanity?

The Greeks had a word for it: *thnetos,* mortal. Humanity is mortality; mortality is the one inescapable universal truth of all human beings. We all die, have always died, shall always die—and we know this in our bones, a knowledge we assume other creatures do not have the same as we do. For other life forms, we assume, dying simply happens, though there may well be suffering in the dying and a sense of loss in others in the group. For us, however, death is given with the awareness of our natures, permeating our imaginations indelibly. Much of what we call "denial," "unconsciousness," and "health"[63] refers to deliberate forgetfulness of the innate knowledge of death. This death-knowledge is most likely the origin of religion from burial rites to sacrifice and ceremony, according to many authorities in this field. The idea that being human means subject to death restores the deeper understanding to the Greek maxim that epitomized Greek wisdom: "Know thyself," which is not merely savvy advice about self-examination of your personality, your deeds, and your motivations. Rather, know your essence; know you are only mortal, which at once restrains the Greek sins of *hubris* (overweening pride), excess, ignorance, and neglecting what is immortal.

Beings that are not subject to death are *athanatoi,* immortals, the term frequently used by the Greeks for their gods. If inhuman means immortal, "of the gods," war's incomprehensible behaviors can be attributed to the immortals, to the presence of an undying, eternal power and not merely to an absence of human virtues. Then war's inhumanity has an altogether different footing, and one that makes much more sense of its extraordinary "inhuman" behaviors and emotions. For instance, the fact that battles so quickly get out of hand, their outcome unpredictable. For instance, the importance of luck, a semi-divine figure the Renaissance addressed as Fortuna and Clausewitz called "chance." For instance, the luck of the weather that postponed D-Day, that prevented Allied sorties and favored the German breakthrough toward and beyond Bastogne, and MacArthur's luck with the tides of Inchon. For instance, Napoleon's oft-cited questioning about an experienced, well-recommended commander, "but has he luck?" For instance, the protective fetishes, totems, superstitions that may keep you safe or bring you luck, and the worldwide customs of haruspicy and the scrutiny of omens before entering into battle. War's unpredictability confirms the presence of its inhuman factor, the immortals.

This inhuman factor must also be taken into account in writing of war. War may be an autonomous phenomenon occurring throughout history, but it may not be subsumed under History as its turning point in decisive battles, the winnings and losings, the origins and consequences, the politics, strategies, and picayune antipathies of its leaders. Battle is the focus of war, and so it must be of war writing as in Marshall's *Men Against Fire* and Keegan's *The Face of Battle.* The study of battle can be severed from war and war from the grandiosity of human history. The writer enters the field of action more a psychologist than a general, a phenomenologist of the human in the midst of war's terrifying and chaotic inhumanity, to stare into the face of battle which is the inhuman face of Mars. The unending, worldwide bellicosity reflects the way of the gods who are themselves—at least the Homeric ones, and perhaps those of the Bible and the Koran too—always at war or in a warlike state, displaying that fundamental germinal principle: war as the father of all things. Our wars on earth must be understood in their divine right, and our impulses of brutality and callousness enact what is already present in the gods. Human "inhumanity" shows the gods in action—perhaps not each and all of the gods, but surely one, the god of war, Ares for the Greeks, Mars for the Romans. They have never left the earth in transcendence (as in some Protestant and mystical theology). They are not unknowable; not wholly other. The gods of war continue to reveal themselves, battling their way through history, drawing blood, scorching earth, and have been blamed for the history of wars through the Renaissance, the Elizabethans, the Romantics, and even into Vietnam as Shay reflects that war as a work of the gods in an all-too-exact enactment of Homer's *Iliad*.

Now we have another way of imagining this "self-replicating pattern of behavior, possessed of a dynamism not unlike that of living things."[64] Comparisons, however, with the predatory autonomy of free-market capitalism, a fictitious meme, or an endemic disease are insufficient because these models do not account for that crucial component of war that Ehrenreich, and this book too, is trying to imagine: "the uniquely religious feelings humans bring to it."[65] Secular models fall short in grasping war's attraction, its cult, and our terrible love for it, which occasion "the 'highest' and finest passions humans can know: courage, altruism, and the mystical sense of belonging to 'something larger than ourselves,'" yet, "we have invested these lofty passions in a peculiar kind of god indeed—an entity that is ultimately alien to us and supremely indifferent to our fate."[66]

In short, unless we imagine war as inhuman in the transcendent sense, inhuman as the autonomy and livingness of a divine power, war as a god, our secular models—as Susan Sontag said—cannot imagine and cannot understand. Now we can see that war's inhumanity derives from war's autonomy and that this autonomy reveals war's nature as a mythic enactment explaining both its bloodletting as ritual sacrifice, and its immortality—that it can never be laid to rest.

A "self-replicating pattern of behavior" echoes words used by Jung for defining archetypes: as well, he writes of them as dynamisms not unlike living forces that dominate human life, societal forms, and as timeless and omnipresent gods erupting into history.

Drawing down the gods into the discussion of war helps account for why wars are mythical, not coherent despite all their hyperrationality, not logical for all their reductions to structural oppositions, not human for all the analyses of their causes in human drives and errors. As Tolstoy said, none of these causes account for war; over and above is some unnamed force not unlike that of living beings.

This transhuman force shows up in the frenzy of combat; one man or a small group become possessed by what General Creighton Abrams calls "a crazy force."[67] A galloping horse can be its instigator, for as any rider knows, a horse can suddenly shy at a shadow or an invisible phantom, become possessed, and wildly panic. The error-filled bravery of the charge of the famous light brigade in the Crimea (1854) was an entangled madness of animal and man. "Horses, some of them uninjured, others with shattered jaws and torn flanks . . . were trying to force their way . . . —but the riderless animals . . . mad with fear, eyeballs protruding, the blood from their wounds reddening the lather around their mouths, they ranged themselves alongside Paget, alone in front of his regiment, making dashes at him [who] soon found himself in the middle of seven riderless animals which surged against him [and] he was forced to use his sword to drive them away."[68]

In Greek myth the horse was a gift of Poseidon (the stormy brother of Zeus), who ruled the oceans and the coursing unstoppable rivers; but it was Athene (daughter of Zeus) who gave the Greeks the bridle. In that Crimean "valley of death" we can recognize divine forces at work. Riderless horse, berserk without bridle.

Mastery of the horse—and Patton was an expert rider, a cavalryman who converted to tanks—means riding the back of unstoppable force by being one with it. Wild horsepower threatens the order of battle as it endangers the order of civilization. From the wild centaurs that menaced Athenian order to the fantasies of Amazons, of Huns, Mongols, Cossacks, to the four horsemen of the Apocalypse, the horse presents the devastating impetus of Mars in animal form. In the Field of Mars outside of Rome each October a proud horse was slain with a spear, offering the god that creature to which he is most akin. Rather than intimate participation with and thereby mastery by the cavalryman of the animal drive, myths of Asian asceticism give it over, as in the very ancient Hindu horse sacrifice (*asvamedha*) and the Buddha's abandonment of his horse, Kanthaka, all fury renounced.[69]

To go berserk means literally to wear the bear coat, from the Norse where *ber* means both "bear" and "bare" as naked, stripped to one's basic mammalian shape. "I became a fucking animal," reports a veteran to Jonathan Shay.[70] "I started putting fucking heads on poles. . . . Digging up fucking graves." Another says, "I was a fucking animal. When I look back at that stuff, I say, 'That was somebody else that did that. Wasn't me.'" Remember the earlier quote from Levinas? "War destroys the identity of the same."[71] "That was somebody else." Only a shell remains of the human person who consists of memories, feelings, words, needs for food and shelter. One participant in the Somme slaughter (1916) writes that it was so "impersonal that one cannot . . . feel any personal emotion. . . . Hope, revenge, anger, contempt: any of these would be a sustaining emotion in action but very few experience them."[72] Vigilant but dead. Death seems to want the *thymos* first, the emotional blood of personal life before death stiffens the body.

The Norse sagas named this death-trance condition "fey," meaning "doomed." Lee Sandlin describes it as "an eerie mood that would come over people in battle, a kind of transcendent despair. . . . They feel something in their soul surrender, and they give in to everything they've been most afraid of. It's like a glimpse of eternity."[73]

The berserk possession of fury takes over the human person differently. "Intoxication of utter fearlessness," "death was beside the point," "disregarding all caution," "I knew I couldn't be killed."[74] "I didn't give a fuck anymore. I didn't give a fuck about anything. They couldn't kill me. No matter what they'd fucking do."[75] "I could not come down from the high produced by the action. The fire-fight was over . . . but I did not want it to be over. So, when a sniper opened up from a tree line beyond the village, I did something slightly mad. . . . I walked up and down the clearing, trying to draw the sniper's fire. . . . 'C'mon, Charlie, hit me, you son of a bitch,' I yelled at the top of my lungs. 'HO CHI MINH SUCKS. FUCK COMMUNISM. HIT ME, CHARLIE.' . . . I was crazy. I was soaring high, very high in a delirium of violence. . . . I was John Wayne in *Sands of Iwo Jima*. I was Aldo Ray in *Battle Cry*."[76]

Commando Kelly, one of World War II's most known heroes: "You get so charged up that often you don't notice your injuries until the tension eases off."[77] "I felt like a god, this power flowing through me. Anybody could have picked me off there—but I was untouchable."[78] Among the immortals. Remember Kevin Costner early in the film *Dances with Wolves* furiously galloping back and forth between the facing lines of Blues and Grays, drawing their fire, contemptuous of death? Untouchable; or in touch with, touched by, the immortals. (The ancient Greek hero, like Hercules, was only part human; as son of Zeus he was half-immortal.)

The notorious German writer and militarist intellectual Ernst Junger describes in his diary the state of the soul as the last push of the German army in 1918 rises out of the trenches toward the enemy lines: "I was boiling with a mad rage, which had taken hold of me and all others in an incomprehensible fashion. The overwhelming wish to kill gave wings to my feet. . . . The monstrous desire for annihilation, which hovered over the battlefield, thickened the brains of the men in a red fog. We called each other in sobs and stammered disconnected sentences. A neutral observer might perhaps have believed we were seized by an excess of happiness."[79]

At Antietam in the ferocious fight in the Cornfield: "Some even noticed a queer phenomenon. Fearful at first of going into battle, some men found that when it began, they lost their terror and, instead, were seized by a peculiar fearlessness and compulsion heralded by everything in sight taking on a crimson hue. Literally, they 'saw red.'"[80]

This "incomprehensible" something "which hovered over the battlefield" General Patton could explain. He said: "Despite the impossibility of physically detecting the soul, its existence is proven by its tangible reflection in acts and thoughts. So with war, beyond its physical aspect of armed hosts there hovers an impalpable something which dominates the material . . . to search for this something we should seek it in a manner analogous to our search for the soul."[81]

Again that refrain: "incomprehensible"; "cannot imagine, cannot understand." Precisely this feeling of astonished confusion descended upon the generals and staff at the battle of Missionary Ridge as the Yankee troops climbed up the mountainside into well-prepared and well-defended positions of the Rebels, who held the heights with some ten thousand men. The Yanks had more than twice that number but the terrain was steep and the soldiers burdened. "Each carried a nine-pound rifle and around eighty rounds of ammunition, plus—this was November in the mountains—a heavy winter overcoat."[82]

> First one, then another, began going up the slope toward the enemy. It was mostly spontaneous. No arm dropped to start the troops forward, no command had been shouted, and no bugle blew. There went a squad suddenly . . . digging in, climbing up—then another, followed by a platoon here and a company there . . . junior officers yelled for these men to stop, but they soon caught the fever and joined the rush. . . . It was now an army of inspiration, not deliberation . . . caught in a dangerous mood of directionless adventure.
>
> Down below at Orchard Knob, Grant . . . foresaw the makings of a gigantic disaster. Sherman, on his left, had been trying all day to go up Missionary Ridge, but had been foiled and humiliated. . . . The blue army was trying to scale a wall in the face of overwhelming firepower. *Grant could see it!*
>
> "Thomas, who ordered those men up the ridge?" . . . Thomas said, "I don't know. I did not." "Did you order them up, Granger?" [asked Grant]. "No; they started up without orders."
>
> Grant began muttering, dissatisfied . . . Several general officers were not as cautious as Grant . . . they also sensed something infectious in the air, some mood.[83]

It is time we looked more closely into this power that brings men to feel they are immortal, this "red fog," this "impalpable something" hovering over the battlefield and permeating also the mood of this book. Let us be clear that each and all of the acts recounted were done by humans—not monsters, not aliens from another planet, not carnivorous dinosaurs, deathless robots, graveyard ghouls, or glistening rubbery creatures from a horror movie. You and me; the boy next door. Also, we didn't have to go back to Asiatic "hordes" at the gates of European towns, "red" Indians on the warpath, headhunters in "darkest" Borneo. These events of war were performed not by atavistic savages following the code of archaic rituals, but usually by trained troops from societies boasting civilized values, humane laws, moral education, and aesthetic culture. Nor were these acts specific to one nation—typically Japanese, typically American or German or Serbian—and therefore characteristic of its ethos. Nor were they confined to exceptional psychopathic criminals among the troops. No: this is what wars do, what battles are; conventions of rampage on both a monstrous collective and monstrous individual scale, implacable archetypal behaviors, behaviors of an archetype, governed by, possessed by, commanded by Mars.

The presence of this ancient god has been intimated from the beginning of this book; now we shall expose his nature more fully, starting off with the epithets or descriptive attributes and "nicknames" commonly used in Roman culture. *Caecus* (blind), *furibundus* (raging), *ferus* (feral, wild), *ferox* (untamable), *nimius* (overpowering, excessive), *insanus* (insane), *sanguineus* (bloody), *sceleratus* (accursed, profaned by crime), *rapidus* (swift), *subitus* (sudden), *atrox* (horrible), *calidus* (vehement), *lascius* (unrestrained, wanton), *hastatus* (spear-carrier), *cristatus* (cock-combed), *ultor* (avenger), *deprensus* (pounce upon, sudden seizure), *turpis* (foul, loathsome, obscene, disgraceful), *asper* (rough, bristling, shaggy), *confusus* (disordered, unarticulated), *saeuus* (savage, harsh), *priscus* (archaic, ancient).

Before Mars, there was Ares of the Greek pantheon, who too had his epithets: *androphones* (killer of men), *aidelos* (destroyer), *miaiphonos* (murderer), *brotoloigos* (fatal to mortals), and *krateros* (mighty; brutally, supernaturally powerful).[84] Others are: *tharsos* (audacity, courage), *lussa* (rabid), *menos* (life force; fierce passion, battle rage).[85] Following Girard's examination of *krateros,* we find it covers precisely the inhumanity we have been witnessing, which is un-understandable without the superhuman meaning of "inhuman." The violence of Ares *krateros* is a sacred violence because authorized by its inhuman proponent and ritualized in the altered states of the battlefield which "displays the conjunction of good and bad violence within the sacred." "Ares is no less divine for being cruel and brutal."[86] Battlefield as place of sacrifice; participation in a sacrament. The whole bloody business reveals a god, therewith placing war among the authentic phenomena of religion. And that is why war is so terrible, so loved, and so hard to understand.

"There are few real Ares myths," writes Walter Burkert, who today knows the sources better than anyone alive.[87] Ares appears in Homer's stories of the Trojan War, but there are few cult places, few temples, few descriptions of rites or mysteries, though warring armies dedicated sacrifices to him. Since the Greek states were so busily fighting one another, and the Persians, too, why is there so little about Ares? It is to be expected, since this god is not finely articulated. He presents himself in action rather than in telling. His legends and myths (tellings) are on display in combat and the sudden seizures of blind, insane fury. We have to think of Ares as a force rather than a figure, in the midst rather than apart. "The style of the Gods and the Gods themselves are one," said Wallace Stevens.

We tend not to think of gods in this ancient way. Our modern god of monotheism is a creator who starts things going and saves them, we pray, from going wrong. He is primarily a maker, the one and only maker; some philosophers have said a clockmaker who may miraculously intercede from time to time. We know what he thinks by studying his book rather than by hearing poetic myths and legends that make no claim to authority or truth and can't be taken literally. We believe, too, that this god of ours, despite all contrary evidence in dreadful events such as war, is fundamentally good. And he is omnipresent (everywhere), which also means nowhere in particular. This absence here and now is understandable to the pagan mind: there is too much ground to cover for one god—too many fields of action and kinds of relations. He can't possibly be everywhere at once. The god present in combat is not the god present in the strategy session (Athene) or in securing the home (Hestia). You wouldn't want Ares there anyway!

So, to think in the pagan way we would say: what happens on the battlefield is Ares; what men do to one another in war is Ares; the possession that makes one insane and inspired, furious and deathless all at once is Ares. The god does not stand above or behind the scene directing what happens. He *is* what happens.

As latecomers (twenty-five centuries or more) to the ancient world, our paganism radically repressed, we have to know the skew history has put into our eyeballs—the secularism that has no room for gods, the Christianity that doesn't like pagan gods, the psychologisms that reduce them to personal complexes and human fantasies. Our insights are slanted by our modern beliefs so that we tend to see what we already know, unable to see what looks us in the face: "the god in the disease" of war.[88] The modern imagination has been trimmed to fit the TV screen; unable to "imagine the real,"[89] unable to get out of the box.

Moreover, we do not approve of war; it's a "last resort" (which also implies that war belongs among first things as the final, most powerful, and ultimately determining real). Besides, we certainly do not like its god, preferring to imagine the god who justifies American wars in particular as a Prince of Peace, baptizing all war's horrors in the name of peace. We go to war "to end all wars,"[90] and our twenty-first-century battalions go abroad "waging peace."

The senior god of the Greek pantheon, Zeus, did not like Ares either—or so he says: "You are most hateful to me of all the gods: forever strife is dear to you and wars and slaughter" (*Iliad* 5, 890). Scholarship takes to the Zeusian perspective, neglecting altogether Homeric irony—for Zeus says this in the midst of one of the greatest and bloodiest chronicles of war of all time in which slaughters abound. It is a book of Ares, its characters, warriors; its language impassioned, physical; its scenes of combat ruthlessly cruel. Yet scholarship takes Zeus at his literal word. The major classical compendium by Farnell reviews what is known of Ares only at the very end of his five volumes, and then with disdain: "In the hierarchy of Greek religion Ares remained a backward god of most limited function, inspiring little real devotion and no affection, associated with no morality or social institution. The civilized art of war, so intimately connected with progress in culture, is not his concern. And the courage which he inspired was not the tempered civic courage exalted by Aristotle and other Greek moralists as one of the highest virtues, but the brute battle-rage, which might at times be useful, but for which the Greeks, who had left the Berserker spirit long behind them, had little sympathy. The monumental representations of him that can be called religious are very few."[91]

The "monumental representation" of Ares is the *Iliad* itself, as well as the Peloponnesian Wars, the wars of Athens and Sparta and Thebes and Corinth, and Alexander's Macedonians, and against the Persians. Ares is to be found not in isolate statues in secluded temples but in the "throng of battle," which is the origin of the word *ares.*[92] Besides, what statue, what temple can encompass his terrifying screams and his stretched-out length of seven hundred feet![93]

Another way scholars deny Ares' significance is by locating his origin in uncivilized Thrace, the imaginal place where Orpheus was destroyed and Dionysos found a barbarian home and also his dismemberment, a region away from the balanced golden mean of

Athenian law and order and Arcadian simplicity. Thus, Farnell asks: "Was Ares a genuine Hellenic divinity?"[94]

To the young men of Athens he most certainly was, for they swore upon Ares their oath to the city. And not only young *men*: the warrior Amazons honored Ares as their special patron deity, and the women of Tegea held a sacrificial feast (from which men were excluded) in the war god's honor. We may not forget that his mother—whom Kerényi says he resembled[95]—was the great goddess Hera, queen of the heavens and wife of Zeus, though Ares was not Zeus's son. Hera brought forth Ares out of herself alone in furious revenge against Zeus for his dallying escapades and prolific offspring. The war god, germinated in her fury, emerges from her wrath.

These tales must be recalled so as to obviate the testosterone hypothesis, that is, everything to do with bellicosity and militarism is the expression of male physiology, both the cruelty and the courage—it's all reducible to glands of gender. The myths and legends tell it differently: the spirit of war and the rage of battle are archetypal, forced upon all animal life, all gender, all societies. No gland can contain it. It is irreducible, a *Ding an sich*. It breaks out in matriarchal and matrilineal societies. No one is exempt. Women cannot hide from it, as its victims know, nor can they hide it. Not only legendary Amazons but modern women in power have been war leaders; women have clamored for admission to military academies and they serve the military with distinction, pride, and killing weaponry.

To imagine war to be a "man's thing," one more example of the abusive, self-inflating activity of "the patriarchy," traps one in the genderist division of the cosmos: all things are either male or female, *tertium non datur.* The genderist division takes on the absolutism of a logical opposition, an either/or which allows no space for the "both" of compromise and ambivalence, and androgyny.

This division then influences our fantasies of primordial societies, reducing war to an activity of violent hunter-gatherers versus gentle cultivator-weavers. If, however, we think about war as an emanation of a god, war as an archetypal impulse, then patriarchy does not originate war but serves war to give it form and bring it to order by means of hierarchical control, ritual ceremony, art, and law. Remember Foucault's idea that law is a continuation of war in another form. Patriarchy makes the forms. Rather than the origin of war, patriarchy is its necessary result, preventing Ares from blowing up the world and leaving a few poor remnants a life that is "nasty, brutish, and short." That this hierarchy, these forms can become tyrannical is evident enough, since cruelties of discipline are often secondary consequents of form. Nonetheless, patriarchal tyranny is not the primary cause of war; that cause is the god.

Ares had two sons who drove his chariot into the fray. We have already met them in the above accounts of battle behavior: *Phobos* (fear), from which our phobias, and *Deinos* (monstrosity), as in our *dino*-saur. *Phobos* shakes the soldier in the Sicilian tent, in the panic flight (*fuga,* Latin), those strange fugue states of wandering, lost, out of oneself. Dread and awe, wondrous and terrifying, present *Deinos.* These sons of Ares have recently reappeared under new names: Shock and Awe, as if the mind of the American nation's capital city, named after the military commander of its great revolution, had been seized by the sons of Ares. As drivers of the force, it is they who are responsible for the inhuman coercion that carries men into the killing zone[96] and the impersonalization that drives men to do what they do there. Field Marshal Haig, the supreme commander of British forces on the western front that averaged seven thousand casualties a day[97] during World War I, said, "Men are not brave by nature." Nor are they killers, said Hannah Arendt. In fact, far too many infantry grunts—to the worry of battle tacticians—never fire their weapons. Without Ares and his sons there would be no urge to battle, though there might still be wars, new kinds of wars: star wars, cyber wars, robotic wars (see De Landa), biochemical wars—wars that call for no bravery yet leave their cruel trails of blood.

A richer differentiation of the war god comes from Rome rather than Greece. Early in Roman history Mars was the second person of an archaic trinity of ruling gods (along with Jupiter and Quirinus),[98] and the thousand-year history of Rome is a history of a thousand battles. Recent writers on our topic mention Mars in passing but leave the reference bare. He is treated as a symbol and of the past. The epithets cited above portray a phenomenon of dreadful power, as do the characteristics assigned to Mars, the red planet, by astrology from Babylonia forward into the Renaissance.

This force had to be held from exploding into civil life. Today, psychologists speak of "anger management," naively believing that the martial fury is merely a trait of character belonging to person-alities with short fuses. The Romans felt Mars to be a collective danger and for their own security placed his cult outside the city walls in the "field of Mars." Even in Rome where Mars was a ma-jor divinity and Roman militarism fundamental to the Republic and the Empire the distinction between the civil and the military was clearly maintained, or at least kept in mind.

This distinction between civil and military is archetypal; it is as basic to society as that between priest, shaman, or medicine-healer on the one hand ("church") and king ("state") on the other. West-ern nations fear the "takeover" by a military junta and perpetuate the Roman distinction by keeping constitutional control over the mili-tary and the declaration of war in the hands of civilian authority.

Like the wall of separation that sets Mars in his own terrain is the cult that surrounds war and the work of war. The military have their own jurisdiction, their own courts, their own prisons; they obey their own codes, observe their own remembrances, march to their own music, care for their own graveyards. Cult is a major attraction of military service in a secular society. Hence the more free and open and unorthodox a society, the more inviting Mars, and the more valid war seems as a mode to purify and rectify, to set society on the straight and narrow path. The specifics of the cult serve as memento mori, because the cult of Mars, for all its nobility, is ultimately a cult of death. Mars brings wars and wars bring death. The civilian soldier doing his time only as an extra may not fully comprehend the hand of death in all the doings until he is called up and sent off. There at dockside, tarmac, or train platform as the units board for distant battles, death is in the parting. A sudden shift in the midst of an embrace—from life here on this side to the undiscovered country from where there is no sure return.

The geographical placement of Mars outside the city walls in a field of his own literalizes the psychic wall between the more human and inhuman areas of our being. Martial training aims to ice away or burn out altogether the more humane softness so that the recruit can get on with his inhuman duty, fix his bayonet. In the Sicilian tent Patton and the draftee were on different sides of the wall, and their conflict, because it is archetypal, has not subsided. The wall must hold for Mars to do his work, even if by the slow deadening process that kills the life of every trace in the heart of "back home." The god whom the soldier serves kills the "life-soul,"[99] and the trooper who survives comes home a revenant.

To say the god is in the style, the style is the god displayed, means Mars is thrust, like the forward, straight pierce of spear, lance, and bayonet. This style turns encounters, including ordinary human relations, into scenes of in-your-face close combat. That Mars is most vivid in immediate closeness raises a question that could shed doubt upon the prospect of this book as a whole.

Why dwell on this archaic god of war when war has moved on, when the entire action of battle has radically changed? Napoleon, Grant, Eisenhower, and Patton too, belong to another era. The fleets of dreadnoughts at Jutland, and the hand-to-hand death struggles at the front—all memories and movies. War is now either devastatingly high-tech and executed by skilled experts with their fingertips, or so small-scale that war is fought by a single person with a bomb under her blouse or a sneaky kid leaving a school bag at a bus stop. "When the Khmer Rouge marched into Phnom Penh . . . the first troops were teenagers. Young girls, young boys, some under fourteen years old, bearing very heavy portable rocket launchers. The girls wore hand grenades around their waists and across their chests like necklaces."[100] "I was ten years old when a Viet Minh convinced me to go to a secret school. . . . At night they took me into a cemetery, behind a gravemound where two people can sit unnoticed. . . . Sometimes they only train a child for one or two months before they send him somewhere with a hand grenade—inside the city or a marketplace."[101]

No more battle rage; cool. Different styles of war under the aegis of different gods with different styles of imagination. Instead of Mars/Ares, the strategies and political indoctrination of Athene, wars of words and leaflets, winning the hearts and minds, conversion to reason, and the long-term planning of countermeasures to the long-term planning of hijackers and plotters. Instead of Mars, Hermes: invisible and instantaneous Internet communications, undercover infiltration, code-breaking, jamming, surveillance with night vision, hearing through walls, bribes, gifts, rewards, and financial laundering.

Yet more threatening is the imagination of Apollo, "the far-darter," as he was called, who killed with arrows shot through the air: the imagination of distancing. Weapons far from the front, the front itself dissolved as war moves upward into the air, to satellites, outer space, transformed by the Apollonic imagination into nuclear visions brighter than a thousand suns.

Where the wars of Mars pit armies against armies on battlefields outside the city, acknowledge "open cities" preserved from attack, the Apollonic style makes war against cities, against civilians, against civilization—cafés, embassies, office towers—against water lines and power lines. Children in schools mere collateral damage.

Meanwhile, the technician sits in his shelter at the control panel and with the push of an orderly series of buttons fires missiles that can take out a town hundreds of miles away. He does not know the name of the place, the people, or see the flames. He has commendably done his duty, obeyed orders exactly, even though he is less an actual combatant than the civilians he has killed. Apollonic distancing. Apollo, remember, could not consummate his relations. He chased but failed in closeness.

The increasing distance between central command and actual engagement is not overcome by speedy communication. The feeling of distance between headquarters and front, between officers and men, that plagues armies with contempt and murderous hatred is reinforced by the Apollonic structure of vertical hierarchy. There is distancing in language with fancy names for special operations, acronyms for war and the places of engagement, and for casualties and death. It would seem Mars has been eclipsed.

Yet the ground must still be held under the soldier's boot. The dead must still be buried. No matter the distance, the abstract language, the covert operations, explosions still blast, firefights erupt in close quarters, house to house, street by street, roadblock, check-point, river bank, thicket. War comes down to ground. Beyond the violent occasions of martial action, the god is also there, and essentially so, in the will to fight, the love of war, the rush to win and the rush of winning. And the fanatic's sacrifice. Mars is the fire that tempers the men and melds them into a deployable team.

His is the vision of war as the last resort that is the final life-or-death determinant, or deterrent, within all strategies, subterfuges, and nuclearism. The impetuous passion of Mars makes war happen in the flesh and blood of history. If war were left only to Apollo or Hermes or Athene, war games, war plans, and maneuvers of the mind would be enough.

EXCURSION:

Down to Earth, Back to the Land

Could the land want war? Why is Ares also an ancient god of agriculture and Mars given his own field in the countryside beyond the walls of the city? When you try to understand the fury of the American Civil War and its somber enduring patient suffering that went on for four years, fought even in Florida and New Mexico—more than ten thousand separate armed conflicts that killed more than six hundred thousand men and boys—the reasons for it are not equal to its bloodshed. I have come to think that an immense inhuman factor was at work beyond the will and vision of Lincoln and the stubborn delusions of Jefferson Davis, and beyond the forces of history—political, economic, ideological, technological—beyond, or below, even the gods of war. So, I began to look at the battles themselves, going to the places where the supposed reasons for the war were enacted, the blood actually shed, and to the cemeteries where the remnants are interred. Instead of searching the minds of men for the reasons for these dead, I wondered if the earth that now held their bodies had asserted a claim to them. Is not the presence of the earth the underlying fact of battle; does not the field participate in the battle? Do not the cessations of hostilities often come about when demarcation lines are laid upon the land: this parallel or that; boundaries, borders, no-man's-land into neutral zone? Out of the land come great walls and forbidding fences. They stand; but the ideals the men fought for and the love for their comrades, the loyalties and miseries all vanish in the aftermath. What's left on the field are the fields and the invisible blood drained into the land.

Suppose the earth, Mother Earth if you prefer, demands blood. Suppose the slaughtered are like offered animals, their heads held down so the blood runs through a trough hollowed into stone, the pouring out of blood like a libation onto the earth; suppose the battles to be terrifying acts of consecration, the fields as sacrificial ground, the specific sites of intensity (marked in the guidebooks) altars. Suppose the entire American Civil War that has permanently marked the land and scarred the character of the American people was a sacrifice by a secular Christian society to a god or gods that had not been honestly remembered until the war, gods of the land, gods honored on that land and kept alive in that land by the peoples who had been there for centuries before the combatants donned the blue and the gray.

Suppose the gods in this "new world" soil were saying: "You may not land here; you cannot claim this land by labor alone, nor by law or treaty, nor even by expulsion of others and the rights of victors. To claim this land you shall pay for it with your own blood, and until you have paid you have not truly landed; you remain colonists, attached still in soul to another mother as refugees from her, rebels against her, secretly fawning upon her, and have not let this land bring forth its birth in freedom."

When historians write that the United States was born at Appomattox, they are confirming my supposition: the Civil War was our landing in America, a landing that took all of four agonizing years. Once landed and paid for, the earth gave itself with incredible generosity, receiving millions of immigrants, yielding up its ores, bearing the railroads, allowing the people to till and take whatever they wanted. Land grabs, land rushes, real estate spreads and holdings. The multiplication of such wealth!—so that within fewer than forty more years America became itself a colonial power. The treachery and genocide in the western plains that followed the Civil War and was carried out largely by its blooded veterans exemplified the colonialism. By means of the Civil War the earth taught its lesson: it will be the third, and silent, partner in every claim to property rights. Inheriting the land, surveying the land, tilling and mining and producing from it—especially producing by means of black hands, imported hands, manacled hands—does not convey entitlement, does not pay the debt. Only blood is the last full measure of devotion.

Sacrificial blood consecrates. Sunday morning's cup of wine brings back the fruit of the earth—and also the blood that must remain vivid in memory as taste on the tongue. The mass is a reenactment. Those reenactors dressed like their ancestors sleep all night on the fields where their Civil War ancestors slept, still sleep. Like the chorus in a Greek drama, the reenactors play their parts in our American epic and its subsequent tragedies of a nation divorced, in race, in class, in family, in soul, and in its central myth of separatism versus unionism that dominates our culture and has spawned both dignified movements and vicious passions. On an early September morning, the mist rising from the exhausted fields of Antietam, haunting reminiscences bring back the incredible valor of the dead. History becomes myth just off the highway; right here, a place of the *Iliad,* and the people know, coming here to walk and study, then raising public clamor to protect the sanctity of the battlefields from the disneyfication of tragedy.

The forces that grant the land, the land-granting authorities, are ultimately the invisible powers that reside in it, one of whom we saw above invoked by Susan Griffin. She wrote of the telluric queen worshipped by many peoples as a great mother who is the earth. Another lord of the land is Mars impelling the aggressivity of his agricultural implements and whose earth is always present in the mind of the embattled from grunt to general.

The earth as presentation of Mars was clear to Machiavelli, who insists the commanding prince "learn the nature of sites—to know how the mountains rise, how valleys open, how the plains lie, and to understand the nature of rivers and marshes—and in this to put the greatest of care . . . by means of his knowledge and experience of these sites, he will comprehend easily any other site that he may necessarily have to examine for the first time . . . this teaches one how to find the enemy, choose encampments, lead armies, prepare the order of battle, and lay siege to towns to your advantage."[102]

Below it all is the elemental earth to which the French

scientist of chemistry and scholar of imagination, Gaston Bachelard, attributes two basic attributes: Will and Repose. Bachelard's two volumes, written late in his life, researched the imagination of the earth element in language, literature, and thought. The mythic power of the earth activates human will. We dig and plow and blast rock from quarries, mold clay into bricks and turn rivers in their beds. The stuff of earth, says Bachelard, is like a primordial paste or dough inviting the imagination of the will to do something, make something, act. In Aristotelian philosophy matter and action are paired as opposites. Bachelard, however, sees the possibility of action already inherent in the matter beseeching the will to act. As well, earth inspires a countertendency: repose, cover, calm, quiet, interiority, depth, concealment, ashes, silence. Although Bachelard does not carry his poetics of earth into the battlefield, it is there that we find the two attributes of earth exposed in their extremes: the fury of battle and the repose of death. Battlefield and war cemetery: the poetics of will and repose.

What might be true for the American Civil War could also apply to Europe where the land has been given so much blood for so many centuries. Could the Pax Romana (going back only that far in time) which fed much of Europe's earth with warrior bodies have laced its soil with the martial spirit? Caesar's legions fought along the Aisne and Sambre, the Rhine. They battled and bled in Alsace, Trier, Aachen, Reims, Flanders, and into Belgium—places contested, fought over, died for, again and again, as late as World Wars I and II. War's seeds have been planted all through Germany where the Thirty Years War between kinds of Christians raged. The troops of Napoleon gathered from many nations marched from Spain to Moscow leaving their blood in the ground. Wars in the Balkans, in Poland; between the states and cities of Italy; along Europe's coasts where Normans raided and set down their towers.

Could the "carnage and culture" of which Victor Davis Hanson writes be so European in essence, unlike any other culture in the world, because one war nourishes the next? As the earth is fed war's blood, its blood soul remembers, addicted, insatiably needing more. We like to believe, following Hanson, that it is the specific quality of Western intelligence, combined with Western ideologies and forms of thought beginning with the Greeks, that has given Europe and now America their bellicose superiority. But could Western bellicosity be compounded through the ages because of what resides in its "civilized" land?

Look to the land of the southern United States. Despite the old generations and their families thinned out or gone, and the fact that the settlers in the big cities of the New South come mostly from the northern regions or foreign ports, the myth of the South, its "lost cause," its angry sense of abuse and militarism continue to inhabit its spirit. The fog of war hangs on as if rising from a soil that harbors belligerent seeds.

There is more buried in the ground than bodies, more danger lurking than from land mines. The earth germinates the dragon seeds of Mars and the fantasy of endless enemies springing up, ready to fight. Does blood transmute to paranoia? Marines learn their martial arts in the Carolinas and Virginia; the Air Force at their training centers in Texas, Alabama, and Mississippi. The Army's big training bases called "forts" are largely in Texas, Virginia, Alabama, Louisiana, Missouri, and the Carolinas. Military schools are mainly in southern states; Texas regularly produces proportionately more inductees than any other state.

Let me remind you of the myth of the dragon seeds. After completing a heroic task Cadmus, legendary king of Phoenicia, intended a thankful sacrifice to the gods, but he heedlessly sent his men to fetch water for it from a source sacred to Mars and guarded by him in serpent form. (Note the element of "heedlessness" already at the beginning of the tale.) The men arrived at the spring . . . But better hear the tale told by Ovid in the brilliantly martial version by Charles Boer in his translation of the *Metamorphoses* (book 3):

> *: old woods, never cut, cave in middle,*
> *low rock-sided arch, lots of sedge*
> *& willow, spring streaming forth: hideout*
> *of the Snake of Mars! gold-scaled & fire-eyed,*
> *body bloats poison: three tongues buzz*
> *through three tooth-rows*
>
> *a bad day, Cadmians, to set foot there!*
> *their buckets bang drawing water: long, blue*
> *snake-head wakes from cave hissing horribly!*
> *they turn white! drop buckets! bones shake!*
> *it coils scales in one enormous arc & leaps*
> *at least half its body height over entire*
> *forest! so big it could fit between Bear-stars!*
> *grabs Phoenicians reaching for weapons, running or standing*

too scared to run: bites, crushes, kills
some with sickening breath

sun now at highest, making thin shadows;
Cadmus wonders: what's delaying the men? investigates
(with lion-skin protection, steel-tipped spear,
knife, & better than weapons: courage!) in woods, sees
slain bodies & giant destructive snake-tongue
lick blood from awful wounds: cries, "Revenge
for your deaths, men, or my death too!"

he lifts rock so big it could crumble
tall towers; a mighty heave: throws: snake's
not scratched! saved by tough black skin's
scaly wall repelling blow; not tough
enough for spear through! he thrusts into coiled back,
plunges into flank: snake snaps head back
in ferocious pain to check wound, bites spear
& barely works it out from behind, forcing handle
from side to side: but steel stays buried in bone

really mad now! throat veins puff,
white foam froths poison jaws, ground
resounds when scales rip! black breath seems
out of Styx mouth, stinks & sickens air

it winds gigantic rolls & stretches beam-straight
slamming belly flood-force at trees in the way;
Cadmus yields a bit: lion-skin for defense;
his lance-jabs hinder jaws: enraged, it takes

tip in teeth, bites stupidly at steel: blood
& poison gush from throat, dyeing green grass;
but only slight cut: head writhes back,
refusing to linger over wound; yields ground
& keeps tip from going deeper; Cadmus at it,
driving iron into throat, backs it against oak & nails
neck to tree; tree bends under snakeweight
& groans, whipped by tail

Cadmus, the winner! checks out size of loser:
suddenly hears voice—where? (sure?) yes!
"Why stare at snake, Cadmus? one day
you'll be one too & stared at yourself!"

cold white fear; his hair stands up

suddenly Minerva, man's friend, glides through air,
arrives, tells him throw snake teeth
in torn ground to start new people: he does,
as if ploughing; scatters teeth in soil as told:
human seed: incredible!

dirt stirs: tops of spears appear in furrows;
colored helmet-crests nod; shoulders, chests,
arms heavy with weapons: a crop of shielded men!
like images on theater curtain, faces rising first,
then little by little the rest; finally feet

another enemy! Cadmus, horrified, prepares fight:
"No!" earthcreature cries, "keep out

of civil wars!" & hacks brother earthborn
with sword; but falls himself on spear; spear guy
doesn't live long either: soon breathes last
(just breathed first!)

These men come to life armed to the teeth, as also other versions tell, and their first perception regards each other as enemies. They are all sons of Mars, brothers born from his teeth, the hardest residue of the decaying body, the ultimate palpable substance of individual identity when all else is dust. The myth tells of the everlasting presence of war in our natures.

I can imagine the earth itself is angry, perhaps revengeful. Does it not bear the imprint of horses, of caissons, the years and years of marching feet? Does it not resent the waste of its topsoil, subsoil in the six thousand miles of trenches dug by the French army during World War I, and another six thousand miles by the British? German trenches were like an interlocked city, with levels, compartments, floorings. Do we owe the earth something, and how can the debt be ac-knowledged? It is as if the enemy has become the earth itself. What do the reports say: "Not a mile gained"; "no ground taken." And the officers shout: "Hold your ground!" "No-man's-land" states the truth: the earth does not belong to us.

Perhaps the cessation of hostilities begins with calming the earth, letting it rest in peace, giving the ground below its due with each footfall, our heads, now and then, slightly bowed, looking down. Maybe, before "going off" to war and sending in the Marines, we should consult the planet, and learn from its patience and slowness.

At the beginning of this book we raised the essential hermeneutic question: why can't we understand war? In his philosophy of hermeneutics (the study of interpretations) the profound German thinker Hans-Georg Gadamer asked the question more comprehensively: How is it possible to understand anything? What is understanding itself? A superficial meaning of hermeneutics reduces it to interpretation, and further reduces interpretation to translation. A closed door means a secret, an open tomb means a resurrection, and a penetrating spear is a phallus is a penis. We move through a series of equivalents that ignore qualitative distinctions. Or worse, we exchange an enigma for a simplification, passing by the lure of the unknown for the already known. We can leave perplexity behind and walk away at ease. But war does not let us walk away from it. We are desperate to understand.

Also above, we read Whitehead saying that understanding proceeds by penetration, pressing ever further and deeper, an interminable method like war without end. Mars is in the method by which he would be understood. Whitehead said that we never arrive at a complete understanding, which implies that something necessarily remains beyond human ken. In the case of war, something must remain unalterably inhuman.

We followed this method in approaching the American Civil War, attempting to imagine it from below. The usual analyses explore the deep mind of the battlers, from field marshals to berserkers. Our hermeneutics tries to penetrate the deep mind of the battleground. We worked toward a different perspective by starting not in the capitols of the states, their debates, their policies, but in the depth psychology of the burial grounds to learn from the slain.

To visit the dead for knowledge repeats a long tradition. The great teachers of culture entered the underworld to gain understanding, sometimes to rescue or repent. Ulysses, Orpheus, Aeneas, Ianna, Dionysos, Psyche, Persephone, even Hercules—all made the descent. Jesus too—but his purpose was to eliminate those depths. To go below is a capitulation to the earth and its inhuman darkness, a move into its will and away from our will. "Understanding involves a moment of 'loss of self,'" says Gadamer,[103] admitting that "we" can't understand. It is an unconditional surrender, a falling from mental superiority to a falling in with, going along with, the peculiarly devious paths of Hermes *chthonious,* the earthy aspect of the god of hermeneutics.

That strange guttural syllable, *chthon* (deep earth) as "that which covers"[104] seems to partake in the same base as the Akkadian *katāmu,* "to cover, to cover with earth," Hebrew *hātam* "to hide."[105] The hermeneutical method follows the downward path (*methodos* in Greek) of Hermes, attempting to get under the covers with war, share its darkening, occulting the kind of understanding that would clear things up. No attempt to get at the real cause, the true message by lifting the cover in a heroic style of muckraking to liberate truth. The true nature of things loves to hide, said Heraclitus, and to stay hidden.[106]

Because war does not yield to the human mind's day-world comprehension, it makes no evident sense—or it makes sense only invisibly, in terms of the buried powers and governing gods whom humans, on the field of battle, meet and at moments become. Therefore, ancient commanders turned to omens and oracles before battles to discover what was hidden from even the best intelligence. So, still, men imperiled in combat turn to prayer and amulet, invoking powers beyond their ken, recognizing that war is out of their hands, that it is a religious phenomenon, mystical, mythical. Whatever understanding we might have of war comes from imagining, and affirming, the presences who give war its inhumanity.

Chapter Three:

WAR IS SUBLIME

W E HAVE NOT DONE with Mars, and now we shall find him with his paramour, Venus. War and Love, battle and beauty, entwined. Right at the beginning of Western fantasy two millennia before our era in Crete, Ares and Aphrodite are configured together in Knossos and in Gortnya and Dreros.[1] Then, in Homer's *Odyssey* (book 8), you may read how they fell in love in the palace of her husband, the armorer-smith, Hephaistos.

The Sun, who sees all, observes them in their illicit dalliance, and tells the husband, Hephaistos, who is often depicted as a limping, introverted, sulky artisan.[2] He immediately plots revenge. The offense must go to the core of his marriage, for how can he with his deformity and heavy-handed drudgery hold faithful Aphrodite, goddess of physical beauty and pleasure, she who authenticates the world of smiles and guiles, promiscuity, seductions, sweet courtesans, and the delights of the senses! In his workshop Hephaistos devises a net of chains woven of invisible filaments and hangs them over the marriage bed. Then, pretending to leave the premises for one of his favorite retreats far away, he hides. The lovers, seeing their chance, rush to the bed, upon which the steel mesh falls. They cannot move, not an arm, not a leg; caught *in flagrante delicto.*

Hephaistos, enrages, shouts at them so loudly—(after all, not only is she his wife, but Ares is his brother, both born of Hera)—that all the gods gather around, that is, all save the goddesses, whose modesty keeps them at home. The gods stand in the doorway, observing, commenting, laughing. If the gods are there, we are there too, for we are lived by forces we pretend to understand, as Auden wrote. Our attitudes and observations are informed by archetypal patterns. The gods laugh to see the helpless pair caught in the brilliant device of the insulted husband, as we are amused by Homer's clever device within this chapter of the *Odyssey*—except for some scholars who have found the story to be a later inauthentic insertion into the narrative, declaring it "scandalous, ridiculous, indecent."[3] Their prissiness enacts the goddesses whose sense of shame keeps them out of the story altogether.

The gods speak among themselves about the bride price and penalties owed Hephaistos for this violation. However, when Apollo asks Hermes how he would feel being in Ares' place, caught and exposed, Hermes says he would be glad to change places with Ares, allowing himself to be likewise on view for all to see, if only he could lie with Aphrodite.

Again the gods break into laughter at Hermes' brazen admission—except for Poseidon "whom laughter did not touch" and who sets out to right the wrong and end the matter by offering to pay the adultery debt in behalf of Ares to Hephaistos. This was done and the two lovers spring apart each to a distant land.

What is this magnetic attraction? What does Love find in War; what beauty does battle afford? What does their copulation mean? To pursue these questions we have to take our cue from Hermes, who among the gods is the one able to enter the image with imagination,[4] taking the fantasy further by placing himself in it, caught by it, and willing to be foolishly exposed.

To be caught in the tale makes it psychological, which helps explain why Hermes is often called a *psychopompos,* guide of psyche. The tale is not merely another story about the gods which the ancient world could spin out and listen to endlessly. It tells not only about them, but also about us, not merely their mythology but our psychology. The characters in myths portray the characteristics of human nature, and psychology is mythology in contemporary dress. So, when the goddesses won't even show up, won't even consider the possibility that there can be beauty coupled with the savagery of war, their denial repeats our shamefaced embarrassment over our fascination with war films, with weapons of mass destruction, with pictures of blasted bodies and bombs bursting in air.

Apollo looks, but with a distant hauteur, disengaging himself by asking opinions. Poseidon looks too, but he is morally affronted, a surprising response in view of the fact that he is a major chaser in Greek myth, with offspring fathered through a wicked variety of copulations and violations. He is not at all amused. He becomes sanctimonious, legalistic. Is this too not a familiar reaction? Do we not try to draw fixed lines between battle and beauty so as to keep our violence violent and our love loving? In short, this little tale of gossip and titillation exposes ways of resistance to and participation in the love of war.

Understanding the fusion between beauty and violence, terror and love—the terrible love of war—is precisely our task. The distinctions between Mars and Venus (Ares and Aphrodite) as opposites and the reason for their mutual attraction as opposites is easy enough. Their natures seem so radically different that this pair is a familiar theme in poems and paintings through centuries. Mars hirsute, Venus smooth. Mars fiery, brash, savage, and red; Venus watery, pale, receptive, and secretive. Mars armored and shielded with earthbound feet; Venus unclothed, vulnerable, lightly grounded. Blood, iron, rams, and horses; roses, pearls, waterfowl, and doves. Mars is the god of rhetorical speed, galloping along in dactyls and anapests, while beauty lingers and, because it satisfies, beauty arrests motion, according to St. Thomas.[5] Thus they balance each other in a compensatory system of mutual concord, each fulfilling a gap in the other, expressed allegorically in the child of their union, Harmonia.

Great idols of war are supposedly given to Venusian pleasure, Caesar and Napoleon for instance, and Nelson too. Cleopatra, Josephine, and Lady Hamilton are essential to the heroes' legends. Great novels of war seem to call on Venus for their aesthetic satisfaction: *A Farewell to Arms, For Whom the Bell Tolls, War and Peace.* The Trojan War arises from the seduction of beauty. Caesar's accounts mention the impedimenta of camp followers. Elizabethan verse employs swordplay and battle as major tropes for the thrust and parry and final conquest of lovers tangled in the hay. Love lyrics speak of "killing" beauty, "slain" by beauty, of heart-stopping beauty much as American teenagers were wont to use the description of "drop-dead" for a gorgeous boy or girl who took your breath away. Even when Mars and Venus make conflicting claims they remain paired, as in *Carmen*: a soldier's duty deserted for his body's passion—and it can be vice versa: the body's passion deserted for the call of duty. Insuperable alternatives are simply another mode of pairing: "Make Love, Not War." Relief and recreation of the combat soldier—from battle to brothel to battle again.

Understanding the pair as opposites is too easy. Even should we sophisticate opposition into its various logics—contrasts, contraries, contradictories, complements, alternatives, polarities, reciprocals—or bring them together as coterminous and corelevant with each other, they remain distinct identities without inherent connection. We still have not got to the internal necessity of the coupling of Love and War.

Perhaps, our habitual mind-set can't think otherwise. We are schooled to believe that understanding results from definitions, each item clear and distinct. We have such hard-edge minds that we escape their narrow confines by falling happily, religiously, for fanciful scientific descriptions of fuzzy sets, indeterminacy and uncertainty, black holes, warps and waves and chaos. Perhaps our Western Christian literalism takes each thing by its word and for what it is and not something else (Mars is war and Venus is love and never the twain can merge). We seem able to think only in accord with our beliefs, atomistically, monotheistically, each thing to itself with a distinct identity, so locked into Leibniz's self-enclosed monads and Aristotle's logic of either/or that we are unable to follow Hermes into the bed of the image.

That bed, that image, belongs in the house of Hephaistos, in a mythical construct in a mythical cosmos of a polytheistic imagination. "Never, believe me, do the Gods appear alone," wrote Schiller during the German Romantic revival of the ancient myths, "never alone," from which Edgar Wind draws the principle "that it is a mistake to worship one god alone."[6] Our present plain style of single-minded unambiguity fails to grasp the "mutual entailment" (Wind) of mythical configurations. We prefer to imagine them each standing like statues in a museum, quite separated, with descriptive labels explaining their traits and domains. But they don't stand still and their domains overlap, since they are necessarily implicated in one another and complicated by one another. In fact, says Wind, complication rather than explication is the preferred method of polytheistic understanding. The pagan divinities are not merely polytheistic because there are so many of them, a multi-plicity of distinct units. They are multiple in essence, unable to be separated out from the multiplicity of their localities, their appear-ances, their names, and the internal confluence with their peers. Polytheism is necessary to their natures, inhering in their images; each is always all.

Mars and Venus are always in the bed of the image, even when the tale says they fly off and away from each other. They remain an inseparable archetypal conjunction. Where Mars is Venus will be. Love and beauty, seduction, glamour, and pleasure, intimacy and softness shall accompany Mars wherever he goes. These camp fol-lowers belong to his battle train. The world of war's horror and fear is also a world of desire and attraction. We have come to another place where understanding our subject is again most baffled: war's beautiful horror, its terrible love and exhilarating fusion called the sublime.

I take my first notion of the sublime from a line in Words-worth's *Prelude*: ". . . and I grew up / Fostered alike by beauty and by fear."[7] And from the fearful symmetry of Blake's "Tyger":

THE TYGER (CONDENSED)

Tyger! Tyger! Burning bright
In the forests of the night,
What immortal hand or eye
Could frame thy fearful symmetry?

In what distant deeps or skies
Burnt the fire of thine eyes?
. . . .

And when thy heart began to beat,
What dread hand? & what dread feet?

What the hammer? what the chain?
In what furnace was thy brain?
What the anvil? what dread grasp
Dare its deadly terrors clasp?

When the stars threw down their spears,
And water'd heaven with their tears,
Did he smile his work to see?
Did he who made the Lamb make thee?

. . . .

(WILLIAM BLAKE)

EXCURSION:

The Catalog of Horrors

It becomes more understandable now why I have had to present so many pages of terrible deeds, and why most writers on war dwell on the naked and the dead as Mailer called his great war novel (1948). I had believed it is our way of "working through" the trauma we know as war, trying to contain its blood in our words: writing as sublimation. But now I recognize the fascination, the delight in recounting the dreadful details of butchery and cruelty. Not sublimation, the sublime.

Partly the reason for the dreadful details is that Mars demands this from us. I like to think he asks to be spoken about, spoken to, in his own style. Any phenomenon inhabited by a particular god must be addressed in the rhetoric of that god. Aphrodite is not present in a sex education course or a sex manual; the language itself must seduce, flatter, and amuse. Neither logical argument nor positivistic evidence carry messages from Hermes; there must be ellipses, reversals, and the lucky strikes of ungrounded intuitive leaps. So, Ares is loud and bloody, demanding from the recorders of his deeds the gruesome display of victims and the language of excess—those huge numbers of casualties, vast armadas, cannons and horses. An archetypal psychology varies its writing style to accord with its topic, following an age-old aesthetic principle of unity, not merely unity within the work as a whole, but an unwavering uniformity of topic, tone, and voice. The rhetorical conformity of an archetypal psychology conceives style to be in service to something further than the reader's pleasure and the writer's vanity. A kind of therapy goes on, a therapy of language. *Therapeutes* referred originally to those in service at an altar or in a ritual; they were caretakers, ministering to the needs of an impersonal, archetypal power. In the case of Ares, the cup runneth over with wrath and blood.

There is, as well, a more personal background to the exhibition of so much brutality in this book. I confessed in an earlier excursion to being a "child of Mars," as the Renaissance humanists described basic kinds of characters with names from the planetary gods. An affinity with martial rhetoric is natural to my method. My path in life and way of being calls up enemies. I like to sharpen oppositions and set fire to the passions of thought; I take pleasure in cracking numbskulls. (Mars finds dumbness everywhere because he is so dumb himself.) It is as if there is a native need to be at war, as if I must enact Heraclitus and not merely consider his words as "ancient Greek cosmology." War thus becomes my constant season of spring, of April, Mars's month; "april" phonetically consonant with *aperire* (to break into, open), aperture, *apertus* (revealed, unprotected, exposed, laid bare, in broad daylight; glaring, flagrant); *apricum* (the light of day, a sunny place); apricot with the connotation of *praecox,* early. And *aper,* the boar; *aperinus,* of a wild boar. April, opening by breaking into, the violence of awakening; slicing plow-blades like the tusks and snout of the boar; spilling hot spermatic seeds, the beaks of ravenous birds and stinging insects returning to feed on the buds blindly forcing their way into daylight. The cruelest month, infectious with the disease of profligate intensity.

A passage from Foucault may more rationally explain the martial need and the martial method: "For Nietzsche, Bataille, and Blanchot, experience has the function of wrenching the subject from itself, of seeing to it that the subject is no longer itself, or that it is brought to its annihilation or its dissolution. This is a project of desubjectivation." Foucault goes on: "however boring, however erudite my books may be, I've always conceived of them as direct experiences aimed at pulling myself free of myself, at preventing me from being the same."[8] What did Levinas say about war? "It destroys the identity of the same." Or, as the British soldier at the front wrote his wife: "I am all right—just the same as ever, but no that can never be . . ." "Which means" (Foucault again) "that at the end of a book we would establish new relationships with the subject at issue: the I who wrote the book and those who have read it would have a different relationship with madness, with its contemporary status, and its history in the modern world."[9]

In this book the madness is war, and a book on war seeks what war achieves: destabilize, desubjectivize, destroy. The writer comes out of the book a casualty, and the reader too, or at least all shook up. "For Nietzsche, Bataille, Blanchot . . . experience is trying to reach a certain point in life that is as close as possible to the 'unlivable,' to that which can't be lived through. What is required is the maximum of intensity and the maximum of impossibility at the same time."[10]

War declared itself the subject of this book, drawing me into an initiatory rite of my later years because war demands a maximum of intensity and impossibility. To write of war is to reach as close as possible to that which can't be lived through. This effort of excess for a Neoplatonist, liberal, democrat, bourgeois, PhD, overage psychoanalyst is a move from sublimation into the sublime.

I had tried to cross this threshold before with my first destabilizing book, *Suicide and the Soul,* and again with a descent into Hades via *The Dream and the Underworld.* These were indeed entries into the sublime, but viewed with the eyes of the soul. Mars has no eyes; it is all engagement. His death-knowledge, and the terror of being led by him, lies in the ultrarapidity of the doing. "The fact is I think I am a verb," said General Grant at the end of his life. Advancing, advancing, despite the thickets and the din, like Patton— which helps account for why that general figures as a red thread marking these pages. Breakneck speed and then after all battles were done, Patton laid flat by a car crash to end immobilized on a hospital bed with a broken neck.

Therefore this catalog of corpses and rapes and body parts. Only these take us below the skin and below the mind of rational understanding and the retrospective mirror of fact-finding and figuring out. Below also the teary vision in the mother's eye and the lover's eye that beholds us human creatures as children of a good god's redemptive love; below the comfort zone of trust in our best selves with virtues at the core of our substance, rather than sinews and intestines propelled by unlivable relentless forces like the tanks called "tigers" carrying their crew into battle, their sacrificial Lamb going on before.

Sinews and intestines under the skin. "It is no longer possible for me to speak, my tongue is broken, a thin fire runs underneath my skin. There is no sight in my eyes, my ears hum, sweat pours down me, trembling seizes my whole body. I am paler than the grass, and I seem little short of dying."[11]

This oft-cited passage used to exemplify the sublime comes from the treatise called "On the Sublime," written in Greek in the first century of our calendar.[12] The unknown author is conventionally named Longinus and the work has become the classical point of departure for thinking about the styles of expression and the psychological experiences called the sublime.

Does the passage quoted from Longinus's treatise refer to a soldier after the clash of combat or one just about to enter the field of battle? Is it the earliest witness to shell shock? Or does it perhaps describe the experience of one lying wounded among his fallen comrades? None of these; nothing to do with war at all. This seizure of the sublime comes from a poem by Sappho, wounded by Aphrodite's divine desire. Ares and Aphrodite indistinguishable.

Death and loveliness held in one vision. A German soldier on the western front in 1914 dreams: "I came into a room and a beautiful, ravishing woman advanced to meet me. I wanted to kiss her, but as I approached her I found a skull grinning at me. For one moment I was paralysed with horror, but then I kissed the skull, kissed it so eagerly and violently that a fragment of its under-jaw remained between my lips."

It is this fusion that makes war so spectacular and terrible, brutal and transcendent within a single moment. To the civilian imagining the land mines underfoot and stabbing bayonets it is un-understandable that so many engaged in war write of beauty, of spectacle, aesthetic delight, and use the word sublime. "Yes, the chief aesthetic appeal of war surely lies in this feeling of the sublime."[13] "The combatant who is relieved from participation and given the spectator's role can nearly sate the eye with all the elements of fearful beauty."[14] Moreover, "men expose themselves quite recklessly for the sake of seeing."[15] Remember the opening of Coppola's extraordinary war film, *Apocalypse Now*. A spectacle of intoxicating power; bursting the limits. When the first nuclear blast blazed its mushroom into the heavens, there flashed in the minds of observers images from Grunewald's resurrecting Christ and holy script from the Bhagavad Gita.

For some, the war years were the "one great lyric passage in their lives."[16] "I shall always remember above all other things in my life the monstrous loveliness of that one single view of London . . . stabbed with great fires, shaken by explosions, its dark regions along the Thames sparkling with the pin-points of white-hot bombs, all of it roofed over with a ceiling of pink that held bursting shells, balloons, flares and the grind of vicious engines. And in yourself the excitement and anticipation and wonder in your soul that this could be happening at all. These things all went together to make the most hateful, most beautiful, single scene I have ever known."[17]

The bombing of London in 1940 impressed Malcolm Muggeridge similarly. Sometimes together with Graham Greene he went into the streets. "I remember particularly Regent's Park on a moonlit night, full of the fragrance of the rose gardens; the Nash Terraces, perfectly blacked-out . . . white stately shapes waiting to be toppled over. . . . I watched the great fires in the City and Fleet Street. . . . It was a great illumination, a mighty holocaust: the end of everything, surely. . . . I felt a terrible joy and exaltation at the sight and sound and taste and smell of all this destruction."[18]

From the chopper, says a fresh rifleman coming in over the rice paddies of Vietnam, "it looked so beautiful. But at the same time I was scared to death."[19]

As the Allied armada moved toward the North African beaches, Ernie Pyle wrote: "Hour after hour I stood at the rail looking . . . and an almost choking sense of beauty and power enveloped me."[20] A member of Patton's staff in Sicily wrote to his wife: "And speaking of wonderful things . . . [t]he high water mark—and perhaps the most beautiful as well as satisfactory sight I have ever beheld— was a flaming enemy bomber spattering itself and its occupants against the side of a mountain. God it was gorgeous."[21] Hateful and beautiful in a single scene. Exaltation at all this destruction. Others write: "the combination of sound and color . . . had a kind of wicked beauty."[22] William Manchester in Guadalcanal refers to Baudelaire's *Fleurs du mal*. "It was a vision of beauty, but of evil beauty."[23] Leon Uris sees Guadalcanal as "the body of a goddess and the soul of a witch."[24]

The British often call a raid or skirmish, even a full-scale battle, a "show." They are right not only because of the English gift for theater but because war is spectacular. A spectacle for all the senses, but especially the eye, which captures the scenes and resurrects them into images. War feeds on and is fed by imagination. Long before enlistment, the images of propaganda and the war games of children have already set the stage. Afterwards, war becomes literature, movies, and is imagined even in its midst into poems and thoughts and tales. The eye cannot help but see: "It must not be forgotten that we imagine with our retina," wrote Bachelard.[25] "Imagination is the faculty," not of forming, but of "deforming the images offered by perception."[26] War offers perceptions already deformed, an imaginative scene just as it is. So witnesses say: it was unreal, fantastic, unimaginable, because war's very explosive unpredictability is imagination itself displayed. "If an occasional image does not give rise to a swarm of aberrant images, to an explosion of images, there is no imagination."[27]

The goddess in the arms of Ares makes her presence known mainly by aestheticizing. "A moonlit night, full of the fragrance of the rose gardens," remembers Muggeridge. A young German near Verdun in 1915 writes: "The moon shone into my mug . . . only now and then a bullet whistled through the trees. It was the first time I had noticed that there can be some beauty in war—that it had its poetic side."[28] Southeast of Ypres another German writes about decorating his trench: "from a pinewood close by, which had also been destroyed by shells, we dragged all the best tree-tops and stuck them upright in the ground. . . . Out of the ruined chateaux, we fetched rhododendrons, box, showdrops and primroses and made quite nice little flower beds."[29] Aphrodite, the lovely one, the smiling one, as she was called, prompts the loving letters to a wife who was hardly known and never loved before. She roofs over Ernie Pyle's scene "with a ceiling of pink," and she is that indomitable something that dominates the material which Patton compares with the soul, much as Plato and Plotinus in another age identified the soul of the world with Aphrodite *urania,* the goddess of the upper spheres and the uplift of love. To the blood of war, she brings the aestheticizing imagination of war.

Pink is the prettier part. There is as well the shudder that Sappho feels, the exaltation at the vast panoply of battle formations, gleam of gunmetal, start-ups of clanking tanks, the surge of joy amid the chaotic rush, and increasing sexual intensity while waiting on picket at night. Attacks begin at the first blush of dawn, the hour of the handsome, amorous, divine Eos. Aphrodite raises the dead into beauty with a few lines by Wilfred Owen and Rupert Brooke. She makes Patton dress up for killing the bastards. Without her, there is no sublime.

The idea of the sublime as an aesthetic phenomenon akin to but distinct from beauty entered modern discourse also via the eye. Longinus was incidental, a text for professors of classics and rhetorical style, because his treatise focused mainly on writing and speaking in an elevated, inspiring manner. Boileau's translation and reflections (1674) on Longinus did not deeply touch the latent romanticism of the English soul. The sublime as a stunning concatenation of the baleful and the beautiful in one elevated moment came from nature, from the earth.

In 1688 an English writer, John Dennis, crossed the Alps into Italy and published what he saw of mountains, precipices, raging waters "that made all such a Consort up for the eye . . . in which Horrour can be joyn'd with Harmony."[30] Sights of alpine nature produced "in me a delightful Horrour, a terrible joy, and at the same time I was infinitely pleased, I trembled." The influential essayist Joseph Addison on his Grand Tour southward wrote of an "agreeable kind of horror" in the nature of the mountains, and he advanced the idea of the sublime further into the vast, the great, stupendous, unlimited, perceived by the eye and strongly affecting the imagination.

As these nature-embedded sprouts of romanticism and the gothic began to burgeon in the English psyche, the sublime reincorporated the literary descriptions of Longinus, and the Horrour overpowered the Harmony until they all but divorced into long-standing antipathy. It was a nineteen-year-old student at Trinity

College, Dublin—Edmund Burke—reading a paper before the philosophically inclined, who drove in the cleaving wedge between the sublime and the beautiful: "whatever is in any sort terrible . . . is a source of the sublime, that is, it is productive of the strongest emotions which the mind is capable of feeling." "All general privations are great because they are terrible; Vacuity, Darkness, Solitude, and Silence."[31] Harmony, agreeable delight, joy, "transporting pleasures" were relegated to Beauty and qualified as smooth, small, delicate, familiar, rather like objects and events we now call pretty. On the other side loomed the Sublime, evoking fear and trembling, and qualified by roughness, great size, difficulty, menace, magnificence, and the awe-ful. "The passion caused by the great and sublime in *nature*," writes Burke, "is Astonishment . . . that state of soul in which all its motions are suspended, with some degree of horror . . . the mind is so entirely filled with its objects, that it cannot entertain any other."[32] For Burke, at nineteen, the sublime was also linked with the more "strenuous purposes of heroism."

Some forty years after Burke, Kant moved reason from its alignment with beauty to the deeper possibilities within the sublime. The valences changed; aesthetic satisfaction resonates because of the sublime, it is a "negative pleasure." This second level adds reflection, thought, structure to the merely pleasing or beautiful. "By infusing the sublime into the beautiful as if to hide it there, Kant laid the basis for the Romantic sense of beauty as an awesome and heart-stopping universal force that stands over the entire universe as a kind of ultimate principle."[33]

This historical digression may help grasp what the witnesses in the midst of bombardment are declaring by saying war is sublime. They are not saying it is only terror; they are not feeling only fear. Nor are they claiming in the manner of sadistic fascism that cruelty is an aesthetic delight. They are with Dennis and Addison, and with Kant in reverse—inside the horror is a spectacular beauty, a beauty of another order. More: inside the utter chaos there is a structure of meaning, of meaningfulness, not to be found any-where else. When an observer such as Sontag stands before the hor-ror finding it beyond understanding and beyond imagining, she is bearing witness to the sublime, a revelation of "an awesome and heart-stopping universal force . . . a kind of ultimate principle," which here we are discovering is war itself.

So we ought not be surprised by the relevance for our theme of the words of these intellectual aestheticians from Longinus through Addison and Burke to Kant. The sublime "forces its way to the sur-face in a gust of frenzy." Images "of War and Havoc and Terror, the lover of blood" reveal the sublime which is characterized by "fire and vehemence of spirit." McEvilley, who assembled these passages from Longinus, sums up his vision in one sentence: "The sublime is sheer chaos, beyond reason, beyond finity, beyond order."[34] Yet alluring with its own beauty, following Kant and pronounced by Wordsworth: "Fostered alike by beauty and by fear."

EXCURSION:

Another Personal Part

Following the trail of war this closely has raised a few more peculiar pieces of biographical memory, releasing them from attachment. In the early 1950s before the south-ern Sudan (Malakal, Juba, Tonj, Wau) was torn by genoci-dal war, I passed two months among the Shilluk, the Dinka, and the Nuer. Warriors. Their stance, their lean nudity, their scars—can I say, their cool—held me in a kind of embarrassed thrall. For three nights camped by the Nile near Terakeka, the Mandari held a tribal gathering of their branches. Spear-throwing contests, tubs of millet beer, incessant drumming, drunken firelight dancing. Ex–college white boy felt the "power."

Still in the 1950s, while I was pony-trekking from the valley of Kashmir north into the high mountains, a tribes-man, probably from Gilgit, or a Pathan, came down the trail on his horse as we were climbing. Thin, hawkish, black beard, a lot of red in his blanket and dress. This single fear-ful moment on a steep trail remains vivid. Again the fierce gravitas, the distinguished high-held head and observing, yet diffident, look. We passed each other in silence.

What was I doing in these places, what was I after?

What makes me watch TV boxing? It began early, on the radio, the imagination of jabs and uppercuts when I was seven or eight. Of all the useless trivia to have stamped into the mind are the names of the heavyweights: James J. Brad-dock, Max Baer, Jack Sharkey, Billy Conn, Tony Galento, and the famous Schmeling-Louis fight. That puny kid (with glasses) already in training for this book on combat. How else understand it. Doesn't *The Soul's Code* say to read life backwards?

Why did I land on Ireland to study, have Irish roommates before that, close Irish friends? That place of wildness, fear, and beauty, pub nights ending in fistfights (I held coats). Ire-land—land of the free and home of the aesthetic brave. Why do I stand in awe under the flags in war museums? The war memorial in downtown Cleveland with its images and names has lasted longer in my memory than their fine mu-seum of art. I began collecting books on war thirty years be-fore beginning my own.

Puzzling pieces constellated by this book must belong to this book. Why the trepidation in telling? In view of my personal predilection or obsession with the alluring dignity of warriors, there may be something beyond coercion that keeps men on the battleground. Though coercion forces them to stay, what gets them there to begin with? Does the sublime figure into it? Is that how I now might read my own pale adventures?

I recall when I was twenty hearing from a good friend who had cracked up in officer's training school about the "Test," searching for that moment or encounter that would be a decisive defining point. I vaguely remember his saying the idea came from Christopher Isherwood. The "Test" had not entered my mind until this writing on war, perhaps prompted by the phrase "The Supreme Test," often used to describe initial combat. Since the Isherwood idea comes to me only now, it must be bringing something to this subject, and bear on my relation with the sublime.

Despite the vagueness, I do recognize the effect of the idea then in accounting for my restlessness and hunger. It made sense of my extra-vagances, wide vagaries, looking for strangeness and surprise. Going around small towns in Mexico with a friend on buses and wooden-benched trains, drawn to crossing borders (into Guatemala, El Salvador) at sixteen or seventeen; hitchhiking sometimes at night on long-haul trucks during the war, up from Laredo to home in the Northeast. I kept a rock in my pocket—just in case. One piece after another rises from dimness, out of the closet of chagrin over one's youthful foolishness. Yes, I had to wander from the train at the Turkish-Bulgarian border in 1948 (a dangerous year in the Balkans), to be picked up and later placed under house (hotel) arrest for six days. Exhilaration and fear, the interfusion of the exotic and the terrifying. Preludes to this chapter?

What is this mythical test? In my case not a hero's quest to recover a grail of great importance, to meet the master of enlightenment, to save a maiden pinned to a rock. I was not brave enough, even if foolhardy. Not on a fool's picaresque journey either, on the road bumping along, let's see what happens next. No, I was too purposeful and wanted too much. I was always "heading" out. Was the test an imagined overcompensation for my physical weaknesses and cowardice? Was I a Lord Jim (which I had also read early) who would fail when the moment came, or D. H. Lawrence driven to escape to the foreign in order to find his own?

What then may have been looking for the test, now comes to mean a search for the sublime. Not to test myself, but to encounter that place, that moment of amazement, to be elevated by traveling to the edge of the bearable where one is filled with fear. Is this longing for the sublime what draws men to war, and drives war journalists addictively to one war after another? When I read the philosopher Alphonso Lingis's two extraordinary books *Abuses* and *Excesses,* which recount his going to the ends of the earth and to extremes with exotics, fanatics, and freaks, is he not testing himself against the sublime? He too seems to be following the path Foucault (above) describes as indicated by Nietzsche, Bataille, and Blanchot "to reach a certain point in life that is as close to the unlivable . . . the maximum of intensity and maximum of impossibility at the same time."

My references here have been literary: Isherwood, Lawrence, Conrad, all the way back to Richard Halliburton. The aesthetic as vehicle of the test, the test as aesthetic adventure. In my case the aestheticism of the sublime emerged from my juvenile heroics during a stay in a Swiss TB sanitorium and the encounter with the sublimity of sickness and the authors of sickness. Up there in the pure air and sunny cold I read both *The Decline of the West* and *The Magic Mountain,* studied *The Waste Land,* and began Proust. This was a very different search for the sublime—the languid beauty of reclining among international patients in dreadful states of decay, mixing morbidity and courage, sputum and erotics. The rough travels and difficult encounters, and the beauty, happened in books; and the test turns out now to be this book, this very chapter in which my history comes out of the too personal closet of chagrin at youthful overreach.

The test continues here. It does not belong only to youth. Now its challenge is standing in my history, for my history with pride and pleasure, an old veteran on parade whose wars were "only" psychological.

Rocky gorges and thunderstorms may have helped invent the modern idea of the sublime, but today you may pick up a fearful beauty that holds Ares, Aphrodite, and Hephaistos all together in a fine piece of metalwork at your local gun dealer. Like the steel net that entrapped the lovers, the weapon is another Hephaistian instrument holding beauty and violence in permanent embrace. Uzi and Colt, Luger and Beretta are contemporary idols: you can hold the gods in your hand, carry death in your purse. Hannah Arendt made the important point that violence depends entirely upon instruments, and the prime instrument that ensures that each individual's life may be solitary, nasty, and short, and at war with every other individual, the instrument that re-creates the original condition of the Hobbesian person, is the handgun.

The legislative and judicial battles over gun control epitomize larger ones of disarmament in general. Research in this field shows a profound psychological resistance to disarmament, as if firearms are unconditionally necessary to the idea of the nation-state and, in the USA, to the citizen of that particular nation-state. The fond belief (verging on paranoia) that one is solely responsible for one's own salvation and that self-preservation is the first law of nature (Protestant Darwinism) in a mobile, anomic, class-ridden society may provide grounds for American volatility and insecurity, but not enough ground to account for the American idolization of the gun.

There must be a myth at work. It is as if the gods have combined to manufacture the guns, are in the guns, as if the guns have become gods themselves. The spear that stood at a Roman altar to Mars was not a symbol; it was the god. When Ulysses and his son hide the weapons from the crowd of suitors with whom they soon do battle, Ulysses reminds his son of the magnetic power in the weapon, "since iron all of itself works on a man and attracts him."[35]

Human beings love their weapons, crafting them with the skills of Hephaistos and the beauty of Aphrodite for the purposes of Ares. Consider how many different kinds of blades, edges, points, metals, and temperings are fashioned on the variety of knives, swords, spears, sabers, dirks, battle-axes, stilettos, rapiers, tridents, daggers, cutlasses, scimitars, lances, poinards, pikes, halberds . . . that have been lovingly honed with the aim of killing. We keep them as revered objects, display old battle tanks and cannon in front of town courthouses, convert battleships and submarines into museums through which tourists stream on Sundays, build gun cabinets in our homes, trade weapons at Sotheby's. How foolish to believe we can enforce licensing and regulation. No society can truly suppress Venus.

As emblem of both death and love, of fear and care, the sublime weapon du jour is no longer the sword over the mantelpiece or the flintlock behind the grandfather clock. It is the handgun in the drawer of the bedside table. Along with sex toys and condoms, the handgun belongs as much to Venus as to Mars. And if to Venus, then to Venus we shall have to turn for "gun control," since only that god who brings a disorder can carry it away.

Venus *victrix* states a fact: Venus will out. She will be victorious and she cannot be suppressed. Prostitution is the oldest profession and blue laws have never been able anywhere to extinguish the red-light district. When suppression does rule for a while under fanatic puritan literalism, the goddess goes to compensatory extremes. She returns as a witch in Salem or in epidemics of hysteria afflicting entire convents. The Taliban keep girlie magazines. She infiltrates the Net with pornography and the free-marketing of children for pedophiles. Or she unleashes sadoerotic cruelties in revenge for her suppression in prisons, schools, and offices.

We must try to enter this love of weapons. Rifle as friend, companion, trusty comforter; no teddy bears here. When the ragtag Rebel soldiers lined up for the last time for surrender at Appomattox, they stacked their rifles. Men kissed their guns good-bye, bid them farewell,[36] spoke of them as their "wives" on whom they had relied during the long years. "Marry it man! Marry it! Cherish her, she's your very own," quotes Paul Fussell from an epic poem of World War I.[37]

Curiously, however, and to the dismay of the high commands, men love their guns but for the large part do not use them in combat. Statistics drawn from American inductees in the Second World War are staggering: perhaps only one in four riflemen uses his weapon in battle, and this fact has been found to be generally true through a variety of wars among Western nations with conscripts. One of war's most thoughtful authorities, S. L. A. Marshall, says, "the average man likes to fire a weapon and takes unreluctantly to instruction on the [firing] range,"[38] yet in the heat of an engagement he does not shoot. Even matured troops who have been through many engagements follow the pattern. Marshall says this inhibition has many causes—from the paralysis of fear in general, to the fear of revealing one's position, to the main fear, not of being killed, but of killing.[39] Ducking for cover to protect oneself comes first, which is why Patton wrote so strongly against hitting the dirt and digging in, and why Marshall entitles his chapter "Fire as the Cure." " 'After the first round the fear left me,' wrote a [Union] soldier to his mother after his initial battle."[40] "The mere rumor that a fight was in prospect would lift [Union] soldiers from the doldrums, and sustained firing on the picket line would affect a camp like an electric shock."[41]

Mars is battle rage, an insane red fury in a field of action. Firing the weapon brings Mars immediately into the scene, saving a man from cowering and trembling, from feeling himself a victim, and shakes him from his self-occupied inertia at a loss to himself and to his unit.

Since the god is in the gun, the passionate love for these weapons may express less a love of violence than a magical protection against it. Handgun—a fetish or amulet to hold at bay the fear of injury or death, the passivity of inertia, and, in ordinary civilian life, to have in one's hands a charm against the paranoid anxieties that haunt the American psyche. The continent is filled with roaming revenants, giant spirits of destroyed forests, buffalo spirits, slaughtered tribes, drowned valleys behind dams, ghosts of the lynched hanging from trees, miasma hovering over rapacious levelings and extractions, unjust executions named "due process," knifings, abattoirs. The land not only remembers, it is humming with agonies, a pulsing layer of the collective unconscious deposited there by American deeds recorded as American history.

"Iron all of itself works on a man." The automatic in my hand brings Mars to my side. God in his heaven may not smile on me or deliver me from the valley of death; he might long ago have forgotten my name and I may not be among the chosen, but so long as my gun is within my reach the ghosts can't get me.

Caputo in Vietnam remembers one of his men who suddenly pops an old woman they were holding. The man later explains, "Phil, you know the gun just went off by itself."[42] Automatic. The autonomy of the god. Because a god is in the gun it is demonic, so that control of the gun in your hand is not altogether in your hands. The question remains whether control of weapons by humans can ever be achieved without a more radical appreciation of the inhuman factor.

If guns are the American medicine against American paranoia (all the while reinforcing the very disease they would counteract— the basic formula of addiction), then how will the United States ever kick the habit and establish gun control? The armaments industry is so entrenched in the United States that its defense extends beyond the National Rifle Association, beyond the gun lobby and libertarians, into the churches and academia. Michael Bellesiles' scholarly, though disputed, assault on the origins of gun culture in America, in which he claims that it is an "invented tradition" not deriving from the historical evidence of America's first two hundred years when guns were, contrary to fond belief, less frequently fired, less popularly owned, less well made, and used less by hunters than trapping, was raked with criticism. Menacing hecklers showed up at his lectures.[43] Bellesiles argues that it was not the Revolution against the Crown that put the gun into the hands of the people, but the Civil War and its millions of combatants.

Part of the "invented tradition" promotes an idea of freedom that requires a vigilant gun-keeping citizenry, pointing, for example, to the heroes of Lexington Green in 1775. Images of these Minutemen, muskets in hand, muskets shouldered, muskets at the ready, costumed and marching to the music of Fourth of July parades, pasted on ads of *real* American products, affixed to menus of New England inns, are an exaggeration if not invention. Of that little band "only seven fired their muskets, and only one Redcoat was actually hit."[44]

The "invented tradition" seems written into the code of the American soul as if an article of faith, a necessity of its religion, sustaining the American predilection for violence, or as it is more happily called, its "fighting spirit." Worldwide violence depends largely on ours, for the United States is gunsmith to the world. While regulations more strictly govern the manufacture and distribution of weapons in most Western-style nations, handguns are so easy to get in the United States that they are part of our shadowy export trade keeping alive terrors in foreign lands, e.g., Northern Ireland. The wars we try to stop, officially, offering our "good services," are aided and abetted by the weapons business at home.[45] "For terrorists around the world, the United States is the Great Gun Bazaar."[46]

If violence is a contemporary curse and if violence by definition depends on instruments (Arendt), and since the most immediate and efficient instrument is the gun, and that gun is loaded with economic profit and religious idealizations—how in any god's name can gun control find its way through the American psyche? No chink in the armor; no weak link in the chain of its logic. The gun answers the fear of vulnerability; it defends against the inevitable victimization that is built into a winner-take-all society; it shortcuts the law's delay. Gun as equalizer is the neatest, fastest, and cheapest expression of the open society and popular democracy. Guns appear to be more necessary to personalized security, individualized liberty, and fungible equality than having your own castle, a roof over your head. The statistical reality that guns make everyone under that roof far more endangered, that they probably increase terror (just seeing them brings death to mind) bears far less psychological weight than the endemic American fears which prompt their purchase, and their use.

IT COULD be claimed that war on TV, in movies, and played on video games offers a window into the sublime. These mediated wars provide an aestheticized terror, battle and death as spectacle. Similar to a work of art, war is framed and plotted, its sequences selected, the whole unified, and limited in time. You can stop it anywhere, turn it off anytime.

Wars available on these media belong to the division in history (or is it in the mind that thinks about war?) between older and newer wars. Newer thinking has come to reverse the process of representing war. Formerly, actual events were recorded or imitated (say, by camera) and presented as documents close to the factual truth. Recently, war's actual events not only use media technology to do the fighting, but also imagine actual events to follow mediated models. The simulacrum governs the real. For instance, war policy and planning relies on aesthetic principles as presented by Weinberger, Powell, Bush, et al.: before committing troops abroad there must be a clear and well-defined purpose, enough force to carry it through, and an exit strategy (a work of art does not just go on and on).

The historical division refers to technology, both how wars are fought and how wars are perceived. Before television, wars were imagined by means of messengers recounting battles, by witnesses and participants, by journalists, poets, and writers. We relied on newspapers, forming our mental images from words. Since television, wars, when not censored, are seen and heard, full front and loud. No more than a sheet of glass stands between couch and trench. Moreover, simulated violence in general, from car crashes, building demolitions, and urban riots to scenes of invasions and shellings displayed on the glass, is difficult to distinguish from one-to-one documentaries.

What criteria differentiate reproductions from the "real thing"? The staged image is more persuasive emotionally, more fully actualized, and more enduring in memory than reportage. The simulacrum implodes with more realism than the "real," providing "unreal" models for measuring the reality of the real. Sophisticated thinkers, writing often in French, have pressed this new determination of the real by standards drawn from the virtual. This twist of the old way of thinking about what is real has weakened our attachment to the actuality of events in favor of their artful hyperintensification. In short, TV violence becomes "the real thing," and war on TV becomes war's "truest" depiction.

The intensification of war's realities did not begin with television. The poetic technique of artfully condensing the images of war was already applied by Brady during the Civil War when he moved bodies and arranged their postures for his "real life" shots of the battlefields. The pregnant images—flag-raising by the grim heroes of Iwo Jima, Russians on top of the Reichstag, Saddam's statue toppling—were staged with the glass in mind (glass of camera lens or TV screen).

The broadcast of violent television images worries citizens. Don't these images stimulate aggression in the viewers, feeding their urges, their hatreds and fears? Don't these images of war transfer from the glass to the streets, providing viewers with accurate models of aggressive behavior that are only virtual, only role-playing by actors (or cartoon figures) faking it, along with the imitation blood and detonations rigged on a soundstage? No one really gets hurt. No one gets blown apart; it's only an extra there in the mud.

The persuasive realism of video games, arcade games, play-stations may be less significant than the learning of skills these games offer. The games are teachers, improving the ability to attend to several locations at once, quicken finger-eye coordination, widen peripheral wariness, and other aspects of visual acuity. Instantaneous reflexes are necessary in combat, especially when actual battle on shipboard, during bombing runs and missile launchings, or at the controls of tanks is conducted on similar equipment. Taking away kids' guns, shutting down violent programs, will not cancel kids' preparation for engaging in war so long as they have access to their digitally manipulated equipment. The obsessed suburban nerd all day Saturday zipping the tips of his fingers like a snake's tongue is already in boot camp. He has a huge advantage, despite never going into the street or seeing an open wound, over the urchins in desperate lands in training for their brand of terrorism by heaving rocks or crouching behind walls with heavy weapons slung over their meager shoulders. The real war is conducted virtually, and the Pax Americana will be maintained by grown-up nerds.

Censorship-prone minds do not focus on the equipment; they see only the "what" and not the "how." So the argument against violence games and TV says that impressionable souls are being prepared in childhood for war, looking at its horrors as entertainment. War is made familiar, exciting, participatory, and harmless. Even if the show is promoted with the overt intention of discouraging violence, you see violence and that's what you get—and become. Violence, they say, breeds violence.

Perhaps violence does breed violence, but most certainly *harm-*

less violence where no one gets hurt breeds innocence, a word that literally means "uninjured."

The main damage done by violent TV images is their contribution to American violence *indirectly,* that is, by maintaining our endemic national disease: the addiction to innocence, to not knowing life's darkness and not wanting to know, either. (How differently children in Palestine, Cambodia, Bosnia, East Africa and West Africa, or in South-Central L.A. learn about violence!) It is by fostering innocence that TV violence contributes to American violence. The innocent American is the violent American—which is usually how other nations perceive us.

Those who pick particularly on TV (and movies, and Hollywood in general) are adamant about exposing children so wantonly to sex and violence. Before this issue can be considered it needs to be taken apart in several ways. First, are children as naive and unknowing as their protectors want to believe? For centuries in Western society they were imagined to be inherently vicious and perverse, requiring every sort of ritual and discipline to bring them from their unruly savagery into civilization. More to the point, however, is the American coupling of sex and violence: why are they paired? Does this linking imply that sex is a kind of violence, essentially abusive, forced like rape? Or are they linked because they are both adult "vices," behaviors of passion inappropriate to the lesser capacities of children?

More likely, the wide unthinking acceptance of the formula "sex and violence" finds its background in moralist repression of the body's libidinal spontaneity. The irrepressible returns, infusing the mind of the moralist with symbolic indistinctions. Sex becomes eruptive like violence, and violence—even skeet shooting and target practice—are conceived to be sublimated ways of "getting off." Media critics who link sex and violence to be jointly at fault for American civil disorder are less objective observers than witnesses to their own subjective roots in their ancestors' suppressive codes brought over from Victorian Ireland, Calvinist Scotland, Cromwellian Britain, Lutheran northern Europe, and the promulgations of papal bull. Once we have disentangled TV violence and the images of war from the peculiarly American sexual anxieties, we can consider TV war-reporting freed of pornographic imputations, no longer symbolizing protruding howitzer barrels into sex organs and explosions that toss bodies in the air into orgasmic climaxes.

Claims that media violence causes or contributes to aggressive behavior do not stand up to scrutiny. Jonathan Freedman at the University of Toronto, who has studied the claims for twenty years, takes them apart and shows the facts are simply not there. Neither the laboratory experiments nor the field studies establish a causal connection between media violence and personal aggressivity. Moreover, it is also possible to conceive this relation to be reversed: aggressive people select for their entertainment the violent shows and games.[47] Yet, the claims are repeated as fond shibboleths of righteousness. So we must ask why the persistence of this belief; what does it serve?

Is there actually more violence now in the society and its youth than formerly in America's history? More than in pioneer days? In Salem days; in the days of the Civil War and afterwards when the buffalo and tribes of the West were cut down and wiped out? Add to those times the period between 1882 and 1937, when 5,112 persons were lynched. On 209 occasions northern mobs attacked abolitionists. Cavalry and infantry fought a mob during the Astor Place riot in New York in 1849. Student riots at universities preceded the American Revolution, a war that too had its precedents in the violence against the French, against the native societies, and against tax collections. The rebellious riots of laborers and the brutal force brought in against them both by owners and government marked the "Golden Age" right up to the First World War. America was at "the brink of anarchy," says Paul Gilje in his study of the nation's explosive aggression. If we do believe that gang wars in a few cities, drug killings in a few neighborhoods, police brutalities caught on camera, and a few governing officials talking tough prove how aggressive behavior dominates the American scene *only now, only since TV,* ask the Chinese in old California, the blacks in Alabama or St. Louis, the young girls in colonial Massachusetts, Mormons in Missouri, plains braves in South Dakota, Irish cops in Chicago or Boston, Italian kids in New York, Jewish boys on their way to school, or Texans anytime.

Let me reinforce my list with one from Michael Ventura:

During the siege of Jerusalem (66–70 A.D.), Jews who sneaked from the city to forage for food were captured and crucified by the Romans (i.e., Italians) at the rate of 500 a day. The Roman soldiers quickly became bored with crucifying them in the usual way, so they nailed their victims in all sorts of pretzel-like postures and then watched the crows peck out their living eyes. These soldiers hadn't OD'd on violent video games.

The Catholic torturers of the Inquisition . . . the Europeans and Americans who, for hundreds of years, burned and hanged uppity women whom they called "witches" . . . the upright Christians who let hundreds of thousands of Africans die in the stinking holds of slave ships, and defended slavery as an institution until their Confederate armies were beaten beyond hope . . . the Anglo cavalrymen who massacred Native American women and children and often cut the genitals from the dead women and wore them as skull-caps as they rode off in victory . . . the Nazis who ran

the death-camps . . . the young airmen who incinerated the
civilian populations of Hiroshima and Nagasaki . . . the rural
boys who slaughtered nearly half the population of Cambodia . . . the rural boys who, this year, cut off the hands and
arms of hundreds of enemy tribes-people in Africa . . . none
of these people watched too many explosion-punctuated
Hollywood movies, sang hip-hop, glommed shoot-'em-ups
on TV, or played *Mortal Kombat* and *Doom*.

Although American violence may be a constant since our arrival
on these shores, why do we now blame it on TV? By pointing the
finger at TV and seeing the cause there, what other possible causes
are we not seeing? Who and what else might be the culprit for
contemporary aggressive behavior (besides the inherited "sin" of our
original colonialism)? Could poverty, insufficient housing, and over-
crowding foster violence? Institutional injustice; inadequate communal child care; civic and corporate corruption; racial oppression;
the worship of success and its correlative, failure; school uniformi-
ties; decline in arts programs; lack of prison reform and rehabilita-
tion; low pay and rank of social workers; the prevalence of guns—in
other words, societal faults? These are complex and hard to remedy
compared with the simplistics of censoring what's available on the
screen. Censorship and prohibition appeal to the moralist, legalist
penchant of Americans; subtle and enduring complexities much
less so. Besides, curbing violence by remedying societal faults tends
to redistribute wealth, offering more to the less advantaged, and
could threaten the established plutocracy for whom TV is only a
lesser opportunity among more opulent channels of recreation.

The prevalence of guns. Unlike power, says Arendt, which depends on support of the people, of courts, traditions, authorities,
or force, which is violence governed by power, violence depends
only on implements. In the United States the gun is the prime

implement. In short, we may more logically lay the blame for the supposed increase in American aggressive behavior on the wild proliferation of America's weapons, thereby recognizing the sub- terfuge in righteously demanding media control in order to escape gun control. The vicious passions aroused by discussions of gun control show how aggressively devoted much of today's citizenry is to keeping and staying armed. Congress may have camouflaged the Department of War (as it was called from the beginning of the Re- public) by wrapping it in a security blanket called "Defense," but Mars remains as dominant a god in U.S. culture as he was in the Roman Republic.

There is more to TV violence than the beatings and the bodies. Besides its content, there is the medium itself described so wittily by McLuhan and by semiologists and virtual realists ever since. This medium is simply glass, and the distillation of physical violence into TV images is analogous to that of alchemy whose events took place in and through glass.

The smith works fire by means of a forge; to cook calls for a pot or pan or oven. The alchemist puts his stuffs in a glass vessel and watches them at one remove. Glass allows sublimation, detached observation, a distanced viewing, i.e., "tele-vision."

The alchemical mind is both engaged participant and dispas- sionate observer, fascinated but not captured. By watching the glass you are able to "see through" and "see into" phenomena, which is also a way of containing them. Seeing through is another term for insight, for transforming empirical events into metaphors, discov- ering further meanings in the facts. The glass alembics, cucurbits, goosenecked flasks, and all the other shapes alchemists invented for digesting and cooling, distilling and sublimating their poisonous and hazardous materials allowed them to hold experiences in sus- pension, safe from the fires of desire, of ambition, of "acting out." Hence, alchemists were widely called "masters of fire." Glass was the means of containing danger, precisely not because it was tough and dense, but because it showed things as images, as phenomena, fostering interpretation, reflection, imagination, and fantasy, the mental operations that keep you on the other side of the glass, out of action.

"Out of action" comes from the medium, not the content. The psychic damage, if any, done by TV to the citizens is not due to TV's violence but to its glass. "Glassy: having a fixed, unintelligent look; lacking fire or life; dull." Vacuous passivity in the viewer works backwards on the content, requiring "shows" to accommodate to dullness on the one hand, and on the other, to light the fire with crazed, manic, hysterically convulsive enthusiasms just to get through the glass.

If now we were to go along with the popular, though unproven, notion that TV contributes to American violence, the culprit may not be the cop shows, the hoarse wrestlers, and bombs over Baghdad. Other programs do the dirty work. Hannah Arendt finds *hypocrisy* to be the principal ground for violence.[48] We respond outraged and want to take action. We want to set matters straight, fight against patent wrongs and slimy falsification of the truth. For Arendt, violence—"acting without argument or speech and without counting the consequences"[49]—is a deep-seated attempt to redress injustice coated in hypocrisy.

"To tear the mask off hypocrisy from the face of the enemy, to unmask him and the devious machinations and manipulations that permit him to rule without using violent means, that is, to provoke action even at the risk of annihilation so that the truth may come out—these are still among the strongest motives in today's violence on the campuses and the streets. And this violence is again not irrational."[50]

The high-paid speechwriters, spin doctors, and the press conferences gauged to conceal and rebuff in the name of higher principles like "national security," the well-groomed, dispassionate news anchors, the noncommital hypocrisy of "balanced reporting," the sentimentalities following accidents, the pharmaceutical ads that arouse fear in the name of healing and relief, the Sunday preachers, the titillation of interruptions ("We're out of time, I have to cut you off") before any satisfactory conclusion can be reached; and above all else the whitewash from the White House . . . The unrelenting bombardment of the people with the toxins of hypocrisy, TV's own weapon of destruction of the masses, may indeed call for sanctions and censorship—not by the government but of the government—because TV hypocrisy evokes a subliminal response of disgust and impotent anger, alienation from civic participation, existential worthlessness, degradation of the citizen's innate intelligence, dignity, and perception of truth, igniting a powder keg of terrible rage. Yes, TV is to blame.

THE TALE with which this chapter began may not deserve the laughter it received. When taken to its fullest consequences it may bear a far more menacing message. Perhaps the goddesses would not partake because they foresaw where the union of war and beauty could lead. Perhaps Poseidon was right in trying to close the matter down swiftly and drive the lovers apart. War too easily becomes beautiful.

After the horror of Antietam, and the reality of McClellan's failure there, he wrote his wife that the battle was a work of art and called it "sublime." Years after the Chickamauga campaign Grant wrote: "The Battle of Lookout Mountain is one of the romances of the war. There was no such battle and no action even worthy to be called a battle on Lookout Mountain. It is all poetry."[51] The intoxication of beauty washes clear the blood, transfigures the facts. Just here a caution from the often aggressive, impetuous Lee is worth recalling: "It is well that war is so horrible—we would grow too fond of it."[52]

Remember that "excess of happiness" Junger felt as the charge began. "If at its start," writes Modris Eksteins, "the [First World] war was synonymous for many Germans with beauty, its ever-increasing fury was regarded as merely an intensification of its aesthetic meaning."[53] The mood, even into 1918, of euphoria and uplift, an elevation like a Hegelian *Erhebung,* or overcoming of all internal tensions and troubles, cloaks war's truth in heavenly raiment. It is much like sudden falling in love, into the arms of Aphrodite, into the blindness of Mars. Russia, too. At the outbreak of war, "women ripped off their dresses and offered them to soldiers in the middle" of St. Petersburg. Later, in 1917, when the United States joined the Allies, "the audience of the New York Metropolitan Opera House stood up and greeted the announcement with 'loud and long cheers.'"[54] "The poet Rainer Maria Rilke and many others bowed in humble and awed obeisance to the 'War God': 'And we? We glow as One, / A new creature invigorated by death.'"[55]

The scholar of Japanese culture Donald Keene has collected *tanka* and hundreds of other writings expressing the feelings of major Japanese authors (including liberals, leftists, and Christians) during the 1941–45 war. The following passages refer to Pearl Harbor. Nagayo Yoshio, author of *The Bronze Christ,* on hearing of the declaration of war with the United States, wrote: "I never thought that in this lifetime I should ever know such a happy, thrilling, auspicious experience." The novelist and critic Ito Sei on the same occasion said: "I felt as if in one stroke I had become a new man, from the depths of my being." Honda Akira, scholar of English literature, wrote: "I have felt the sense of a clearing. Now the word 'holy war' is obvious . . . a new courage has welled up and everything has become easier to do."

Beauty is more than, other than "everything is easier to do." What is this euphoric simplification that war seems to offer? Is it because human responsibility has been surpassed and we have entered the sublime and are closer to the gods, and therefore beyond any considerations of good and evil? No need to consider anything except action. Advance, advance, as the French military motto, championed by Marshal Foch, commanded, and Patton endorsed. Advance, advance into tomorrow's news, escaping from the undigested remnants of today and yesterday. Forward action justifies and purifies by forgetting. There is freedom in chaos, joy in unconsidered spontaneity. Anything goes. This was the beauty promulgated by the cultists of action in Western Europe—Italy, Germany, France—and which also fed the Marxist idea of perpetual revolution.

Action per se, for its own sake, brings ends and means together. To do, or not to be; and the doing is sanctified by the cause and the command. I am absolved so long as I act, and therefore my actions cannot sin. This kind of reasoning and state of soul belong to the cult of Mars. Perhaps it is essential to every cult, where one turns human perplexity over to the god, who may be represented by the leader, the cause, or the nation, thereby releasing one from Hamletian hesitation, a liberation from the human into the sublime, which Eksteins calls "aestheticized brutality."[56] When Italy attacked Ethiopia in 1935 and waged war with bombers and modern weapons on natives armed often only with spears, Fascist writers vied with each other to evoke the "beauties" of this conflict. "Do you want to fight? To Kill? See rivers of blood? Great heaps of gold? Herds of female prisoners? Slaves?" asked d'Annunzio. "War is beautiful," bellowed Marinetti in turn, "because it combines the gunfire, the cannonades, the pauses, the scents, and the stench of putrefaction into a symphony."[57]

Now we are nearer to the transcendence offered by cults to the followers of the Thugs in India, Jim Jones in Guyana, and to prison camp guards and torturers. Yes, they are inhuman because the cult to which they belong, the god which they monocularly serve, absolves them of human concerns, and their actions are sublimed into a religiously enacted service.

We are nearer, too, to understanding the worst behaviors in war, where all civilized leashes are loosened and we become as utterly free as ecstatic children. "It made us feel like kids letting loose," writes an American soldier of a moment in the Philippines as they destroyed a Japanese installation. "We sprayed gasoline around . . . and ran along, touching matches here and there and feeling crazy."[58] An American lieutenant describes a similar moment in the Huertgen Forest: "Now the fight was at its wildest. We dashed . . . from one building to another, shooting, bayoneting, clubbing. . . . The wounded and the dead . . . lay in grotesque positions at every turn. . . . Never in my wildest imagination had I conceived that battle could be so incredibly impressive—awful, horrible, deadly, yet somehow thrilling, exhilarating."[59]

"There was no other place in the world that I would have preferred to be," writes war correspondent Anthony Loyd about his feelings just before an engagement in Bosnia. "There can be few instants in life that a man is lucky enough to feel so at one with his time and place. It would have been a good moment to die. . . . I cannot apologize for enjoying it so. . . . It was like falling in love again, a heady sensual rush that I wished only to clasp unquestioningly."[60]

"My wildest imagination," "like kids letting loose," "like falling in love"—is this not like being in bed with a lover and rediscovering in crazy abandon the infantile libido of Freud? An "excess of happiness" in the garden of lawless paradise before the fall into the human condition. The myths tell us that this "polymorphous perverse" child, as Freud named it, is little boy Amor or Eros, the son of Venus/Aphrodite. What about her role in war? What about the martial component in her nature, and how does she contribute to the sublime? That she does contribute in a grand way was already attested to by Homer, for it was Helen, an incarnation of Aphrodite's beauty, whose face launched the thousand ships that carried the Greeks to fight ten years at Troy. Helen's face, or Aphrodite's, folded into a wallet or Bible, her scarf tied to a knight's armor, her body pinned up in the barracks locker, pasted on the nose of a bomb, the fuselage of a jet, or vividly imagined in daylight and dream, still launches a thousand ships toward war.

Both Hedges and Gray point up the erotics of war. Women want men in uniform, badly; especially bad men in uniform, like the notorious Arkan, "one of the most desired men in the country,"[61] like Marko, Milosevic's son. "The erotic in war is like the rush of battle."[62] War transforms the ordinary into lustrous idols of beauty. During the civil war in Angola, a legendary twenty-year-old Carlotta was endowed with "elusive charm" and "great beauty." Later, when Hedges's friend developed the photos he had taken of her, automatic slung over her shoulder, he saw "she wasn't so beautiful. Yet nobody said as much out loud, so as not to destroy our myth."[63]

Mars does not go it alone, despite our images of the austere general, like MacArthur, jaws clamped on a corncob pipe; like Montgomery, bone thin, snappy and taut. Mars needs, wants Venus and will invent her presence somehow. During World War I, although the grimness of "brothels were regular appurtenances of base camps,"[64] it was the elusive charm of the imagined that fed the erotic flame like the blonde hairpieces Italian prostitutes laid on their pubises to give the GI (and the German?) the imagination of the girl back home. War needs a constant supply of imagination, and eros is imagination's fuel. This is more than a charge of libido to raise phallic verve, more than the eros of despair in the brutal arena of Thanatos, as if eros were only a life force that surges to compensate the loss of so many virile youth, fulfilling a demographic statistic: because so many men die, more semen must flow. Because desire flourishes in the midst of war and drives war with its imagination, our task doubles. Not only to imagine war with the help of Ares, but also in terms of his union with Aphrodite, her passion for war and her infusion into the whole body of the armies.

Alone, Homer's Aphrodite has little bellicosity. Zeus pulls her off the battlefield, saying: "Not to you child have been given the works of war."[65] Nonetheless, Aphrodite did have fierce epithets. Roscher and Kerényi have collated many examples: "the dark one," or "the black one," associates her with the three-faced figure of Hekate of whom the witches are fond and to whom dogs were sacrificed, and also the terrible Erinyes among whom she was named as one. The goddess of delicacy and roses was also called *androphonos* (killer of men) and *anosia* (the unholy) and *tymborychos* (the gravedigger). As *epitymbidia* she is "upon the graves." There is also a black-bearded Aphrodite; and in Sparta and Corinth "there was a local cult of warrior Aphrodite."[66] Concealed within the golden, smiling one, so "feminine," as we like to say today, are strange images, such as a little terra-cotta of the seventh century BC which shows a bearded Aphrodite emerging from a scrotal sac; and the play on words: *philommeides* (laughter-loving) and *philommedes* (to her belong male genitals).[67] In Ovid's tale of Anaxarete and Iphis (*Metamorphoses 14*), Iphis suffers the killing cruelty of the goddess.[68] And we shudder at her deadly revenge on dashing young Hippolytos for neglecting her.

Julius Caesar, man and legend, exemplifies the man of war with Venus in his inheritance, for Caesar's grandmother was Venus herself!—a belief he held along with ancient biographers and the populace. Before his crucial victory in the great battle of Pharsalia, which gave him dominance over Pompey and consequently Rome,

Caesar's watchword was Venus *victrix*. In her name he fought and won, though it was Pompey who had dreamt the night before of offering the spoils of war to her in her temple. But these were the remnants of defeat, himself as one of the spoils. Before the battle Caesar makes offerings to Venus and at midnight sacrifices to Mars. Both. "Son of Ares and Aphrodite," so states an inscription honoring Caesar in Ephesus.

Besides blessing him with victory, there are many fine traces of a Venusian infusion in his nature. For instance, unbounded promiscuity, for which he was called "the rooster." Suetonius lists his wives and mistresses, many of whom were other men's wives. He lingered in Egypt with Cleopatra for nine months, and the tale of their legendary liaison goes on lingering in imagination through centuries. Unbounded promiscuity is also is in his dreams where once he saw himself in bed with his mother (or raped her, in another version).[69] The liaisons were urged as much by political ambition as by desire, for Caesar was politic, charming, wily, resourceful, and had a brilliant way with words. Intricate connections, affecting others from within: here is Aphrodite maneuvering her artistry of war. Despite Caesar's devotion to Mars—he did conceive the largest temple ever to be built in that god's name—and his notorious martial ability, the hand of Venus shows in Caesar's "great moderation in victory and the numerous pardons he granted,"[70] leading to the erection of a temple named in honor of Caesar's clemency.

An unsurpassing love opens in the heart of war. Under the compression from which there is no escape, caught in the vice between duty on one side and death on the other, binding strictures give way and the heart opens to a love never known before or to be known again. When Patton (in the film) says, "God help me I love it so," his avowal occurs together with kissing the wounded officer. Love of war and love of fellows, together. Love in war and love for war join to form the love of war. To die for love—we say it, but soldiers do it.

The love of the regiment's name and its colors may raise the pitch of an individual's strength beyond his meager and tired capacity. At Waterloo the regimental colors of the British were "enormous, six feet square, and requiring considerable strength to handle in any sort of wind."[71] A sergeant called to carry them forward took the job, though that day fourteen other sergeants had been disabled or killed doing the same job, and the flag itself tattered almost to pieces. In combat at Waterloo and in other battles when men fought close at hand, the fight over the colors, the attempt to capture them and their defense, brought on intense heroic butchery. Keegan infers a connection between "the solidarity of groups and the power of symbols"[72] so that to this day solidarity has come to be invested in the flag, although the group of loving brothers has expanded into millions and millions and been diluted by the vast colorless wash of insipid patriotism.

Patriotism and symbolism aside, within the narrow compass of actual emergency, altruistic love comes unbidden. The desperate American retreat from the Yalu after the failed invasion of North Korea had to pass into a tight, ice-cold ravine under enemy fire through which funnel the only escape route lay. "From end to end this sanctuary was already filled with bodies, the living and the dead, wounded men could no longer move, the exhausted . . . and able-bodied driven to earth by fire. It was a sump pit of all who had become detached from their vehicles and abandoned to each other . . . 200 men in the ditch so that their bodies overlapped, Americans, Turks, ROK's. . . . Yet there was cooperative motion and human response. Men who were still partly mobile crawled forward along the chain of bodies. . . . As they moved, those who were down and hurt cried: 'Water! Water!' . . . Long since, nearly all canteens were dry. But the able-bodied checked long enough to do what bandaging they could . . . some stripped to the waist in the bitter cold and tore up their undershirts for dressings. Others stopped their crawl long enough to give their last drop of water . . . the wounded who were bound to the ditch tried to assist the able-bodies seeking to get out. Witnesses saw more of the decency of men than ever had been expected."[73]

There is tenderness. One man diverts another from self-centered preoccupation. A man helps another man to die, talking him into letting go. Another assuages guilt for a costly fuckup. Medicine of the heart given in thoughtful doses. Men in small units care for each other, cover for each other. "The ties of comradeship that exist in a good tank crew or infantry section can attain an intensity that is, in Kipling's words, 'passing the love of women.'"[74] *Kameradschaft* is the German word for this kind of intimacy. A French soldier spoke of feeling in the trenches "the most tender human experience that he had every enjoyed."[75] Men who had been only lightly wounded or briefly relieved sometimes sneaked back to their units, called by solidarity with their buddies, or called by the impossible possibility of dying together. To be close to death is close to immortality. Gray calls it "communal ecstasy."[76]

There is the edge, the ultimate limit which one British soldier calls the Line, touching on that word's double meaning, a place where soul is already loosed from its trappings. "You may say we were spiritually drugged and pathetically deluded. But . . . there was an exaltation, in those days of comradeship and dedication, that would have come in few other ways. And so, to those of us who had ridden with Don Quixote and Rupert Brooke on either hand, the Line is sacred ground, for there we saw the vision splendid."[77]

There is an unquenchable desire to help. A veteran of Vietnam twenty years after the ugly wounding and dying of men around him says, "There was nothing I could do to help. . . . Sometimes my thoughts take me right back to what happened to the guys there. I wish I could have helped them."[78]

There is the terrible love that breaks out in mourning, a sobbing passion for a mate suddenly taken. Already in Homer the term *himeros* appearing in Aphroditic contexts means both "the desire to weep"[79] and the sweet desire of sexual urgency. Grieving in war is one of the ways the love goddess works in the soul.

There is bravery for the sake of another. To take the point; to volunteer; to just go on so as not to let your bunch down. Men are not brave by nature, said Field Marshal Haig.[80] Somehow love makes them brave.

There is simply love for war itself. One man who received three Purple Hearts and survived 175 battle patrols in Korea volunteered for more, again, and again. "I had the feeling I had missed the complete experience."[81] The possibility of triumphant being over death or in death offered by union with the god. Martha Bayles calls this dimension "the war sublime."[82]

There is love for a leader. A sergeant in hospital at the end of World War II wrote a letter to his former company commander. "Dick, you are loved and will never be forgotten by any soldier that ever served under you. . . . You are the best friend I ever had and I only wish we could have been on a different basis. You were my ideal and motor in combat. . . . I would follow you into hell."[83]

There is psychological insight: A nineteen-year-old corporal explains how men help those on the edge of collapse:

"You can see it commin' on, and sometimes the other guys can help out."

"How do you mean, you can see it coming on?"

"Why, first they get trigger happy. They go running all over the place lookin' for something to shoot at. Then, the next thing you know they got the battle jitters. They jump if you light a match and go diving for cover if someone bounces a tin hat off a rock . . . you can just about see them let out a mental scream to themselves. . . ."

"How can the other fellows help out . . . ?"

The corporal looked down at his hands a little sheepishly.

"Aw, you can kind of cover up for a guy like that before he's completely gone. He can be sent back to get ammo or something. You know and he knows he's gonna stay out of sight for a while, but you don't let on, see? Then he can pretend to himself he's got a reason for being back there and he still has his pride."[84]

The circumstances of war may initiate a person into a new sublime level of care, as if the terror constellates a gentle beauty, another kind of love where one soul's love responds to another soul's terror. This therapeutic love often lasts into war's aftermath. In a novel of supreme depth and brilliance, *The Human Stain,* Philip Roth offers a long scene of this kind of love. First we must remember that the term "therapy" does not have to designate only the contemporary practice of professional problem-solving in offices and public health agencies by licensed, organized "care providers." Psycho (soul) therapy (service) is a broadly applicable term, descriptive of any activity by anyone or anything that attends to the needs of the soul and performs rituals (deliberate acts addressed to powers beyond the human) that minister to the soul.

Roth sets the scene of war's aftermath in a Chinese restaurant, The Harmony Palace, with its terrifying evocation of the enemy—the "gooks," their eyes, their smells, their cooking, their menace—and the murderous insanity still lurking in the veterans after so many years. Louie, who runs this recovery group, and three others are taking Les for his first foray into this territory. Les had not been able to sleep for days and nights; he knew that this meal out among Asians was preparatory to his facing one day the black wall of the war memorial engraved with the names, the names . . .

"You can let go of the menu now. Les, let go of the menu. First with your right hand. Now your left hand. There. Chet'll fold it up for you."

The big guys, Chet and Bobcat, had been seated to either side of Les. They were assigned by Louis to be the evening's MPs and knew what to do if Les made a wrong move. Swift sat at the other side of the round table, next to Louie, who directly faced Les, and now, in the helpful tones a father might use with a son he was teaching to ride a bike, Swift said to Les, "I remember the first time I came here. I thought I'd never make it through. You're doin' real good. My first time, I couldn't even read the menu. The letters, they all were swimmin' at me. I thought I was goin' to bust through the window. Two guys, they had to take me out 'cause I couldn't sit still. You're doin' a good job, Les." If Les had been able to notice anything other than how much his hands were now trembling, he would have realized that he'd never before seen Swift not twitching. Swift neither twitching nor bitching. That was why Louie had brought him along—because helping somebody through the Chinese meal seemed to be the thing that Swift did best in this world. Here at The Harmony Palace, as nowhere else, Swift seemed for a while to remember what was what. Here one had only the faintest sense of him as someone crawling through life on his hands and knees. Here, made manifest in this embittered, ailing remnant of a man was a tiny, tattered piece of what had once been courage. "You're doin' a good job, Les. You're doin' all right.

You just have to have a little tea," Swift suggested. "Let Chet pour some tea."[85]

More than tea and sympathy; this is tea and active, intelligent, respectful, insightful, courageous, committed, decent, imaginative, particularized, patient, sensitive, responsive love. Real love, true love, long-lasting love that meets madness and death and does not retreat from the memory of ghouls or harpies descending, and it begins in war and does not end when war ends.

Some observers suggest that the intensity of war's love arises from the collapse of all others. All the former attachments in the roles of husband, father, son, even sweetheart faded and forsaken. (The evidence for female military personnel is less plentiful, less sifted and abstracted into conclusions.) These faded loves flare for a moment in a letter or a dream. But they no longer have palpable power, whereas buddy, comrade, mate, and the endearment expressed in nicknames of the guys in the platoon, the shared bitter amusements and cosmic griping, compresses all human love into these few with whom I watch on guard, skirmish, cower, as well as eat, piss, and sleep. Talk has little to do with it. Idiosyncrasies do. The peculiar mumbo-jumbo that bans fright, the odd way a person holds a mug or worries about his feet, the bandanna, the cigarette or joint—these are intimacies that foster the annoying lovableness that makes for comradeship. Talk? What is there to talk about? Home? What is that? Who was that? Me? Psychotherapy may know what talk can do for love and how right Freud was to call his medicine "the talking cure." Psychotherapy may not know that love does not need talk—the less said the better—the rhythm of a small group moving forward, in stealth all day, all night, covering for another; the shared physical imagination of danger, exhaustion, boredom, and obliteration, and the strung-out nerves, yield an unspeaking and unspeakable kind of love between men pulling the same load, caught in the same despair.

Love in war exposes one of our fondest false notions. We like to believe that death is private and solitary, each departs alone. We believe we are owners of our "own" death, the possession of which we confirm by "will" with binding instructions that include the disposal of our remains. Is this idea of death not corollary to the bourgeois sanctity of private property? The mental set that constructs the isolation of our dying is the same bourgeois mentality that builds our individual living spaces with doors of separation to guarantee privacy and single beds in which to die, alone. So conceived, death is a lonely thing, all your own, and this conception finds its intellectual reinforcement in the existential philosophy of Heidegger and Kierkegaard and Sartre and their somber affection for dread, angst, and abandonment.

The study of religion also adds its academic authority in support of the privacy of death by claiming that religion itself arises in the minds of the earliest humans in their puzzlement over death, which invites fantasies of terrifying powers, reincarnations in afterlives, and distinctions between mortal body and immortal soul. By offering protection to the individual soul against the terrifying powers and by teaching about the soul after life, religion keeps itself alive by means of its thanatology, its privileged death-knowledge. The individual faced with death in battle turns to religion because of its claim to special protection and the prospect of individual salvation. Soldiers, however, do not die in the arms of their god; they are cut down amidst their brothers splashed with the blood of their dying comrade. Insistence on the separate individuality of dying denies the facts of battle and the life of war. Searching for the one common denominator that all battles share, Keegan writes: "What battles have in common is human . . . above all, it is always a study of solidarity and usually also of disintegration—for it is toward the disintegration of human groups that battle is directed."[86] It is disintegrative, and disrespectful of the emotional facts of human conduct in war, to maintain that we die alone and shall be laid in a private grave. Yet the mass grave is one of war's horror stories, an anathema to both religious and bourgeois convention.

We do not bury men as they lived and died in solidarity, but each apart in his own marked and numbered grave, rows and rows of them like suburban plots in meticulously bordered war cemeteries. This despite the witness of comrades who may "visualize death as a companionable experience," says Linderman, reporting on a paratrooper who said, "'if it were my destiny to die in battle,' it would come 'by T.L.'s side, surrounded by Berkely, the Arab, Duquesne, Casey, Gruening and the other stalwarts of the platoon.'"[87]

The bullet may have found only one man in the platoon; he may have been "singled" out by a sniper, but neither his death nor his body belong to that one man alone. Buddies go to extremes to bring a body back from where it fell, not letting it lie alone, denying the singleness of death by their communal enterprise.

There is community in dying, and if your death belongs to others, we are essentially not alone—that is one of the great teachings of war.

DEATH

. . .

With our feet we walk the goat's earth.
With our hands we touch God's sky.
Some future day in the heat of noon,
I shall be carried shoulder high
through the village of the dead.

When I die, don't bury me under forest trees,
I fear their thorns.
When I die, don't bury me under forest trees,
I fear their dripping water.
Bury me under the great shade trees in the market,
I want to hear the drums beating,
I want to feel the dancers' feet.

(KUBA, ZAIRE; *English rendering by Ulli Beier*)

According to old folk sayings, to die is to join the ancestors, which means that you become an ancestor yourself and, if having died in uniform, in battle, you remain a member of the innumerable troop of the war dead who may still be at war. Swiss fighters in one of their early battles felt the presence of their ancestors in the lines beside them, behind them. Those who die in war may never be dead to war; war may bring them back and they may be continuing to motivate wars "through the ages" in different guises, encouraging wars' perpetuation. The Armenians and the Serbs, and the Irish too, and men and women in the Deep South of the United States, sense their ancestors stirring in their oppressions and resentments. Who knows how many more incitings of wars are started up by the fresh maimings and murderings in Iraq, Afghanistan, Bosnia, Chechnya, Guatemala, El Salvador, and all through Africa? War's perpetuation by fallen comrades in the ranks of the ancestors who, by dying in war, never leave the battlefield behind.

They do not depart, their spirits are not buried. They work like a prompter out of sight below the stage, remembering, remembering each particular, filling in the lines of the actual actors in the drama of a war with habits and reasons and mistakes from the same old archetypal script. That's what is meant when they say "all wars are the same." That's why theorists of war strategies complain that new wars are fought with the last war's ideas—the Maginot Line, carpet bombing, blockades, starvation and disruption to break civilian morale. The same, again and again. The dead hand of the past honored by the name, tradition.

An eon turned between 1999 and 2001. The revolution in warfare promised by technicians will obviate bayonets and dry socks. Farther and farther away from the blasts they launch, the killers can sit clean and comfortable, soundproof and odor-free, attentive only to pixels. War imagined as encounters between robots aimed to take out "nerve centers" and only tangentially, collaterally, bodies.

But conflicting decisions remain, unclear orders, confusions, fuckups, breakdowns, rivalries and precious vanities, and the reappearance in the blood, despite intensive specialized training, of hatred and paralysis and nightmares and suspicion. The leaders' paranoia does not change, the belief in God, the trust in weapons, and the sublime cruelties humans can invent and inflict upon one another, especially upon those they do not know or ever care to know, or know about. And, will not old men still send the young to fight for the same, old, unchanging, indestructible, archetypal reasons?

WAR

Old age in the towns.
The heart without an owner.
Love without any object.
Grass, dust, crow.
And the young ones?

In the coffins.

The tree alone and dry.
Women like a stick
of widowhood across the bed.

Hatred there is no cure for.
And the young ones?

In the coffins.
(MIGUEL HERNANDEZ, *translated by Hardie St. Martin*)

The persistence of the dead in keeping war alive shows in the attempts, long after, to right a wrong, to correct history, to revisit the tragedy and play the game again. Hedges tells briefly of the Armenians: two million people forced into exile in 1915 by the Turks, hundreds of thousands killed, the facts consistently suppressed, breeding "seeds of resentment that will not be squashed."[88] More than resentment; revenge. Gournig Yanikian was among that number. He witnessed his brother's murder in 1915, and because he was a pacifist he sought no revenge and arrived eventually in the United States. He wrote several books of the massacres, the genocide, and he achieved a successful life—though tormented by nightmares of his brother's death and what he felt to be his guilt regarding his failure to avenge it. James Hersh, who recounts this story, reports that in 1973 (nearly sixty years later!) Gournig Yanikian, in an "act of 'good will' invited two Turkish diplomats into his hotel room where he was to present them with two rare paintings. When they arrived he shot them both. Immediately, he phoned the police and told them very calmly what he had done, explaining that he had committed the murders in order to stop the nightmares. It worked. Before he died in February 1984, he claimed that after the assassinations he never again suffered a nightmare related to the death of his brother."[89] At the time of Hersh's essay (August 1984) "thirty-five Turkish diplomats have been slain for the avowed purpose of drawing the world's attention to the Forgotten Genocide."[90]

Hersh gives fateful significance to Yanikian's revenge much Shay deepens the extreme behaviors in Vietnam: both turn to Greek myths. After a blood-crime the ancient Greek Furies (Erinyes) demand vengeance. They do not let go and they work by disturbing the mind.[91] There is no escape from their pursuit. Heraclitus says that if the sun itself were to leave its ordered course, the Furies would find him.[92] To forget a major wrong is to neglect the laws of the cosmos, which are also reflected in the order of the family. Yanikian's crime was one of omission: an omission of love not avenging his brother's murder, and some scholars explain the Erinyes as ghosts of the one slain.

The classic example of the fateful Furies is their challenge to Orestes to avenge the murder of his father. Aeschylus has Orestes saying: "The accusation came upon me from my dreams, and hit me as with a goad . . . deep beneath lobe and heart."[93] Hersh adds that in early Anglo-Saxon, revenge was an anger "trapped like wind in one's stomach." He cites an Armenian who said there is a "rage trapped under the skin."[94] As with Orestes, the Furies pressed Yanikian with dreams, until the rage was released and the nightmares ceased.

The explanation of unusual human behavior requires that thinking too reach toward the sublime. We must be "amazed" and "transported with wonder" rather than merely "persuaded."[95] The entire context of understanding becomes elevated, gnostic even, which means a thinking that changes one's being. Understanding then is no longer couched in the language of problem-solving, instead becoming more like aesthetic appreciation, revelatory, yet effortless and completely absorbed into one's nature. One's psyche has been elevated by the amazing event it now understands.

Equally lasting and compelling and profoundly puzzling as vengeance is the unquenchable desire to help, that dying for love

men brave beyond normal comprehension. To un-
means understanding the quality, the nature, of love
unlike any other and which veterans report they
only in the midst of war's terror, a love that creates a potency
of one's self that is at the same time the sacrifice of one's self. "I'd
do anything for these guys." "I'd follow you into hell." "God help
me . . . I love it more than my life."

To penetrate into the mysterious love concealed inside war, I
turn again to the philosopher Emmanuel Levinas, who set us on
our way in chapter 1 with his cryptic, "being reveals itself as war."
His examination of altruism makes clear that the idea of a separated Hobbesian subject leaves unsolved the love for the Other.
Why does "I" care at all about, let alone die for, another? Our ac-
cepted idea of the Other places him or her outside our essential
subjectivity. Foreign, alien, ontologically apart from the "me."
Even when my subjectivity is tied in friendship, marriage, or par-
enting, or by oath, the Other stands external, defined as not-I. In
order to find reason for altruistic behavior, ruthless ego psychology
conceives the Other as necessary to fulfill my needs, someone to
benefit from, to gratify desire, to dominate, and also to satisfy my
needs to care and sympathize and save. But the need remains mine
and the other can be any Other so long as he or she or it offers opportunity to meet my needs. Or, as Hobbes says, I may find common cause with another for our mutual welfare and protection. In
every case, altruism is reducible to self-serving.

We can immediately see that the unquenchable desire to help
on the battlefield (which may plague one for a score of years afterwards), this altruism, contradicts the root idea of a subjectivity
based on itself and its ego psychology. Survivors insist that their war
experience was sublime in its transcendence of their usual feelings
and sense of themselves.

Although the following passages from Levinas present a metapsychology or a cosmology of altruism, they are particularly useful in regard to love in war. His "total altruism" means, "The I is bound to the not-I, as if the entire fate of the Other were in our hands. The uniqueness of the I consists in the fact that no one can answer in his or her place. . . . This signifies the most radical commitment there is, total altruism." "The I . . . is infinitely responsible," and my "subjectivity is in that responsibility," which is "irreducible" (and I would say inescapable). "That is what constitutes the ethical." As infinitely responsible, I am infinitely myself in my fullest potentiality: I am all I can be; and, "death is powerless, for life receives meaning from an infinite responsibility."[96]

When we read these words in the context of war, the love that there takes hold becomes cosmological in importance. It is there, under fire in the mud, that I become a supremely ethical person. I become altruistic in essence, not by obeying a commandment to love, but by the ontology of war, war as being itself revealed, which calls forth my fullest potential of responsibility, the responsibility unto death whose terror and ugliness is not the slightest transformed by love. Rather, that terror and ugliness serves to intensify altruism and therewith the fullness of my being. My truest subjective person, lamely conceived as the ego or self in psychological theory, is the responsibility called out by the Other to whom no one else can answer. This response reveals being, not as brave, dutiful, compassionate, or heroic, but as ethical. "To be myself means to be unable to escape responsibility." The *extremis* of battle renders plain and naked the inability to escape. Battle becomes the paradigm of the ethical, of altruism, of love.

No other love can be equal. It is a love sublime, a love in terror. It is unspeakable. The veteran does not, cannot talk about these moments both because it was so terrible and because it was so loving. Should he talk, it can be only with those who have been there, most of whom, closest of whom, may be blown to pieces, often as bodies unrecoverable. How does one return from this sublimity, as if from a spiritual retreat on the mountain or seized by an angel? This is not the love we usually speak about; it is not friendship, as Hedges says disparagingly, because it does not evolve into relating and living out into life. There is no way down to the valley, and besides, who is there to receive? Only those who cannot understand, cannot imagine.

Love, the Ethical, the Other—huge abstractions. The combat unit is merely these few others who are here now: "Berkely, the Arab, Duquesne, Casey, Gruening." The Other is them; these simple concrete correlates of the metaphysical abstraction. They are the cosmos. We few become a community based on altruism which is our strength. War writers call it solidarity; the commanders call us a unit. Because war reveals our being, we are brutal and insane in action and we are ethical and loving in essence. We compose a polis, a utopian polis that is ethical, responsible, and loving, though we shoot to kill. Is this what is meant when the idea is advanced that societies are founded on war and that the state begins as a warring body? Is the Bible's God a warrior God, not only because of his striking force of death, but as well because of the extraordinary, sublime love that is found only in war?

EXCURSION:

Giving up the Gun

A beautiful example of gun control occurred in Japan between 1543 and 1879. The phenomenon is perhaps unique in world history and yet it is also rarely discussed. Guns were first introduced into Japan in 1543 by three Portuguese freebooters (pirates? soldiers of fortune? traders?) who shot a duck. A local lord bought the guns and took lessons in handling and firing the weapons. Within six years some five hundred copies had been ordered and were in stages of production, so that by 1560—only seventeen years after the first gun was ever seen in Japan—they were fired in battle and, by 1575, had become the decisive weapon.

The excellence of metallurgy in Japan and its high culture of war combined to establish Japan as an exporter of a variety of weapons, already in the 1400s. We must remember that Japan in the sixteenth century was a rich land of twenty-five million people, while France numbered but sixteen million inhabitants, Spain seven, and England not even five. The Japanese at that time used more guns in battles than any European country even possessed! They became masters: "They developed a serial firing technique to speed the flow of bullets. They increased the caliber of the guns to increase each bullet's effectiveness, and they ordered waterproof lacquered cases to carry the matchlocks and gunpowder in. . . . [Japanese gun-makers . . . developed] a helical mainspring and an adjustable trigger-pull and . . . a gun accessory which enabled a matchlock to be fired in the rain."[97]

Reeling forward three centuries to 1853, when Commodore Perry arrived and the treaty of Kanagawa was signed, "opening" Japan to foreign trade and its influences, there were no guns! No cannon protecting the harbors, no sidearms, no escorts firing volleys in salute. The very word (probably *teppo*) had become a scholarly remnant. Its referent, the gun, was absent from consciousness. What had happened in the intervening years while Japan was insularly closed in on itself?

Reasons for this reversion from guns back to swords and spears are several, and they are speculations that I have taken from Perrin's elegant little study. Sensible speculations however, and well worth digesting slowly by our trigger-happy society and its difficulties with gun control, since each of the reasons affecting Japan may suggest further speculations that we have not yet considered in the United States.

First, the skill of engagement moved away from the soldier to the manufacturer, and from the soldier to his commander, because "weapons tend to overshadow the men who use them."[98] The weapon and reliance on weaponry dominate the thought and action of war. Before the gun, people often paired off in close individual struggle, and stories emerged from every battle nourishing the myths of folk heroes. But guns made fighters all equal—one man with his gun and at a distance was as good as the next, providing his weapon was operational.

So, equality is a second reason. Japan's warrior class numbered around eight percent of its population (compared with Europe, whose warrior class at that time composed hardly one percent). Suddenly the gun elevated a lowly peasant equal to his noble lord. This the lords did not like; the gun threatened their rule. Third, Japan had no external "gun" enemies and so they had no need of coastal batteries or battlefields with artillery as in Europe. They had no need of an armaments industry. Fourth, guns came into Japan from foreigners and were tarnished by Japanese xenophobia. They were an "outside idea"[99]—and one associated in Japan particularly with Western missions and Western business, activating an archetypal feeling of dislike between the merchant and warrior psyches. This distinction in kinds of soul occurs in Plato's *Republic,* in the Hindu caste system, and appears in the Sicilian tent between Patton and the GI he slapped.

As the gun is more than a symbol, so too the sword in Japan. "For a thousand years, Japanese men of the upper class wore no signet rings engraved with their coats of arms, no jewels, no Order of the Golden Fleece, no military dec-orations, no gold epaulets. All that was concentrated into the beautifully worked handles and guards of the swords they fought with. . . . You couldn't even have a family name unless you also had the right to wear a sword."[100] "The sword was the visible form of one's honor—'the soul of the samurai.'"[101]

I have taken this excursion to dwell on Perrin's study of Japanese "gun control" in order finally to arrive at this last, most intriguing, reason for the absence of guns for so many years in Japanese wars. The cult of the sword was ancestral, symbolic, and religious—and also aesthetic. "Swords happen to be associated with elegant body movement. A sword sim-ply is a more graceful weapon to use than a gun, in any time or country. This is why an extended scene of swordplay can appear in a contemporary movie, and be a kind of danger-laden ballet, while a scene of extended gunplay comes out as raw violence."[102]

Manuals of the time complain that soldiers "must get in such awkward kneeling positions to shoot guns; their elbows hurt. Hips get strange muscle pain. . . . *Must* separate knees to kneel and fire." One instruction from the 1595 firearms manual reinforces the awkwardness that contravenes digni-fied body comportment: "Keep seven inches between big toes as you kneel. One more inch does not look good."[103] Venus *victrix!* It is more important for a person to maintain the aesthetic principles that hold the internal strength of the body's force in harmonious balance by posture, place of hands, elbows, and legs than to lose this for the sake of the practicality of guns.

A distinction between the practical and the beautiful runs deep in Western Christian culture. Venus is suspect; real beauty is angelic, after life in another world; so, while you are here in Caesar's world, render unto him, practically. Yet, in the Renaissance and the Baroque superb walls and bastions of severe beauty, and weapons, were designed and built by the greatest artists, such as Leonardo, Brunelleschi, Michelangelo, Buontalenti. Beauty and usefulness together. But then, according to John Nef, the Protestant Reformation forced the aesthetic and the practical apart.

For example, before the Reformation European warships were carved and gilded and even crammed with sculpture. Colbert, the finance man (read: money manager, state economist) of Louis Quatorze, cut back on the aesthetic. Colbert looked to the Protestants for his model: "The English and Dutch have scarcely any ornaments, and they have no arcades at all. All these large pieces of work serve only to make vessels much heavier, and subject to fires."[104] He gave orders to the king's shipbuilder to eliminate the fancy-work.

Guns were never banned in Japan; they simply faded away. The government's centralized monopoly on firearms and explosives made control of weapons simpler, so that when the governing power no longer ordered guns, there was no demand for them and the gunsmiths began to make swords again. Only four families of gunmakers existed by the end of the seventeenth century. Not only did the Japanese not want to use guns, or manufacture guns, but as the centuries went by, says Perrin, "they came to dislike even *seeing* them."[105]

It all changed with Commodore Perry, who convinced the ruling powers that the best way to keep future Commodore Perrys from entering Japanese harbors was to set up large naval guns themselves. That was in 1853—and the rest is history. Within fifty years the Japanese had enough firepower to sink a large Russian flotilla and then join the arms race, colonialism, and "progress."

Although commentators agree that only after Perry did Japan rearm, the idea of Western-style fortification had previously found an aesthetic expression. In 1846, a young American mate whose whaling ship had run aground made it to an island port. "As we approached, we saw what appeared to be a fort . . . but on coming nearer we found it was a piece of cloth extended about three-quarters of a mile, and painted so as to represent a fort with guns."[106] Trompe l'oeil as homeland security! Is there a lesson here for contemporary America?

The story told so elegantly by Perrin (and with illustrations from old Japanese firearms instruction manuals) need not be read as a return to primitivism or that the Japanese were stuck in hyperformalized feudalism. In fact their civilization "progressed" technologically, and in many other areas, beyond Europe of the time—even as they "regressed" in regard to guns. Nor should we read this piece of history as nostalgia for the good old days with less-deadly weapons. Warfare and slaughter (including foreign invasions) and samurai cruelty did not abate. The absence of firearms does not equate with the presence of gentleness.

We can learn, however, that progress in weaponry is not irreversible, and that the weapons we invent may negatively affect the men who employ them and not only those devastated by them. We may further learn that inventiveness and precision tend to move from the front to the rear, from rifleman to manufacturer, so that the soldier who does the shooting is lessened in value compared with the arms merchant and procurement department.

My reason for the excursion to Japan is the lesson that matters most: the aesthetic is also a force. There may be no inverse proportion between beauty and war: the more beauty the less violence; but Perrin's account introduces an idea worth pondering. Military aesthetics may further display the conjunction of Venus and Mars and, moreover, be a manner of "taming" the madness of the god with highly fashioned, ritualized, overindulged aesthetics.

In 1918, Patton writes his wife: "I often think with regret of how badly I used to dress. . . . Now I am a regular Beau Brummel. I wear silk khaki shirts made to order, khaki socks also made to order. I change my boots at least once during the day and my belts are wonders to see they are so shiney and polished. I have the leather on my knees blancoed every time I ride and my spurs polished with silver polish. In fact I am a wonder to behold."[107]

From the first salute in boot camp to the last decoration, a love for aesthetics is on parade. "Little patches of colour and braid and lace distinguished regiments in almost all armies; the Austrians meticulously differentiated between ten shades of red, including madder, cherry, rose, amaranth, carmine, lobster, scarlet and wine . . ."[108] Standing on the civilian sidewalk, military rites and rhetoric seem high pomposity and kitsch, even though we feel stirred by a marching band, the banners, and the rhythm of the feet. Aesthetic details unabashed and everywhere: the postures, the spit and polish, the chickenshit regulations and stylized speech. Why do they drill, why do they march, why do they forever clean latrines, shine banisters, oil parts, polish floors, precisely fold their gear, pack their sea-bags, trim their hair? "Spahis in streaming scarlet cloaks, Bengal lancers in turbans of peacock hue, Madrassis in French grey and silver, Skinner's irregulars in canary yellow. . . . [T]he Prussian *Garde du Corps* wore helmets crowned with a winged eagle, burnished breastplates and glittering jackboots, reaching to the thigh."[109] Imagine, too, the horses, their manes and tails, the accoutrements, the brasses. Remember the swagger stick, ivory-handled pistols, epaulets, decorated sleeves, bamboo baton? All the hats, the feathers and braids, crushed peaks and brims. The music: reveille and mournful taps, fifes and drums, bugles, the marching songs, choruses. Military tailors: Wellington boots, Eisenhower jackets, Sam Brown belts. "Tomorrow I shall have my new battle jacket. If I'm to fight I like to be well dressed," said Patton.[110] And in later wars' deliberately bland uniformity who designs the desert camouflage; where the line between function and fashion? Formations, orderlies, ranks, promotions. The military mess—its postures, toasts, table setting, seating codes. The manners: salutes, drills, commands. Martial rituals of the feet—turns, steps, paces, warriors' dances. Of the eyes—eyes front! The hands, the neck, the jaw, the voice, ramrod backbone: "Suck in that gut, soldier!"

If this aesthetic excess serves merely to embellish war by dressing it up, or worse, to mask its ugliness, then the display is a seductive deceit of Venus, one of her treacheries. Could it, might she, however, serve a better purpose? These forms and formalities might be following a profound function. They place the mad dog in an Aphroditic halter. There may not be a moral (as William James sought), but an aesthetic equivalent of war. John Nef's book *War and Human Progress* suggests just this.

Nef's analysis of war prior to nineteenth-century industrialism and Napoleonic enthusiasm indicates that wars were less violent and less significant and were subject to cultural restraints. The previous century's religious wars between Protestant and Catholic armies that tore the continent apart and the horrific brutalities of colonialism somewhat subsided in the Age of Enlightenment. The eighteenth century (ca. 1670–1780) in Europe showed a "distaste for bloodshed," a decrease in the mistreatment of captured prisoners, and a reluctance "to kill fellow Europeans."[111] The period was marked by the influence of the royal and princely courts upon decorum and manners, of the salons on conversation and the expression of emotion, of cities on a differentiated elaboration of the senses, and by freethinking philosophers less gripped by religion, "weakening the will of organized fighting" and questioning its purpose. "Europeans were falling in love with the perfections of the mind . . . and, in proportion to the number of people alive (especially to the number of people with political influence), a much larger audience for *serious* thought and art" than in our day.[112]

Serious thinking was carried on by Thomas Paine, Voltaire, Leibniz, Hume, Diderot, Swift, Samuel Johnson, among scores of others who were critical, skeptical, radical, political, advancing a kind of intellectual guerrilla warfare against the cant and hypocrisy that form the fabric of nationalist patriotism, sentimental personalism, and light-headed religiosity so signal in our times. Diderot, who believed in the absolute authority of the people and is a spiritual father of American democracy, said on his deathbed: "I do not believe in God the Father, God the Son, or God the Holy Ghost."[113] These many men and the many women with whom they conversed, corresponded, and slept were not institutionalized academics but intellectually alive citizens forming the minds and tastes of the courts and the expanding middle classes.

This same period did see increases in the standing armies; Frederick the Great wrote on war and developed the military strength of Prussia; France and England fought big battles against each other; and Spain was still colonizing. Yet, "the poetic virtues were more respected than the military virtues."[114]

"It was an age when contemporary art was a part of contemporary history." There are numbers to support this demilitarization. The proportion of combatants to the total population dropped from 500 in the seventeenth century to 380 in the eighteenth. More people alive in Europe, but fewer engaged in European wars.[115] It goes without saying that European bellicosity did not disappear; it was exported in exploitations abroad, naval rivalries, and slave-trading. There were still pirates to conquer and duels to fight, though here, too, Louis Quatorze in 1679 "prescribed the death penalty for all principals, seconds, and thirds"[116] in an attempt to end the hugely popular practice.

"The growing sense of restraint and proportion . . . was encouraged by the love of metaphorical truth, of wit . . . as an intimate part of life, a love which the Reformation and Counter Reformation had threatened to destroy."[117]

It is usual to judge the Enlightenment as an age of Apollo (Durand), but the intimate underside was Venusian through and through. The ascendancy of Venus affected the martial spirit, now more dedicated to battles of wit, diplomacy, finance, the clash of ideas, the rivalry of lovers, composers, and poets. The Sun King himself "refused to have the French armies adopt a newly invented gunpowder, with more murderous properties . . . on the ground that it was 'too destructive of human life.'"[118] Late in his life he declared, "I have been too fond of war."[119]

Some would contest Nef's reading of that historical period. Has he not idealized an oppressive system, an "ancient regime," that necessitated the overthrow by the French and American revolutions, by Napoleon, and the stupendous militarism that followed until today? Besides, we are certainly not in an age of enlightenment! Science is no longer a humanist's pursuit persuaded by moral and aesthetic considerations. Technical devices rather than "serious thought and art" occupy the mind. The principals of power no longer dance; taste is nowhere on the agenda. The sublime, cut off from beauty, becomes an end-of-the-world exhilaration, vast, dark, and unimaginable, reverting to Burke's adolescent distinction, while beauty is romanticized to impotence, a concern not even for the arts, and aesthetics is now generally an unpronounceable word. None of the trilateral ruling powers of the United States—Religion, Economics, Science—give a hoot for culture, ignoring its record as a lasting strength let alone an ennobling progressive value. Certainly, investing in the constraining and optimistic potential of culture is worth a try, since ethical shock, natural cataclysm, statistical probabilities, Christianism's Armageddon—the horror, the horror—have been unable to collar Mars and pull him back from the brink. The idea that aesthetic culture can put some curbs on explosive violence, as in Japan after several hundred years and in eighteenth-century Europe, prompts the mind to think anew an old-fashioned idea.

For the great power that the United States has become, whether long-lived or short, the flagrant imperialism of Louis and Frederick, as well as the other Greats of that period—Peter and Catherine and several Charleses—may be aped; but the amazing power of aesthetic culture which they each fostered is so obviously lacking that the United States seems now partially crippled if not fundamentally retarded. Even in its own defense, it cannot find the linguistic talents to read the enemy's messages.

A War of Words

Aesthetics is so absent from American considerations that the Western engagement with Islam is misread in the light of America's own religious and political devotions. "You can read through reams of expert writing on the modern Near East," writes Edward Said in his landmark work *Orientalism,* "and never encounter a single reference to literature."[120] Supposedly, the West is again on the ramparts defending Christian values as at Poitiers/Tours (732), Lepanto (1571), and Vienna (1683) against an enemy that has made no progress for a thousand years because it is said to be stuck in narrow scholasticism and feudal tribalism without benefit of self-division, reformation, and tolerance. We scour the Koran for proof of jihad, instead of grasping that the essence of the Koran is its language much as the essence of the King James Bible is its language, not the truth of its word so much as the majesty of its song.

One factor alone unifies the Arab world, and that is not simply its belief in the same one God as an abstract idea but the manner in which this revelation was presented by Mohammed: poetic expression. "The exaltation experienced by the Prophet . . . found expression in the very form of his discourses, the bold images and rhetorical diction which are full of rhythmic movement and are marked by genuine poetic feeling."[121] "There can be no doubt but that the Arabic language is the most potent factor in both the creation and maintenance of this over-riding myth of Arab nation, Arab unity, Arab brotherhood."[122] "The Arabs owed their awareness of constituting a people, in spite of tribal contradictions, principally to their most important common spiritual possession, their poetry."[123] "Any explanation of the Arab mind must take into account the profound effect of language and literature on individuals and the whole Arab race."[124] "Poetry today, as it was thirteen hundred years ago, is a part of everyday living. . . . Arabic's wealth of synonyms provides unrivalled possibilities. . . . It has many innuendoes . . . phonetic beauty . . . rhythm and majesty."[125] "Arabic can be compared only to music."[126] "Song language . . . became the mother of classical Arabic, which Islam made into a world language."[127]

My argument here makes no claim that the writers just quoted are objective and not racially prejudiced as Said believes, or that the Arabic mind is less bellicose because of its aesthetics. In fact the Arabic language in the mouths of populist preachers and in religious schools has suffered the cheapening of its imagery to better sell politics, and to buyers whose age and educational level is steadily declining. For instance, almost two-thirds of activists arrested by the Egyptian government in the 1970s had university degrees compared with only 30 percent in the 1990s.[128]

I am not focusing upon the influence of aesthetics on the Islamic mind, but upon the omission of this influence upon the American. What the United States sees of them only reinforces its convictions that the cultivation of their "song language" with its emotional reverberations and exaggerated rhetoric excites mobs to violence and individuals to terrible acts. The course guide (1975) for undergraduates at Columbia College, for instance, said "that every other word in the

[Arabic] language had to do with violence, and that the Arab mind as 'reflected' in the language was unremittingly bombastic."[129] Or, as the influential text by Shouby declares, "Arabic is characterized by General vagueness of Thought . . . Over-assertion and Exaggeration."[130]

Although the art of language mollified the eighteenth century's spirit of war, Americans feel safer in the land of literalism and the plain-speak language of commerce and car repairs. The people of the United States prefer by far the almost unspeakable prose of its leaders, mocking the excesses not only of Islamic speech but of Castro, and earlier, Khrushchev, finding more homeland security in the flat tones of its Secretary where apathy takes comfort, anxiety allayed.

The advocacy of democracy on the listless tongues of American leaders cannot carry the heart of its hearers in Islamic lands. There, what is offered is heard in terms of the rhetoric in which it is presented. If bringing democracy kills off gorgeous speech and reduces inspiration to sociological facts and economic numbers, "democracy" strikes the poetic ear as simply crude, dumb, and ugly. The insult of ugliness may itself be a *casus belli*. The Greeks fought the barbarians—and who were the barbarians? Those who did not speak Greek, a definition which has come down through the ages to be deposited in the dictionary as "the absence of cultivation in language." Besides, since a fundamental tenet of Islam holds that all believers are ipso facto brothers, they could argue that democratic equality brings nothing essentially new. It is merely a legalistic formulation of what already exists within the heart, if not in government, ever since the Prophet's original revelations.

The question which opened this book—how do we imagine and understand war?—becomes immediately practical once a war has begun. Then imagination focuses upon the enemy's mind and culture, since the worst mistake, say the textbooks, is underestimating the enemy, in particular his intelligence. What if the imagination brought to this estimation has inferior instruments of assessment? One such inferior instrument is the very idea of foreign language study which bases itself in the schools set up during World War II and the Cold War, where language study is a "working tool of the engineer, the economist, the social scientist, . . . certainly not for reading literary texts."[131] Yet, "to be a case officer," said the eminent strategic analyst Edward Luttwak, "you have to be a poet. You need to romance and seduce."[132] "Empathize with your enemy," now advises the eighty-five-year-old mastermind of the Vietnam horror, Robert McNamara.[133]

Since "the Arab mind"—to continue with this example—is enthralled by the culture of its language to which we are stone-deaf, because our ears pick up flowery poetry, lengthy harangues, exorbitant fantasy, ancient similes and aphorisms, innuendo and curses, as well as the sound of words, as inessential ornamentation, has our side not been misled by its own ignorance?

If the United States wants war with Islam and cannot imagine war without winning it, then its war party would have to go back to the drawing board, designing new ways of assessing intelligence. By sophisticating American intelligence the United States might find a new compatibility with the culture of the enemy, even to affecting the unnecessary assumption that Islam is the enemy. Were the deeper passion of Islam's soul appreciated and spoken to with imagination there might be a better chance of affecting the minds and hearts of the "enemy," reaching their intelligence with a fresh respect. Isn't the only definition of a victory that lasts just this winning of the mind and heart?

While European and Asian imperials fought their wars they built their cities whose culture outlived their reigns and their names. In the United States, Nef's idea that culture restrains war is being proven in reverse. Along with the American state's promotion of bellicose militarism, it withdraws from the arts. That impoverishment is furthered by debasing the language, neglecting education beyond occupational training, and narrowing the rich complexity of religious studies to one's own favorite brand.

A cultural clumsiness affects American relations with Aphrodite in the affairs of love and in the ways of war, where subtle intelligence is of first importance. Military intelligence must be able to imagine the other as another state of mind with its own affinities and propensities. Eisenhower's intelligence failed to imagine the German winter attack through the Ardennes; MacArthur's intelligence could not imagine the Chinese crossing the Yalu. Pearl Harbor, Tet, Twin Towers—un-imaginable surprises. Sizing up the enemy requires more than measuring forces with high-tech surveillance, cracking codes, and connecting the dots. Imagining the enemy means allowing the other to enter and occupy whole areas of your soul, to submit, to be penetrated, but not possessed. This too is Aphroditic. She took all lovers into herself but was never herself taken.

The culture of the United States since its colonial days has been faithfully promised to the plain style of Protestant literalism: direct, unambiguous, uncompromising. We think in rules and laws, and an aura of righteousness overhangs our decisions in which destiny has a hand, leaving no escape from our own words. "Unconditional surrender," rather than back-door diplomacy that might stave off more casualties and more waste. "Unconditional surrender," however, has proven to be a delusional slogan altogether contrary to the American withdrawals in Korea, and from Vietnam, Lebanon, Somalia, and Iraq (1991). Without the subtle feints and seductive shifts of Venus (basic to boxing and the martial arts), retreat means rout, defeat. We seem able to recognize only Venus *victrix,* which is but one of her many guises that include Sun Tzu's modes of deception and Trotsky's emphasis upon maneuverability. Remember, the gods cannot appear alone. Hermes-Mercurius is mutually entailed with Aphrodite so that she is also hermetic, that is, secretive, duplicitous, unable to be pinned down. And, she is hermaphroditic, an imagined bridging of unlike differences, a flagrant metaphor beyond logic and fact. To a Venus-deprived society, underhanded methods appear depraved, and when they are applied, they become vicious and heavy-handed because of the righteous rule of law. How can wit and metaphor survive in a cosmos simplistically divided between "for" and "against," good and evil, Christ and Antichrist? Yet, the softening, bridging pleasures of poetic discourse were essential to eighteenth-century culture, acting as an indirect force "weakening the will" of aggressive war. Similarly, wars between the Italian cities in the Renaissance were often saved from the madness of battle by the formalisms of display and the artfulness of language.

American imagination in dance and writing, in music and painting, receives worldwide recognition, but the penetration of this culture into the popularism of the American political mind arrives only in the armored car of money delivery. The civilizing influence of aesthetic imagination never makes it to the mall. It is as if the nation as a whole is immune to culture, protected against it as something freak, unnatural, a disease of decadence, a corrupting of what Americans live by and live for: their religious beliefs in God and America, forward marching under the flag and the gun-toting Minuteman into a bright future against all enemies, against all: enemies. "With the cross of Jesus going on before. Christ, the royal Master, leads against the foe; / Forward into battle see his banners go!"[134] Culture which could possibly leash the violence of war with a love of equal strength is so blocked by the American ways of belief that we must conclude that war's sinister godfather and secret sharer in its spoils is religion, to which we have now finally come.

Chapter Four:

RELIGION IS WAR

A s people used to live in God, I live in the war," said
Marcel Proust in 1915.[1] War replaces religion, becomes religion. "War is a force that gives us meaning,"[2] because war does
what religion is supposed to do: raise life into *Importance,* that crucial category of existence defined by Whitehead as "the immanence
of infinitude in the finite."[3] The sublime presence of an other dimension in the finite entrapment of a muddy shell hole, or Proust's
secluded chamber.

Ceremonies of military service, the coercion by and obedience
to a supreme command, the confrontation with death in battle as a
last rite on earth, war's promise of transcendence and its sacrificial
love, the test of all human virtues and the presence of all human
evils, the slaughter of blood victims, impersonally, collectively, in

the name of a higher cause and blessed by ministers of several faiths—all drive home the conclusion that "War is religion." Yet that conclusion provides little for fresh thought. We need to pass beyond what we know to imagining what we may not want to know.

"War is religion" takes us only halfway. Beyond is a far graver proposition: "Religion is war."

Before this chapter can elaborate the idea that religion is war, we have to observe crucial psychological distinctions between myth and religion. Although a god is named all through these pages, this god, Mars or Ares, remains the mythical personification of the archetypal force of war and of a host of martial attitudes and behaviors. He is not a god of religion. He has no church, no congregation, no priesthood, no holy text, no theology. Above all, he does not ask for belief.

Mythical gods differ from those of religion because myths are stories and their gods are "styles of existence," in the words of Carl Kerényi. These gods have no dated origins in history, no authorized mode of approaching them or understanding them, and the stories are not considered to have happened literally, even when they are sometimes set in a specific locale and historical persons may be interwoven in the tale. To paraphrase an ancient Roman defender of myth, Sallust: the gods of myth never happened but always are. Myths provide archetypal ways of insighting the human condition; they present psychological truths such as we discover when turning to war with Mars/Ares in the background of our minds.

Religion, in contrast, encodes a particular story as the revelation of a particular god's own word of immortal truth to a historical human in a specific place at a specific moment. The revelation of this truth to Moses, Jesus, Mohammed, and Gautama too, are set down in books which then, themselves, take on the sacredness of truth. Scholars speak of "book religions" and "oral (storytelling) religions." Religion reads the words literally; myth hears the words literarily. Myths ask the psyche to invent and speculate, to listen and be amused; religion, first of all, calls for belief.

And belief brings with it trouble, because belief posits the reality of its object! This startling idea, logically elaborated by the father of phenomenological philosophy, Edmund Husserl (d. 1938), implies that it is not the god of a religion that brings the soul to belief, but that the psyche's "will to believe" (William James) posits the god in whom the soul believes. More crassly stated by the virulent discounters of all religion: all gods of every sort are inventions of human belief to satisfy human needs, and religion is but the opium of the people.

There need be no conflict between mythical gods and those of religion, because myth never insists its gods are "real." They need no proofs and they do not depend for affirmation of their reality on the faith of their devotees. Besides, myth makes no claim to truth. Some of the major thinkers, during the Renaissance particularly, were ordained Christians in religion and equally serious in regard to the ancient pagan pantheon. They paid tribute to the spirit in their Christianity and to the soul through the imagination of classical gods and goddesses.

When a god speaks in the Greek of Homer and Sophocles or the Latin of Ovid and Vergil, the words carry a huge presence—but that is all. They are borne through the ages by the aesthetic powers of their authors, not by divine authority. They are not words of religious revelation. The Greeks did not have a word for "religion." They did not believe in their gods; they lived with them as myths. The Romans did not believe in their gods; they swore oaths to them in service to the state. There is no "I believe" (*credo*) necessary to Judaism, Shintoism, Taoism, Buddhism, Hinduism, or to the animistically inclined peoples who still inhabit much of the earth. But, when a particular god is especially the one and only Supreme God, transcendent, unfathomable in essence, unnamable, yet capitalized, the connection with this almighty supreme being depends mainly on his generous grace, his epithanic revelations in miracles, tongues, and visions, or finally upon your absolute unwavering faith. Or secondly upon the intercession of an institution, a book, a cult, a prophet, or an incarnation as the literal emanation of the original hidden and transcendent being.

This one Supreme God's transcendence means there are no gods in the doorways as in old Rome, no gods in the gardens, in the cupboards of houses. There are no audible presences of the gods: the owl's hoot (which is Athene), the blasts of north wind (which is Boreus), in the sea-storms and riptides (which is Poseidon), in the sudden flame of erotic passion (which is Eros's arrow striking flesh). So evidently present in the animation of life where life is lived in myths, these gods do not need belief.

Belief is, however, the essential psychological component of religion. Sacrifice, prayer, devotion are hollow motions without belief. And it is belief that brings us to war. An analysis of belief by the philosopher Bertrand Russell gives a definition in terms of its "efficacy in causing voluntary movements," "a content is said to be believed when it causes us to move."[4] Regardless of whom or what you believe in, belief as a psychological phenomenon urges action. We act our beliefs; do because we believe. The stronger the belief, the more action takes over, the more motivated we become and the surer and narrower our justification for what we are doing. Even believers in peaceful nonviolence assemble, march, and demonstrate. Belief is the short fuse that sets off Mars's archetypal force and war's unpredictable devastating course.

When the claims of any divinity such as Jahweh or Allah or a semi-divinized leader like Hitler or Mao or Khomeini, or an abstracted idea of a people, a class, a race, or a nation is believed to be the prime reality, truth, goodness, and power, it will fight against the claims of all others to the same rank and status. The borders which singleness of belief defends may be both geographical and doctrinal; in either case transgressors shall be expelled, imprisoned, converted, or put to death. Believers become martial in defense and martial in their mission. "Go ye therefore, and make disciples of all the nations, baptizing them into the name of the Father and of the Son and of the Holy Ghost: teaching them to observe all things whatsoever I commanded you" (Matt. 28:19–20). Toleration is compromising, inclusion treacherous, coercion to the point of violence necessary.

Theology of god and psychology of belief reinforce each other. On the one hand, belief is validated by the absolute superiority in the object of belief, the god or leader or idea; for who would believe in a lesser god? On the other hand, the hyperirrational extremes attributed to the divinity fuel the faith of believers, who prove their faith by fighting ever more strongly for their cause, even if lost, just because it is beyond reason. In the oft-cited words ascribed to an early father of the Roman Church, Tertullian (d. 222), *"Credo quia absurdum est."* I believe because it is absurd.

So when war clouds gather, religious belief electrifies the air. When our belief is in the republic and the republic is declared endangered, we rally around the flag "for which it stands." Whatever the object of belief—the flag, the nation, the president, or the god—a martial energy mobilizes. Decisions are quick, dissent more difficult. Doubt which impedes action and questions certitude becomes traitorous, an enemy to be silenced.

The single focus on One True God requires that belief be cohesive, organized. The psychology of Christian monotheism, for instance, strives to maintain a defined coherence of its object (God) and a cohesion of belief among believers. "There is one body, and one Spirit . . . one Lord, one faith, one baptism, one God and Father of all." (Eph. 4:4–6) Already in the year 325 the Council of Nicea gathered the educated and leading Christians from diverse places and professions of faith to formulate one agreed definition of Christian belief as a credo (and we still call religions creeds); yet, ever since, the texts of that creed as well as the words of the scriptures have been battled over, slaughtering sister and brother Christian believers through the ages in attempts to determine the final authorized version of what is correct to believe.

Because a monotheistic psychology must be dedicated to unity, its psychopathology is intolerance of difference. Hence the issue of toleration has plagued theological thinkers for ages, leading to schisms and more schisms. As long as you hold that your god is the perfect supreme deity, all other gods will be lesser. There are no several truths, no other roads to the Kingdom. The Roman Catholic Church has not renounced its claim to exclusivity, officially asserting to be "the one and only Church of God." "It is through Christ's Catholic Church alone, which is the all-embracing means of salvation . . ."[5]

Moreover, as long as the others, the lessers, continue to practice their precepts and believe in a different god (or a slight variation in the nature of your god), they exhibit in their very existence a denial of the complete truth of your god. It is a necessity of your truth and your faith to war against them, because no matter how quietly they live or how far away their territories, their existence places in essential doubt the foundations of your belief in your god. "The existence of many churches in one community weakens the foundations of them all."[6]

The psychology of Jewish monotheism differs radically from Christian, putting the lie to that hyphen which attempts to fuse the two into "the Judeo-Christian religion." The raging intolerance of the biblical God of the Jews was mollified through hundreds of years and hundreds of thousands of pages of interpretations and commentaries, leavening the literalism with metaphorical, mystical, and many-leveled meanings. Biblical Hebrew consists in clusters of consonants without definite vowels so that a text may and does support widely different connotations, favoring uncertainty and rich obscurity. Punctuation is also seriously missing. All this together allows an amazing freedom of hermeneutic fantasy and almost comical hair-splitting. Literalist singleness of meaning becomes but one fantasy among others.

The warlike spirit of ancient Judaism—until the literalist revival focused in Orthodox Israel—dissipated in the diaspora of the Jewish people and fragmented under scholarly dispute. That spirit, however, found another home when the Bible was transported into Christianity as its "old testament." The bellicosity of the Prophets and Judges and Kings became part of the new religion, and also of the new religion of Islam which also incorporated biblical figures and motifs into the Koran (e.g., #61, "Battle Array"). The appropriation of the Jewish Bible, unmitigated by later centuries of differing rabbinical options, favored a more militant literalism in the new reading.

In contrast to that Christian literalism, a 1990 survey in the United States found that only 14.2 percent of those declaring themselves Jews consider "the Bible to be the actual word of God."[7] Whereas 90 percent of American Christians believe, for instance, in the Virgin Birth of Jesus, which Hans Küng, a major Catholic theologian and scholar, has declared is "a collection of largely uncertain, mutually contradictory, strongly legendary" stories.[8] To consider the events in the Bible as legends, myths, and stories, or as exemplary lessons for learning life's truths, opens the mind to imaginative speculation, shaking belief in the Bible's revelation of the true words of its God. Can one march off to war in the name of a story? But truth goes marching on.

The uncertainties of text and the centuries of exhaustive study of the Bible succeeded in avoiding for Jewish monotheism the necessity of heresies, anathemas, apostasies, and also the inquisitional

tortures in the name of one true meaning, avoiding as well the coercive demand to believe literally in the Bible at all. Therefore, it is
Christian monotheistic psychology that is the one for our culture
to focus upon and fear.

There is much to fear! First, the sheer numbers of believers
among the population; second, the literalism of their belief; and,
third, the impregnable innocence of belief, as if the commitment
to the doctrine of love prevents awareness of the facts of war and
the terrible truth of a militant monotheistic psychology enacted by
Christian civilization.

Western Christianity's god comes front and center when war is
in the air. War brings its god to life. In World War II this god was a
co-pilot on bombing runs, as one book title declared, and a popular song turned a chaplain into a "helluva gunner." In World War I,
"Clergymen dressed Jesus in khaki and had him firing machine
guns." The bishop of London exhorted his Christian fellows to
"kill the good as well as the bad . . . kill the young men as well as
the old . . . kill those who have shown kindness to our wounded as
well as those fiends . . ."[9]

On the eve of the battle of the Somme (July 1916) which cost
on the first day alone sixty-two thousand British casualties,[10] Field
Marshal Haig wrote his wife: "I feel that every step in my plan has
been taken with divine help."[11] If Haig is right, his god wants war;
if Haig is wrong, the general is deluded.

Another supreme commander, Douglas MacArthur in his
farewell address to the United States Congress, considered his sacred duty "to carry to the land of our vanquished foe the solace
and hope and faith of Christian morals."[12] The traditional pattern:
conquest and conversion.

In the midst of a more recent war, a ranking American lieutenant general declared in uniform to a church congregation that
the satanic foes in Islam "will only be defeated if we come against

them in the name of Jesus." In that general's statement—"If there is no God, there is no hope"—we can see how the values of religion can fuel the will to fight.[13]

In Sarajevo Peter Maass talked religion with a Catholic couple, wanting to know, "How can you believe in a God who permits such things to happen?" The young wife "looked at the statue of the Virgin Mary [and said] 'I believe more strongly than before . . . I have more faith now. I pray more. I believe more, and I believe that this is all God's will.'"[14]

In the trenches of World War I French, German, Russian, Italian, English, Scottish, Irish, Austrian, Serbian, Bulgarian, Canadian, and American—to name but a few—engaged in killing each other, invoked the name of one and the same god. Northern and Southern armies of the War between the States killed each other, calling on the same one god. The god of Israel and the god of Palestine and the god of Iraq is this same one god, and is also the very one invited to White House prayer breakfasts.

The religions of Jahweh, Allah, and God the Father, with all their twiggy denominations, are sister branches of the one monotheistic root of which each claims to be the one and only true daughter. All place Abraham/Ibrahim among the founding patriarchs, and all point to his willingness to kill his son for the sake of their common god as an exemplary lesson. All regard Jerusalem as their own holy city. All still declare that their god is compassionate and have been killing one another for centuries. Of course Jesus is not divine for the other two and Mohammed is not a prophet for the other two, but they all begin in the Bible, grew first in the same religion-bearing earth of the Middle East, and have the strength of monotheism in common. But the commitment to the singleness of vision that monotheism inflicts has them each inflicting centuries of terror on one another, and even on others in distant lands not concerned with their god or their disputes.

In view of all the appeals for peace addressed to this one Supreme God for deliverance from the evils of war, why does he let them go on? This simple question comes from the heart of those under torture, devastated by bombing, herded into concentration camps. War presents theological dilemmas about the nature and intention of a one and only almighty God whose goodness and mercy are exalted by the three great monotheistic religions. By definition this God has the greatest power; there is nothing that he cannot do—that is what his omnipotence means. So why does he not put a stop to war? Why is he not cognizant of the appeals for peace since there is nothing he does not know—that's what his omniscience means. Either he can't stop war or he doesn't want to. The first rebuts his claim to almightiness and the second implies that he likes war, or at least by not stopping it, he sustains it.

The supreme commander of Western "carnage" is the supreme commander of Western "culture"—to use the words from Hanson's book title—and that is why Christian belief is our focus and not other monotheisms, for they, except as enemies, are irrelevant to the Western war machine. Of course the divine name of Allah urges jihad, and the divine name of the emperor inspired kamikaze pilots, but our concern is with the divine name of Jesus Christ. Carnage and culture, yes; but not mainly because the Western mind was raised in Greek thinking, Roman practicality, and the disciplined will, but because we in the West have worshipped at the altar of a militant god ever since Joshua blew his horn. To learn more about biblical terrorism, slaughter and war, read Bruce Lincoln's *Holy Terrors,* Rodney Stark's *One True God,* Regina Schwartz's *The Curse of Cain, The Violent Legacy of Monotheism,* or Millard Lind's *Jahweh Is a Warrior.* Just read the Bible.

Christian thinkers have wrestled with the terrible militancy of their loving religion. Quietists, Pietists, Quakers, Franciscans, silent Trappists, mendicant friars, Orthodox monks and desert anchorites retreating to extremes of Mount Athos and patches of Egyptian sands, have sought ways to turn from the militancy of the martial Christ. But ascetic denial and deliberate self-inflicted punishment are also styles of belligerency. One is still at war with the world, the flesh, and the devil, projected, often too easily, upon other peoples, nations, religions, and even barely differing religious sects.

EXCURSION:

A Third Personal Part

Four months or so into my Jungian analysis in Zurich fifty years ago, I saw in a dream a Christ figure on a cross, or at least pinned upright, with the point of a spear coming out from his side. (The traditional image shows the wound in the side of Jesus where he had been pierced by the spears of the Roman soldiers.) Together with my dream image was the dream sentence: "See (or get) the point from the inside."

I was then young, neurotic, and complaining of a duodenal ulcer. I got the message: I had to become more introverted, feel things more deeply, pointedly, precisely inside myself. My understanding then suited my Jungian ideology of that time, and it suited my identification with the suffering servant of the analytical process, the suffering Jesus, nailed between all sorts of opposites and pulled in different directions. I heard the dream sentence from the position of a man on a cross and missed the point of the spear.

Jesus has since passed on; his worldwide importance no longer embodies personal significance despite my interest in the texts relevant to Christianity to which I have given thought since university days. The appeal of Jesus during that phase of my analysis seems now to be as comforter of neurotic suffering, ennobling passivity with a megalomanic Christ-identification, much as with many writers like Nietzsche and Lawrence and Gibbon who were so despising and contemptuous that as if by attacking Christianity they could free themselves from their own imprisonment in it. So, I could reduce this chapter's "denial of Christ" to a counterphobic compensation for my earlier attraction.

More important now, because of this book, is the point of the spear. The dream was killing the life of this god-figure and my *imitatio Christi* by means of a weapon of a different god, Mars, an initiatory weapon, for instance, among the Nuer where it was like an extension of the right hand.[15] The point of the dream was the spear; I was being moved from the cult of Jesus, as some Jungians then presented him, to a cult of Mars. I did not get that point. Nor until now did I recognize that I had been captured by a central myth of Christianity—not the evident crucifixion but the latent presence of Mars within the wounded, suffering victim. The passive sacrificial lamb, in all innocence, conceals a spear's aggressive iron. The dream exposed the passive-aggressive hypocrisy of my posture.

To see the point from the inside is now this book, the driving emergence of Mars from within my body and my own right hand, my ulcerating anger at my compromises with the Christian compact, so that this chapter could be named, following Kierkegaard, "An Attack upon Christendom."

The fact is clear: Western wars are backed by the Christian God, and we cannot dodge his draft because we are all Christians, regardless of the faith you profess, the church you attend, or whether you declare yourself utterly atheistic. You may be Jew or Muslim, pay tribute to your god in Santería fashion, join with other Wiccas, but wherever you are in the Western world you are psychologically Christian, indelibly marked with the sign of the cross in your mind and in the corpuscles of your habits. Christianism is all about us, in the words we speak, the curses we utter, the repressions we fortify, the numbing we seek, and the residues of religious murders in our history. The murdered Jews, the murdered Catholics, the murdered Protestants, the murdered Mormons, heretics, deviationists, freethinkers . . . Once you feel your own personal soul to be distinct from the world out there, and that consciousness and conscience are lodged in that soul (and not in the world out there), and that even the impersonal selfish gene is individualized in your person, you are, psychologically, Christian. Once your first response to a dream, a bit of news, an idea divides immediately into the moral "good" or "bad," psychologically you are Christian. Once you feel sin in connection with your flesh and its impulses, again you are Christian. When a hunch comes true, a slip-up is taken as an omen, and you trust in dreams, only to shake off these inklings as "superstition," you are Christian because that religion bans nondoctrinal forms of communication with the invisibles, excepting Jesus. When you turn from books and learning and instead to your inner feelings to find simple answers to complexities, you are Christian, for the Kingdom of God and the voice of His true Word lies within. If your psychology uses names like ambivalence, weak ego, splitting, breakdown, ill-defined borders for conditions of the soul, fearing them as negative disorders, you are Christian, for these terms harbor insistence upon a unified, empowered, central authority. Once you consider the apparently aimless facts of history to be going somewhere, evolving somehow, and that hope is a virtue and not a delusion, you are Christian. You are Christian too when holding the notion that resurrection of light rather than irremediable tragedy or just bad luck lie in the tunnel of human misfortune. And you are especially an American Christian when idealizing a clean slate of childlike innocence as close to godliness. We cannot escape two thousand years of history, because we are history incarnated, each one of us thrown up on the Western shores of here and now by violent waves of long ago.

We may not admit the grip of Christianity on our psyche, but what else is collective unconsciousness but the ingrained emotional patterns and unthought thoughts that fill us with the prejudices we prefer to conceive as choices? We are Christian through and through. St. Thomas sits in our distinctions, St. Francis governs our acts of goodness, and thousands of Protestant missionaries from every sect you can name join together to give us the innate assurance that we are superior to all others and can help them see the light.

EXCURSION:

Martial Christianism

How did this happen? When did our Christianized psyche become so belligerent? It goes back to the early years of the Christian era. The wars of religion to which we are heirs and are still fighting today began in the battle of the Milvian Bridge (AD 313). There, Constantine, soon to be Roman emperor, had his soldiers before the battle inscribe on their shields the cross and the phrase "in this sign you shall be victor." The men needed a divine name to fight for and be inspired by.[16] Constantine decided upon the cross of

Christ, following upon a vision or a dream on the eve of battle. Those who were inspired by the cross won the battle; Constantine became Christian; the Empire followed. The rest is your history.

Even earlier, the god who has inspired these pages and who ruled before the conversion of Rome was infusing Christianity from within. Mars did not just go into exile now that a new god took over; he converted. Christendom's conquest of the old Mediterranean gods was an engulfing amalgamation of many into one. The research of scores of scholars has laid out in detail how the old gods were fed into the image of Jesus. The cult of the new god incorporated Sol Invictus, the one unconquerable, daily resurrecting sun god;[17] the suffering and wine of Dionysos and the ecstasies of his followers; the healing gifts of Aesculapius; the wounded sweetness and early death of Adonis and Attis; the imperiled infancies of Zeus, Dionysos, Hercules; the illumination and hymns of Apollo and Orpheus; the triumphant strength of Mithra and Hercules; the divine son, Horus, in the lap of his mother. And of course Venus *victrix,* now wearing a cross around her fetching throat or on her shield.

The early Christians were not merely meek and mild victims; they called themselves soldiers of Christ, *milites* (2 Tim. 2:3; Phil. 2:25), and St. Cyprian (d. 258) used the term *militia* for the Christian's "service against the world." That martial spirit through the following centuries helped accomplish the takeover of the old gods, their cults, their temples, their images, their adherents. "We take prisoner every thought for Christ," wrote Gregory of Nazianzus (d. 390), one of the important fathers of the Roman Catholic

Church, referring to the transmutation of Greek philosophy into Christian apologetics. Christian teachers reduced the old gods and their myths to embellishments upon the lives of historical persons, a technique called euhemerism. "Those to whom you bow were once men like yourselves," wrote the early father, Clement of Alexandria (d. ca. 215).

Manuals collecting the classical myths were popular in the early Renaissance, but Jean Seznec (who has traced the ancient gods' course into later Western civilization) says the pagan world, due to these manuals, became "bookish and barbaric . . . forc[ing] the gods back into the matrix of allegory." The Jesuits later perfected the method of using the gods and their tales for teaching Christian dogma, especially the morals of dos and don'ts in the Jesuit schools.

There burned within these changes a zealous fire much like that which swept the people of Moses centuries earlier and the followers of Mohammed centuries later, a fire that transformed so much of the globe. A consistently critical, and antagonistic, analysis of Christian rise to power is published in Gibbon's *The History of the Decline and Fall of the Roman Empire* (1776–88). For Gibbon, Rome fell, and with it the classical world, not because of the youth and truth of the new dispensation, but because of Christianity's aggressive passion. Gibbon lays out his arguments against the martyrs for provoking the acts against them; against the monks and clergy—"a swarm of fanatics incapable of fear, or reason, or humanity" whom the Roman troops feared more than they feared the fiercest barbarians on the frontiers. He mocks the intra-Christian controversies among its sects, an intolerance deriving from the new religion's congenital fault:

bigotry. He notes that "the degrees of theological hatred depend on the spirit of war, rather than on the importance of the controversy."[18] Moreover, the Christian theology of faith, whose dogmatics are lodged in revelation, mystery (superstition for Gibbon), and personal witness, dodges the classical weapon of rational debate.

Though Gibbon's huge study is infected with the zeal he rails against, that zeal gives him the strength to make his case without fear of what he is taking on. He writes in the independent spirit of the freethinkers of his time. As the contemporaneous American Revolution defied the British Empire and the Parisian populace challenged the established court of France, Gibbon took on Christianity.

Not only Gibbon's main opponent, the Roman Catholics, burned with Christian zeal and promoted Christian carnage in the defense of Christian culture. Cromwell leading his Roundheads; Zwingli, the Swiss reformer, killed while battling Catholics; Swedes rampaging down into Europe's heartland; the Dutch Protestants, the German principalities; Calvin, who burnt the independent thinker Servetus after first tearing out his tongue for having spoken honestly of the Holy Land as barren rather than a land of milk and honey which literalists insisted it must be; this Calvin, behind much early American religiosity, was congratulated for this deed by Melanchthon, Luther's humanist educator. "Basically, Luther's whole life was marked by controversies." From the age of thirty-four (1517), "Luther no longer experienced . . . a time of rest."[19] He called himself "the messenger of God," a god more likely Mars, for he was "ill-tempered and by his own confession, never wrote or spoke as well as when he was at the peak of rage: 'In my prayers, in my sermons, in my writings, I never succeed so well as when I am angry. For anger cools my blood, sharpens my mind, and drives out assailing criticism.'"[20] Anger supports monotheistic psychology by driving out other voices, keeping one narrowly focused on one's personal intolerance.

When Luther defends killing in war, is the god to whom he refers Mars or Christ? "The very fact that the sword has been instituted by God to punish the evil, protect the good, and preserve peace [Rom.13:1–4; 1 Pet. 2:13] is powerful and sufficient proof that war and killing along with all the things that accompany wartime and martial law have been instituted by God."[21]

Mars continues to furnish Christian faith with fundamentalist fervor. He was born again in 1920 when a group of evangelical Protestants presented themselves as militants willing to do "battle royal" in the name of the "fundamentals" of the Christian faith.[22] American boys from obedient Lutheran, Congregationalist, Methodist, Baptist homes shooting up foreigners in the Caribbean, the Philippines, *semper fides,* keeping the faith, from the halls of Montezuma to the shores of Tripoli. "Marines for Christ."[23] The Yanks are coming, the drums drum-drumming. Spread the word; we're coming over, and it'll soon be over everywhere.

"The bombs bursting in air"—give proof that our flag is still there. Words that became the national anthem arose like oracular predictions nearly two centuries ago (in 1814), as did "The Battle Hymn of the Republic" (1861) that came, miraculously on awakening at dawn's early light[24] to Julia Ward Howe, complete in five passionate, religious, bellicose stanzas, e.g., "I have read the fiery gospel writ in burnished rows of steel . . . He has sounded forth the trumpet that shall never call retreat . . . Our God is marching on . . ." Vatic words from the daimon of the collective American soul.

I am bearing down on American Christianity in particular because the United States wields the most military power and is at the same time the most Christian of nations. If religion is war, then contemporary America presents a paradigm of my thesis. Not only contemporary America. Free-ranging violence and religious sectarianism ride side by side through United States history and manifest its destiny since the earliest colonials, who were not only pious pilgrims and wigged gentlemen of Virginia and Massachusetts. Felons, too, were this nation's forebears: "From 1619 to 1640 all pardoned felons were sent [from England] to Virginia. From 1661 to 1700 more than 4,500 convicts were sent to the colonies."[25] Later, another eight or nine thousand were deposited in Maryland. Others came over hopefully to escape English law, which made nearly three hundred offenses punishable by hanging, and those pardoned took off for the new lands of wild freedom that later became Tennessee, Arkansas, and Texas. The "worst representatives of the white men's society went into the wilderness first." By 1812, one observer noted, "the lower order of the white people in the United States of this new world are, if possible, more savage than the copper-coloured Indians."[26]

When Martin Luther King Jr. said, "The greatest purveyor of violence in the world today . . . is my own Nation," did he link this with his religious faith? The courage Reverend King showed in leading nonviolence in the face of the ghosts of ancestral felons reborn as white racists still leaves unaddressed the deep-seated incubus of violence in the American nation: the religious zeal which all parties share.

Violence may depend on implements (Arendt), but before the implements the urge to reach for them. Belief is the Prime Mover (Russell). Mars is loaded and ready, just waiting for the primer. The Christian's task—and we are all Christians—is digging below the blanket of hypocrisies to expose the dragon seeds. The blame for war no longer may be laid on others—*their* holy books, *their* inflammatory priests, *their* history of belligerency. Psychoanalysis has moved civilization to where it must do what its patients do: take back easy blame from out there in search of the more difficult blame in here. The role of religion in providing the motivating trigger for war is not in *their* religion, but in literal monotheistic religion as such, anywhere.

Dare we imagine the history of Reverend King's violent nation, since its earliest colonial times, fearful in a sublime wilderness and among the enslaved, to be the case history of a loner among peoples, psychologically an isolate dreamer of the American dream, a true believer and a serial killer, both? How else live the unbearable cross of the Christian paradox of arrogant intolerance and cruel suppression while professing goodwill, charity, and salvation by a merciful Lord except by virtue of hypocrisy?

Hypocrisy in America is not a sin but a necessity and a way of life. It makes possible armories of mass destruction side by side with the proliferation of churches, cults, and charities. Hypocrisy holds the nation together so that it can preach, and practice what it does not preach.

A foundation for the hypocrisy is revealed in the New Testament's final chapter, Revelation, where the veils fall (apocalypse) that hide the final truth. This truth is the terrifying wrath of the Divine Lamb[27] who wreaks havoc on the world in a conflagration that "owes its fire and energy to the passion of hatred which runs through it."[28] Armies, horsemen, trumpets, swords, iron scepters, killings after killings. The earth is burned up in stages—"all the trees and every blade of grass."[29] Hailstones, falling stars, lakes of fire. Plagues of insects to torture the enemies of the Lord with "the pain of the scorpion's sting."[30] Battles upon battles. Armageddon.

Then in the middle a song to the Lamb:

> Great and marvellous are thy works,
> O Lord God, the Almighty;
> righteous and true are thy ways
>
> . . .
>
> for thou only art holy;
> for all the nations shall come
> and worship before thee
> for thy righteous acts have been made manifest.[31]

More scenes of horror with "birds consuming the flesh of all men, both free and bond, and small and great."[32] The Lamb becomes an avenging Horseman (like the "flaming charger" in the "Hymn to Ares"), Christ himself as the Word of God, his white robe dipped in the blood of his enemies in a passage which "gives vent to feelings so vindictive and cruel as to be offensive to many Christian readers."[33]

"Offensive, too, to the Mullahs abroad who study closely the authorized texts that may lie unread by Christians at home. For here are the grounds of total—totalitarian—destruction for the sake of "a new heaven and a new earth . . . and [a] new [Christian] Jerusalem."[34]

Blake could only have been sadly ironic, asking the tiger "in the forests of the night," "Did he who made the Lamb make thee?" Blake had praised the tiger's kind of wrath in one of his proverbs, and he must have known the Apocalyptic Lamb to be a world-exterminating force, even if disguised as Mary's little lamb white as snow. The "fearful symmetry" between Tiger and Lamb, Wrath and Love, Satan and Christ, Revenge and Justice, Violence and Redemption, becomes hypocrisy when only the Lamb is worshipped and its Wrath ignored. It is ignored. Seven in ten Americans when given a list of characteristics that best describe their God, chose "loving."[35] The hypocrisy of willful ignorance gives sanction to innocent violence and violent innocence. Wrathful lambs of terrible love.

In a Christian civilization the facts of war restore the Lamb to the full image that includes its Wrath, making war all the more unbearable for Christians because war reveals Ares in the depths of their faith. The restoration of the full image *before* war occurs, *before* the prophesied end of the world, is what Revelation offers and what this chapter expands upon. For all its ruthlessness, this chapter is a move of prevention, an attempt at shock therapy. The task is to imagine the real.

Is a therapy possible at all? Six tenths of the inhabitants of the United States "believe that the events of Revelation are going to come true."[36] They believe this mythical annunciation of carnage is the truth of the culture's end. If belief posits the object of its belief (Husserl), then our lives and our works and all the planet shall be burned to nothing simply by the strength of belief. Some call this prophetic foretelling; others the "five hundredth monkey"; others, magical thinking or wish-fulfillment by those who cannot imagine more productively and less nihilistically. If belief sets us in motion, then the push toward annihilation is already going on.

A vision of the end of the world occurs in other myths—the Koran, Ragnarök among the Norse, Great Floods, Nuclear Winter, Black Holes. But where else is it so strongly believed, institutionally authorized, and with such specifically detailed viciousness?

Myth, thank the gods, is not fate, nor prophetic of destiny. In this case, however, because so many in our culture do not receive Armageddon as myth but as the word of the Lord, it is believed, not imagined.

"The greatest harm," wrote the Roman Seneca in his book *On Anger,* "comes from readiness to believe things." "I have read the Book of Revelation and yes, I believe the world is going to end— and by an act of God I hope—but every day I think that time is running out." This from former secretary of defense Weinberger, the man in charge (1982) of the national arsenal of mass destruction. "I do not know how many future generations we can count on before the Lord returns," said President Reagan's secretary of the interior; and Reagan himself said, "I sometimes believe we're heading very fast for Armageddon right now."[37] Presidents Carter, Clinton, and Bush are each committed, praying, churchgoing, Bible-reading believers in the Christian faith. But is Ares enough acknowledged as a determinant in that faith?

Mark Twain wrote a long narrative poem on the relation between lamb-like religion and the wrath of war, which he did not want published until after his death. Did he feel it too strong, too revelatory for the lambs to whom his poem is addressed?

The poem begins with a preacher responding to the nation's enthusiasm by calling for victory and asking protection from a loving god for the young bright-faced soldiers about to go to war. Then, a spectral figure (echoes of Coleridge's ancient mariner) enters the congregation, a messenger of the Lord's truth, explaining that prayers often ask for more than the devout realize. He then unloads upon the assembly the unspoken implication of their innocent beseeching, laying bare the full import of war prayers: every prayer for victory and every blessing of a nation's patriotic soldiers also tacitly beseeches a loving god to ordain and inspire war's terrible acts.

O Lord our God,
help us
to tear their soldiers
to bloody shreds
with our shells;
help us
to cover their smiling fields
with the pale forms
of their patriotic dead;
help us
to drown the thunder
of the guns
with the shrieks
of their wounded
writhing in pain;
help us
to lay waste
their humble homes
with a hurricane of fire;[38]

. . .

There remains the wish at the end of every war that this not happen again, that war must find its stopping point before it ever again begins. We know from what we have read of the history of war and the nature of battle that this wish is only a wish, that war is at the foundation of being, as are death and love, beauty and terror, which find magnification in war; and we know that our thought and our law build upon war as do the beliefs which nourish its ceaseless continuation.

What is then to do? We cannot dismiss the wish for war's end, nor can it be satisfied, nor perhaps ought it be satisfied. The wish to stop war is like any genuine psychological problem: it cannot be satisfied, it will not be repressed, nor will it go away of its own accord. The final sentence of Jeremy Black's thorough study, *Why Wars Happen,* concludes: "The techniques of diplomatic management can help some crises, but others reflect a willingness, sometimes desire, to kill and be killed that cannot be ignored." Ares is ever-present; he belongs in the scheme of things.

A method of classical therapy turned for a cure of a problem to the problem itself. The power that brings a disease is the very one that can take it away. *Similis similibus curantur* is the old motto: cure by means of similars (rather than by means of opposites). Since Ares/Mars puts war in our midst, we ask the same source for relief. For clues to how Ares might help, we look to the oldest text describing the specific characteristics of the different gods and goddesses, conventionally called the *Homeric Hymns,* although their attribution to a person named Homer is but a useful simplification. What matters is not their author(s) but their content. In the content of the "Hymn to Ares" we catch a glimpse of ways to "cure" war.

THE HYMN TO ARES

Ares, superior force,
Ares, chariot rider,
Ares wears gold helmet,
Ares has mighty heart,
Ares, shield-bearer,
Ares, guardian of city,
Ares has armor of bronze,
Ares has powerful arms,
Ares never gets tired,
Ares, hard with spear,

Ares, rampart of Olympos,
Ares, father of Victory
who herself delights in war,
Ares, helper of Justice,
Ares overcomes other side,
Ares leader of most just men,
Ares carries staff of manhood,
Ares turns his fiery bright cycle
among the Seven-signed tracks
of the aether, where flaming chargers
bear him forever
over the third orbit!
Hear me,
helper of mankind,
dispenser of youth's sweet courage,
beam down from up there
your gentle light
on our lives,
and your martial power,
so that I can shake off
cruel cowardice
from my head,
and diminish that deceptive rush
of my spirit, and restrain
that shrill voice in my heart
that provokes me
to enter the chilling din of battle.
You, happy god,
give me courage,
let me linger
in the safe laws of peace,

and thus escape
from battles with enemies
and the fate of a violent death.
    (*translated by* CHARLES BOER)

Some basic lessons can be gleaned from this hymn since it directly responds to the wish to escape from battles and violent death. First: honor the phenomenon, even if it be the dreaded god of war. Give praise and thanks to Ares who is called, without a trace of irony, "helper of mankind." As we said at the start of this book, the first psychological step in coming to terms with any phenomenon—no matter how much you may hate it—requires imagination and understanding, some of which is offered by this hymn in its catalog of specifics.

So, second, understand what Ares offers, where he helps. He defends the city, civilization itself, as shield bearer on the ramparts. He stands and fights for justice, gives courage, has a mighty heart, is tireless, and "hard with spear," driving home a point with superior force.

Also, as Kant explains, the martial spirit constructs civilization by promoting internal dissension between conflicting parties. "The means nature employs to accomplish the development of all faculties is the antagonism of men in society; since this antagonism becomes, in the end, the cause of a lawful order of this society." "Man wills concord; but nature better knows what is good for the species: she wills discord."[39] This appreciation is written by perhaps the most humane and gentle philosopher who ever thought his way into the heart of things.

War defends civilization, not because a war is claimed to be a just war, or a justified war. The just cause lies not in the end—overcoming evil, repelling barbarians, protecting the innocent—but in the way the entry into war and the conduct of the war maintain the steadfast virtues, the "gentle light" shone on them by Ares.

If you look to Mars for help, it is well to be courageously hon-est; to be in mind of civilization, its history, its frailty, its culture; to know more about justice than merely what the law says; and to make your points in support of war, not with repetitious jabs and insinuations but with straight, hard argument. Why not expect those who lead nations to war in the name of helping mankind to read further than the machinations of Machiavelli and Mao, and to study the oracular phrases describing the archetype of war itself?

As "rampart of Olympos," Ares, third, defends the other gods and goddesses. They are not imagined to be enemies, rivals, oppo-sites. His is the archetypal tolerance of polytheism—each god, each goddess entails another. They are all enfolded together in the great bed of myth, and their tolerance is essential to their natures. When, however, the martial spirit is confined within any single-minded belief, the result is domination, intolerance, and suppression of other ways of being, and we suffer the horror of war from which we seek escape.

We can find, fourth, a yet more subtle implication in the Homeric ode: it is to Mars we turn to diminish the "deceptive rush" into war. Stopping war once it has begun belongs less to his capacity than preventing war from ever starting. The hymn answers the age-old question: how do wars begin? They begin in the shrill voice in the heart of the people, the press, and the leaders who per-ceive "enemies" and push for a fight. The deceptive rush and a rush of deceptions promote each other, so that we are deluded by feel-ings of urgency and cover ourselves with the hypocrisy of noble proclamations.

The rush of deceptions was known and mocked during the high tide of Christendom by the learned and peaceful Catholic humanist, Erasmus (d. 1536). "But seek the reasons that drive Christians to take up arms; there is no injury, however insignificant it may be which does not seem to them sufficient pretext to start a war."[40] "They suppress and hide everything that might maintain Peace; they exaggerate excessively everything that would lead to an outbreak of war."[41] "These gentlemen invoke the Christian religion and even claim they are extending the empire of Christ by such means! What a cruel monstrosity to believe that one is never of such use to the Christian cause as when destroying from top to bottom."[42]

After five hundred years, Erasmus, this ancestor of the therapeutic calling, all the more deserves our ear because he was a passionately believing Christian who demanded more of his fellow believers than mere belief. As an eminent editor of the New Testament he brought both a critical and an aesthetic eye: "Religion he loved for the sake of letters rather than letters for the sake of religion."[43] He used knowledge, irony, and a critical mind to keep the soul honest in the midst of hypocrisy as current then as today. He attacked Christians not by deserting the fold, but by trying to awaken them to themselves.

Another translation of the "Hymn to Ares" (by Evelyn-White) phrases the same lines as: "drive away bitter cowardice from my head and crush down the deceitful impulses of my soul." Deceit, cowardice, and the headlong rush to war are all of a piece, an archetypal constellation, that we see all too clearly as wars are about to begin. No one has the courage to retreat from the brink; everyone is afraid of appearing cowardly. The fog of war spreads through the mind, stupefying, desensitizing, long before the battles begin. Witness Tuchman's *The March of Folly: From Troy to Vietnam*; witness Taylor's *How Wars Begin*. Witness the demonstration of the "deceitful impulses of the soul" that rushed the American nation to war against Mexico, against Spain, and into Iraq.

Mark Twain would have nailed the hawks: "next the statesmen will invent cheap lies, putting the blame upon the nation that is attacked, and every man will be glad of those conscience-soothing falsities, and will diligently study them, and refuse to examine any refutation of them; and thus he will by and by convince himself that the war is just, and will thank God for the better sleep he enjoys after this process of grotesque self-deception."[44] "The people can always be brought to the bidding of the leaders," said Hermann Göring at his trial at Nuremberg. "This is easy. All you have to do is to tell them they are being attacked and denounce the pacifists for lack of patriotism and exposing the country to danger. It works the same in every country."

Who would have imagined that restraint is what Mars offers, the restraint of awareness at the beginning? Restraint produced by a sensitive kind of intelligence that feels the rush; resisting the divine possession and the high-pitched shrillness crying for action, which can be met with the courage to "linger," to hold back and "keep your head when all about you / Are losing theirs . . . and not be tired by waiting." Kipling's "If," like the "Hymn to Ares," presents this kind of courage as a sign of "manhood."

Such steady courage is also Christian, and the "Hymn to Ares" can be heard with Christian ears. Like a long-drawn-out bass chord on the church organ reverberating through centuries, there is a profound retardation in the Christian traditions, sounding steadfastness of soul in the individual person against mob panics and enthusiast hysteria. The prolonged theological debates, the testing of evidence for suspect claims of miracles and visions, the unbudgeable dogmas, the collections of elders, hierarchies, the rhythm of calendars and the deliberations over language—all for the sake of slowness, from which the impatient would be reborn to be free. The oldness and the weight of institutional religion and the unconscious burden of the Fall can gentle the wild horses that want to rush to war. These reins are applied not by reason, but by something in the Christian soul itself—the hesitation of doubt, the scruples of conscience, and the responsibility to the protesting voice of one's daimon.

Though we cannot stop war, we might at least slow its start. The "Hymn to Ares" gives clues. The same virtues needed to fight are also means of restraint.

It goes against reason to speak in the same breath of Mars the mad berserker and martial restraint. But war is not a product of reason and does not yield to reason. During the decade after World War I, the reason of treaties reduced arms and reinforced rational conventions regarding prisoners of war, noncombatant civilians, weapons such as gas, attempting to put limits on war's inhumanity. Later, attention turned to restraining a far greater madness: the proliferation of nuclear weapons, their numbers, their striking power. Peace institutes, arms limitation, new university departments—still the wars have gone on to massacre as many and as terribly as ever.

Mars cannot be held by rational agreements in reasonable language. Clausewitz and Eisenhower, as we saw above, both said there is no limit to war's force. It goes on and expands its range and finds ever new objects of enmity. Like the manic syndrome, war eventually exhausts itself. The men in the lines refuse to move out, and the people at home simply get tired of war. But the civilian population cannot be hurried into exhaustion. The Civil War burnings of Shenandoah farms and the wide swaths of ravage in Georgia, and during the early 1940s in Russia and the Ukraine, the fiery bombing of Hamburg and Dresden and Tokyo, only stiffened civilian resolve. Save for a decisive battle and one party's collapse, the process of war's unraveling is slow. Accumulated lethargy at home; here and there desertions of troops as they dissolve into civilian camouflage. This is neither surrender to the enemy, nor defeat, nor even satisfaction of war's gluttonous appetite for human flesh; simply the fact that war's ferocious momentum has run down in the sands of time.

Restraint, limitation, prudence—these are seldom found in the American character. Were Americans to set up statues, as did the Romans, to the personified characteristics that move its national behavior and are idealized as virtues, one of them would surely be Rashness, the god of Haste. Quick, Fast, Instant, Flash, Time-Saver, One-Liner, Sound-Bite—are some of this god's epithets. This is the figure who makes one act before thinking and lets action determine what to think: when a problem occurs, it is Haste who asks, "What do we do about it?" "What are you taking for it?"

Prudence no longer appears on the American calendar of saints. Once upon a time it was a popular name for a daughter. Quakers, Methodists, and Calvinists cogitated for the long haul, and their laconic well-paced style continued to feature heroically in movie men from Gary Cooper through Wayne, Bronson, Ladd, Eastwood, Ford, Stallone, even Willis, to Connery, until the hero, too, has had to catch up with the speeding vehicles and flaming explosions in which he is set. The speed of martial implementarium ricochets into the action heroes; even as they age, they have to run faster and faster. Emotion has shifted; few daughters are now named Constance, Honor, Modesty, Patience, or Sweet Charity.

Prudence is out the window. When new equipment on which a soldier's life depends is procured, careful testing submits to early delivery date. One moves from one rash decision to the next in a game of increasing hurry in order to "get there first with the most" (in the famous words of General Nathan Bedford Forrest), even though the wrinkles aren't yet ironed out. Investigate after the failure; slowly, painstakingly, and at great expense piece together all the wreckage of Haste. (I recall hearing Aldous Huxley remark that moderns have been able to add only one sin to the traditional Seven Deadlies: Haste.) We pay for this sin with inevitable retardation that has to clean up the waste, repair the damage, count the casualties of mistakes as the point moves forward: "Damn the torpedoes! Full speed ahead," said Admiral Farragut in Mobile Bay.

The invasion and conquest of Afghanistan and Iraq are tributes to the god of Rashness. Move in, take over, but then come the retarding complexities that do not yield to haste. In fact, the war for Iraq began actually when the United States government declared it concluded, for Haste with its promise of quick victory had been driven from the field by the long-festering spirits of revenge, wounded pride, and seething hatred. We may garb the statue of Rashness in the robes of boldness and point to Patton's amazing speed in pivoting an entire army to win the Battle of the Bulge (winter 1944–45), but a quick masterstroke that saves a battle does not serve as a general rule for engaging in a war. Rashness can carry the day and mobilize the patriotic rush to arms, but war plants so rich a field of dragon seeds that days and days and days of death follow in the mopping up.

So it is not war that needs to find a cure, but its haste, that shrill cry in the heart brought on by Mars's fury. In that same heart, fortunately, there is another voice of restraint: Venus *victrix*.

We might assume that recoil from war's devastation, as well as sympathy for the wounded and the widowed, would restrain the deceptive rush to war, that Aphrodite, goddess of love who shrinks from battle, would hesitate at the threshold. But this conclusion is again to think in opposites, to look for an antidote to war in love.

Love is not an answer to war. Love is not a policy, nor can love be enacted in a public program. When love is declared, it is a private matter. Love may be the greatest of virtues and can be practiced by turning the other cheek, the patience of long-suffering, and by forgiving others who have sinned against you, but to employ love to end violence as did lesser followers of Gandhi and King turns love into an instrument—effective perhaps; but is this love? President Carter may have gone to Camp David in the spirit of love, but he also brought a plan. Begin and Sadat accomplished an accord, but did they depart in love?

A vague idea of love tends to whitewash the mind in innocence. It becomes an all-purpose remedy that gets you out of trouble and makes things come out all right. Love as salvation. Such love is another monosyllabic, open-mouthed, vowelly word that keeps the mind simple, without bite or hiss. This is hardly Aphrodite and Venus: for them love is the beginning of trouble, the necessary delusion that keeps one from seeing what's coming.

Thus Hedges's educated and deeply felt book on war fails finally because it ends with the usual Christian paean to love: "To survive as a human being is possible only through love. . . . It alone gives us meaning that endures. . . . Love has power both to resist in our nature what we know we must resist, and to affirm what we know what we must affirm. And love, as the poets remind us, is eternal."[45] Hedges falls back upon the same classical pair of opposites that Freud resurrected: Eros versus Thanatos, Love versus Death (War); whereas I have sought to show that love can be found inside war, (the *philia* that Shay emphasizes in *his* educated and deeply felt book), a love of the most profound sort. And also of the ugliest sort—necrophilia, sadism, exuberant murder, morbid prurience. Moreover, I have insisted that war must be embraced by a loving imagination to be understood. Otherwise, we are fighting war in our approach to it, at war within our own constructs and using love to conquer war. Love in the hands of innocence is just more trouble.

The retreat to love leaves untouched the important question that each of us as Christians must pose: why is Christianity, which entered the world as a religion of love and has distinguished itself from other world religions by the message of love in its founder and its apostles and exemplified in its martyrs and saints, also so martial? Its notion of love has not converted the god of war, and in fact the Christian culture has inspired the greatest long-lasting war machine of any culture anywhere. Does this not demand from our educated Christian minds a sharper examination of Christian love?

Instead: Venus *victrix* who brings a passion and a sensate fury hardly different from that of Mars. Their coupling presents a union of sames (not opposites) which suggests war may be restrained by aesthetic passion, which does not mean merely protection of cathedrals and libraries. Coventry, Louvain, Cologne, Leipzig, Monte Cassino, Bamian, Hue, were ruined after due decision. No, not the shield of aesthetic value, but the fury of aesthetic engagement.

In the previous chapter Nef's evidence from the eighteenth century (when orthodox faith was giving way to freethinking) suggested that aesthetic passion restrains war. All the arts and sciences, and the intimacies of talk, letters, and diaries, lived on slowness and its pleasures. I do not mean the lingering indolence of the leisure classes, but the slow aesthetics of workshop, studio, husbandry, garden, and laboratory, taming haste but not its passion. Venus *victrix* still wants to win and conquer the task at hand. Aesthetic intensity draws Mars onto a parallel path.

The old saying, "The pen is mightier than the sword," is not true, a writer's delusion. Ask Lorca or Ovid, Giordano Bruno or Walter Benjamin, or the multitude of murdered intellectuals in the last century alone from Stalinist Russia to Pol Pot's Cambodia. Yet that old saying does attempt to make an equivalence, and it recognizes that culture is a martial art, requiring tirelessness, the hard point of the spear into the bowels of philistinism, and the courage to hold back the temptation to deceive.

Not art objects made in response to war—*All Quiet on the Western Front*; the *1812 Overture*; *Guernica*. Not art objects at all; but rather concentration upon their making. *Natura naturans,* as philosophers call nature's process of creating, rather than *natura naturata,* the made, finished product.

The making invites martial metaphors: slogging through and sticking it out; cutting, breaking, tearing, rending; suffering wounds and defeat; uncontrollable rage at obstacles. Intermittent sleep. Images, shapes, lines pop up out of darkness as to pickets on night watch. The verge of madness. The loss of self on the continued adventure into no-man's-land.

Aesthetic intensity offers an equivalent of war by providing an obdurate enemy—the image, the material, the ideal—to attack, subdue, and convert. Venusian passion also offers the erotics, the sacrifice, a devotion but without doctrine, and a band of comrades dedicated to the same search for the sublime. As war is beyond reason, and religious faith is beyond reason, so too must be the aesthetic parallel to war.

Although these romantic and heroic notions of aesthetic endeavor compel the individual and draw him or her into do-or-die emotions, civilization which mobilizes wars is not moved by the same aesthetic passion. Art-making is on the sidelines, an inessential diversion; Venus reduced to cheerleading propaganda to boost the real thing: war.

Rather than cordoning off the magical power of making cultural beauty, civilization can find demonstrative modes of realizing the passionate Venus. When both accidental and intentional catastrophes hover over our heads, over the planet itself, we must imagine other ways for civilization to normalize martial fury, give valid place to the autonomous inhuman, and open to the sublime. Is civilization so dedicated to repression that it fears an outbreak of culture? Imagine a nation whose first line of defense is each citizen's aesthetic investment in some cultural form. Then civilization's wasteful "stress" converts into cultural intensity. All the diabolic inventiveness, the intolerant obsession and drive to conquer compelled toward culture. Would war lose some of its magic? Culture generates from excesses of imagination which Mars's narrow focus on its notion of victory completely occludes.

If we cannot let private fantasy play with far-fetched ideas in search of parallels to the passion of war, civilization remains delivered over to the suppressive regularity of the usual which it worships as "order." In sum, the aesthetic passion of Venus can disrupt war's source in peacetime monotony "in which nothing happens" (as Gray found), which affords no true "meaning" (as Hedges says), and promotes "psychic numbing" (which Lifton fears). Aesthetic passion provides multiple fields for engagements with the inhuman and sublime certainly less catastrophic than the fields of battle.

THERE IS no practical solution to war because war is not a problem for the practical mind, which is more suited to the conduct of war than to its obviation or conclusion. War belongs to our souls as an archetypal truth of the cosmos. It is a human accomplishment and an inhuman horror, and a love that no other love has been able to overcome. To this terrible truth we may awaken, and in awakening give all our passionate intensity to subverting war's enactment, encouraged by the courage of culture, even in dark ages, to withstand war and yet sing. We may understand it better, delay it longer, and work to wean war from its support in hypocritical religion. But war itself shall remain until the gods themselves go away.

This last chapter has been contending that religion does not want war to stop, nor does belief want a psychological awakening. You can believe your way out of war's realities, believe yourself to sleep. You can make believe you have found a practical solution to war by choosing one of the three propositions stated in the foregoing chapters:

If war is normal, then it has been and will always be no matter what we do.

If war is inhuman, then we must counter it with humane structures of love and reason.

If war is sublime, we must acknowledge its liberating transcendence and yield to the holiness of its call.

The practical consequences drawn from any one of these propositions prevent awakening to the real. The real, the truth of war, is the insoluble perplexity presented by all three chapters *together,* obliging the mind to engross itself in war as such, to imagine and understand philosophically, psychologically, theologically. "To streamline the theories of war by artificially eliminating contradictions is dysfunctional, unrealistic, and counterproductive," concludes Handel at the end of his exhaustive study of Sun Tzu and Clausewitz.[46] By imagining the real and standing in the conflict of its complexity, in willing suspension of the practical urge, we may awaken. Ever since Heraclitus and Socrates, the awakening of the deepest mind continues to be the main purpose and pleasure of psychological inquiry.

Psychological inquiry makes peculiar demands. The validity of its understanding depends on the exposition of the case *and* on the exposure of the inquirer. This book bowed to that requirement by means of personal excursions revealing remnants of the author's history and the torsions they left. The movement back into the skewed subjectivity behind the eye of the objective observer is an interiorization of awareness, a method discovered by Freud in personal psychoanalysis and since extended to cultural analysis by postmodern criticism. Revelation of the gods comes not only from outside and above but from within the perspectives of the observer.

The person in a psychoanalysis can deny awareness by projections onto others outside. Far more comfortable to see the mote in the other's eye than the beam in one's own (Luke 6:41). Similarly an entire culture can prefer blindness to itself allowing it to rest assured in its worldview. The more clearly it sees and judges, and confirms its judgments by what it sees in other peoples and religions, the more it is exterior to itself, and asleep.

The comfort of sleep cushioned by the teddy bear of innocence is precisely what war awakens us from, and to. So, this book has tried to emulate the god of war's startle and shout. It has taken deliberate aim at our culture's monotheistic psychology and the Christianity which upholds it, rather than trying to make its case in the examples of others we cannot interiorize, or in generalities about all wars everywhere and of every kind. Other wars with other-named gods among other peoples are no less terrible, but ours are ours. Our book of war cannot deny its own context, that religious context which is interior to both the culture and the author.

I have tried to expose the unacknowledged force of Ares/Mars within Christianity ever since its origins. The historical and psychological truth must be acknowledged, else the hypocrisy in the depths of Christianity keep its believers ignorant of the wrath of the Lamb in which they place their trust. Only a contrite awakening to Christianity's hypocrisy in regard to peace and war could release a new dispensation, a new reformation to rid monotheistic religion of its roots in war and the roots of war in monotheistic religion.

The bugle blows. Wake up, said Paul Revere; and Marx to the workers of the world: "You have nothing to lose but your chains." "Awake, awake, put on strength," exclaimed Isaiah (51:9). "You gotta get up, you gotta get up . . ." Wake up, said Plato; we are all in a cave watching shadows on the wall, believing them to be reality. But Socrates was put to sleep by the civilized keepers of the cave.

What use one more wake-up call? Reveille has been trumpeted from every pulpit and politician's platform and after each catastrophe year after year. Complacency, apathy, sloth, diffidence, resignation are also shadows on the wall because these are the illusions the alarmists rile against. Behind them is the real satanic seducer: *avidya,* as the Hindus call willful ignorance, arrogant stupidity; the coward's retreat from awareness. The call to wake up goes by unheard, and so "most men lead lives of quiet desperation" (Thoreau). Why? Simply because they believe simply. Most men, the huge majority, in fact all of us, are dyed-in-the-wool Christians, fully immersed in hope. We are unconsciously converts to the hopeful illusion. But hope itself converts into what it covers, its everfaithful nighttime companion, despair, and we have been instructed, deceitfully, in only the upper half of this truth: Look up; a new day is coming!

"Surely some revelation is at hand," said Yeats in his great prophetic poem "The Second Coming," only to conclude: "The darkness drops again." The future of religion is the future of illusion, wrote Freud. New day? New wars. More self-righteous killing, more gut-wrenching fear, more earth despoiled in the name of the nation, the leader, the cause, the god. And more prayers. Wars will go on; they will not cease and they will not change. The dead will fall as ever. At least we can imagine and therefore understand—not all of it, but enough to step away from delusions of hope and love and peace and reason.

The bugle blows; but we have heard Reveille too often. Instead, the few piercing tones of "Taps." They hit the right pitch, recalling Hobbes, "and the life of man solitary, poore, nasty, brutish, and short"; recalling Arnold, "And we are here as on a darkling plain . . . Where ignorant armies clash by night." Recalling Hernandez, "And the young ones? In the coffins."

Acknowledgments

With thanks to Diane Hassin, who turned my messy pages into clean copy, to Meredith Blum for her patience in seeing the book through the press, and to Kate Gorczynski and the helpful, intelligent staff of the Thompson Public Library.

Notes

CHAPTER ONE

1. Levinas, *Totality and Infinity,* 21.
2. Ropp, 508a.
3. Sontag, 2002, 98.
4. Lifton and Falk, 111–25.
5. *The New Yorker,* February 10, 2003, p. 42.
6. Ibid.
7. Tuchman, 383.
8. Tuchman, 377.
9. Sereny.
10. Sun Tzu (fourth to third centuries BC), in Handel, 77.
11. in Handel, 44.
12. Handel, 50.
13. Tolstoy, *War and Peace,* Louise and Aylmer Maude translation. NY: Simon & Schuster, 1942, p. 1359.
14. Whitehead, 63.
15. Whitehead, 66.
16. in Gray, xii.
17. Keegan and Holmes, 161.

18. Hedges, 31.

19. Levinas, *Totality and Infinity,* 21.

20. Plato, *Phaedo,* 66c–d.

21. Plato, *Laws,* 1.626A.

22. Kant, "Perpetual Peace," #365, p. 123.

23. Arendt, 62n.

24. Marshall, 1947.

25. in Handel, 68.

26. in Handel, 68.

27. Caputo, 120.

28. Blumenson, 1972, 368.

29. Eksteins, 172.

30. Eksteins, 172.

31. Heraclitus, 38.

32. Eksteins, 212.

33. Levinas, *Totality and Infinity,* 21.

34. Griffin, 245.

35. Maass, 254.

36. Hedges, 47.

37. in Hedges, 60.

38. Plato, *Laws,* 1.626A.

39. Hobbes, *De Cive* (1642), ch. 13.

40. Matt. 10:34.

41. Linderman, 350.

42. Eksteins, 292.

43. Ambrose, 304.

44. Ambrose, 306.

45. Witkop, 151.

46. Stafford, 177.

47. de Tocqueville, 304.

48. Machiavelli, xiv.

49. Lifton and Falk, 104.

50. Hobbes, *Leviathan,* I:13.

51. Freud, *Collected Papers IV,* 316.

52. Foucault, 35.

53. Foucault, 34–37.

54. Foucault, 116.

55. Foucault, 116.

56. Bobbitt, 336.

57. Aristotle, *Politics,* 1253a.2.

58. Lind.

59. Witkop, 60, 42.

60. Semmes, 6.

CHAPTER TWO

1. *Science News* 154 (August 8, 1998), p. 87.

2. *Newsweek,* August 7, 1972, p. 25.

3. Harnley, entries 0419–0684.

4. *Newsweek,* August 7, 1972, p. 26.

5. Eksteins, 218.

6. Eksteins, 146.

7. Griffin, 234.

8. Caputo, 117–18.

9. Cunliffe, 194.

10. *The New Yorker,* April 7, 2003, p. 39.

11. Hillman, *The Dream and the Underworld,* 45, 114.

12. Hedges, 13.

13. Terkel, 213–16, condensed.

14. in Weigley, 152.

15. Linderman, 177.

16. Linderman, 182.

17. Linderman, 180.

18. Keegan, 320–31.

19. Keegan, 330.

20. Guénon, p. 9f.

21. Shay, 37–38.

22. Shay, 134.

23. Chang, 119.

24. Beevor, 70.

25. Eisenhower, January 12, 1955, in Walzer, 23.

26. Lingis, 57.

27. Brownmiller.

28. Maass, 54–55.

29. Maass, 56.

30. Maass, 56.

31. Loyd, 234.

32. Hochschild, 294.

33. Hochschild, 303.

34. Blumenson, *Patton,* 210.

35. Keegan, 334.

36. Patton, 1947, 362.

37. Patton, 1947, 353.

38. Dean, 127.

39. Walzer, 138–43.

40. Walzer, 140.

41. Kugelmann, 253–61.

42. Keegan, 335.

43. Hedges, 164.

44. Keegan, 309.

45. Linderman, 356.

46. Linderman, 357.

47. Hedges, 164.

48. Shay, 168.

49. Dean, 116; Wiley, 275–92.

50. Griffin, 243.

51. Caputo, 265.

52. Patton, 1947, 337–38.

53. Constance Garnett translation.

54. Clausewitz, I.3.

55. Loyd, 303; Hedges, 162–63.

56. Ehrenreich, 232.

57. Ehrenreich, 232.

58. Ehrenreich, 232.

59. Walzer, 30.

60. Ehrenreich, 235.

61. Ehrenreich, 236.

62. Ehrenreich, 234.

63. Ziegler, 21–23.

64. Ehrenreich, 232.

65. Ehrenreich, 232.

66. Ehrenreich, 238.

67. Linderman, 261.

68. Harris, 227.

69. Hillman, 1997, 47–52.

70. Shay, 83.

71. Levinas, 21.

72. Eksteins, 180.

73. Sandlin.

74. Shay, 80.

75. Shay, 90.

76. Caputo, 268–69.

77. Linderman, 261.

78. Shay, 84.

79. Gray, 52.

80. Davis, 80a.

81. Patton, *The Secret of Victory.*

82. Bowers, 230.

83. Bowers, 228–29.

84. Girard, 263–64.

85. Vernant, 254–55.

86. Girard, 264.

87. Burkert, *Greek Religion,* 169.

88. Jung, 37.

89. Lifton and Falk.

90. Woodrow Wilson.

91. Farnell, 407.

92. Burkert, *Greek Religion,* 169.

93. Kerényi, 150.

94. Farnell, 396.

95. Kerényi, 150.

96. Keegan, 330.

97. Fussell, 41.

98. Dumézil, vol. 1, 205–46.

99. Hultkrantz.

100. Santoli, 7.

101. Santoli, 59–61.

102. Machiavelli, chap. 14.

103. Gadamer, 51.

104. Semerano, 71.

105. Semerano, 71.

106. Burnet, frg. 10.

CHAPTER THREE

1. Willetts, 286.

2. Stein.

3. Friedrich, 64.

4. Lopez-Pedraza, 62.

5. Thomas Aquinas, *Summa Theologica,* I.q.5/1.

6. Wind, 198.

7. Wordsworth, *Prelude,* I/305.

8. Foucault, 241–42.

9. Foucault, 242.

10. Foucault, 241.

11. McEvilley, 58.

12. Chapter 10.

13. Gray, 33.

14. Gray, 32.

15. Gray, 36.

16. Gray, 28.

17. Pyle, 21–33.

18. in Linderman, 242.

19. Santoli, 127.

20. in Linderman, 243.

21. in Linderman, 244.

22. in Linderman, 354.

23. in Linderman, 354.

24. in Linderman, 354.

25. 1934, 132.

26. Bachelard, *On Poetic Imagination and Reverie,* 19.

27. Bachelard, *On Poetic Imagination,* 19.

28. Witkop, 176.

29. Witkop, 62.

30. in Nicolson, 333.

31. in Nicolson, 337.

32. in Nicolson, 336.

33. McEvilley, 71.

34. McEvilley, 59.

35. *Odyssey,* 16.294.

36. John L. Smith.

37. Fussell, 153.

38. Marshall, 1947, 70.

39. Marshall, 1947, 78.

40. Wiley, 71.

41. Wiley, 76.

42. Caputo, 313.

43. Wiener, "Fire at Will."

44. Wiener, "Fire at Will," 31.

45. Brown and Abel.

46. Brown and Abel, 281.

47. Freedman, 194–210.

48. Arendt, 65.

49. Arendt, 64.

50. Arendt, 66.

51. in Bowers, 212.

52. in Gray, 31.

53. Eksteins, 201.

54. Ehrenreich, 13.

55. Eksteins, 193.

56. Eksteins, 316.

57. in Eksteins, 316.

58. in Linderman, 245.

59. in Linderman, 244–45.

60. Loyd, 303.

61. Hedges, 103.

62. Hedges, 101.

63. Hedges, 102.

64. Eksteins, 224.

65. *Iliad,* 5.428–30.

66. Friedrich, 96.

67. Burkert, *Greek Religion,* 154–55.

68. Bettini, 152–57.

69. Dumézil, 544.

70. Dumézil, 546.

71. Keegan, 186.

72. Keegan, 188.

73. Marshall, 1953, 300–301.

74. in Keegan and Holmes, 52–53.

75. Eksteins, 231.

76. Gray, 46.

77. in Eksteins, 232.

78. in Kulka et al., 50.

79. Friedrich, 99.

80. Keegan and Holmes, 39.

81. in Russell, 94.
82. Bayles, 18.
83. in Ambrose, 1992, 290.
84. Linderman, 272.
85. Roth, 219.
86. Keegan, 303.
87. Linderman, 272.
88. Hedges, 123.
89. Hersh, 56–57.
90. Hersh, 57.
91. *Odyssey,* 15.233.
92. Burnet, frg. 29.
93. Aeschylus, *Eumenides,*
    II.155–61.
94. Hersh, 59.
95. Longinus, ch. 1.
96. Levinas, *Noms Propres,*
    107–9.
97. Perrin, 17.
98. Perrin, 24.
99. Perrin, 42.
100. Perrin, 36.
101. Perrin, 36.
102. Perrin, 42.
103. Perrin, 43.
104. in Nef, 245.
105. Perrin, 70.
106. in Perrin, 71.
107. Blumenson, 1972, 608.
108. Keegan, 1999, 76.
109. Keegan and Holmes, 92.
110. in Province, 180.
111. Nef, 255.
112. Nef, 256.
113. in Nicolson, 1961, 270.
114. Nef, 257.
115. Zeldin, 213.
116. Baldick, 60.
117. Nef, 261.
118. Nef, 260.
119. in Nef, 261.
120. Said, 291.
121. Brockelmann, 15.
122. Patai, 42.
123. Brockelmann, 11.
124. Laffin, 62.
125. Laffin, 69–70.
126. Patai, 48.
127. Brockelmann, 12.
128. Gaffney, in Appleby,
    288–89.
129. Said, 287.
130. in Said, 320.
131. Said, 291–92.
132. Luttwak.
133. in Angell, *The New Yorker,*
    January 19, 2004.
134. Sabine Baring-Gould, "On-
    ward Christian Soldiers,"
    1864.

CHAPTER FOUR

1. in Painter, 223.
2. Hedges.

3. Whitehead, 28.

4. B. Russell, 244–45.

5. in Stark, 239–40.

6. Walter Lippmann (1929), in Stark, 249.

7. Stark, 213.

8. in Kristoff, *New York Times,* August 15, 2003.

9. in Eksteins, 236.

10. Middlebrook, 243.

11. in Griffin, 231.

12. in Wintle, 436.

13. Thompson, in *Time,* November 3, 2003.

14. Maass, 131.

15. Evans-Pritchard, 236.

16. John Holland Smith, 48.

17. Afföldi, 57.

18. in McCloy, 20.

19. Lohse, 76.

20. Chapiro, 101.

21. Lohse, 60.

22. Almond et al., 2.

23. Almond et al., 45.

24. Silber, 10.

25. Osborn, 72.

26. in Osborn, 72–73.

27. Revelation 6:16.

28. Scott, in Turner, 924g.

29. Rev. 8:7.

30. Rev. 9:7.

31. Rev. 15:3–4.

32. Rev. 19:18.

33. Turner, 918e.

34. Rev. 21:1–2.

35. Kurs, 28.

36. McAlister, 33.

37. in Lifton and Humphrey, 66–67.

38. Mark Twain, *The War Prayer.*

39. Kant, "Idea for a Universal History."

40. in Chapiro, 158.

41. in Chapiro, 171.

42. in Chapiro, 158.

43. Fairbairn, 697.

44. Twain, "The Mysterious Stranger," 726–27.

45. Hedges, 184–85.

46. Handel, 305.

Bibliography

Alföldi, Andrew. *The Conversion of Constantine and Pagan Rome,* trans. Harold Mattingly. Oxford, England: Oxford University Press, 1969.

Almond, Gabriel A., R. Scott Appleby, and Emmanuel Sivan. *Strong Religion: The Rise of Fundamentalisms around the World.* Chicago: University of Chicago Press, 2003.

Ambrose, Stephen E. *Band of Brothers: E Company, 506th Regiment, 101st Airborne from Normandy to Hitler's Eagle's Nest.* New York: Touchstone, 2001.

Anderson, Jon Lee. "Ill Winds." *The New Yorker,* April 7, 2003, p. 39.

Angell, Roger. "Late Review." *The New Yorker,* January 19, 2004.

Arendt, Hannah. *On Violence.* New York: Harcourt Brace Jovanovich, 1970.

Aron, Raymond. *On War,* trans. Terence Kilmartin. New York: Doubleday, 1958.

Art, Robert J., and Kenneth N. Waltz, eds. *The Use of Force, International Politics and Foreign Policy.* 2nd ed., Lanham, MD: University Press of America, 1983.

Bachelard, Gaston. *Earth and Reveries of Will: An Essay on the Imagination of Matter,* trans. Kenneth Haltman. Dallas: The Dallas Institute Publications, 2002.

———. *La Terre et les rêveries du repos.* Paris: José Corti, 1977.

———. *Le nouvel esprit scientifique* (1934). 10th ed. Paris: Presses Universitaires de France, 1968.

———. *On Poetic Imagination and Reverie,* trans. Colette Gaudin. Dallas: Spring Publications, 1987.

Baldick, Robert. *The Duel: A History of Duelling.* London: Chapman & Hall, 1965.

Bayles, Martha. "Portraits of Mars" (on Hollywood war movies). *Wilson Quarterly,* Summer 2003, pp. 12–19.

Beevor, Antony. *The Spanish Civil War.* New York: Penguin, 2001.

Bell, Catherine. *Ritual Theory, Ritual Practice.* New York: Oxford University Press, 1992.

Bettini, Maurizion. *The Portrait of the Lover,* trans. Laura Gibbs. Berkeley, CA: University of California Press, 1999.

Black, Jeremy. *Why Wars Happen.* New York: New York University Press, 1998.

Blumenson, Martin. *The Patton Papers, 1885–1940,* and *1940–1945* (2 vols.). Boston: Houghton Mifflin, 1972.

———. *Patton: The Man Behind the Legend, 1885–1945.* New York: William Morrow, 1985.

Bobbitt, Philip. *The Shield of Achilles.* New York: Knopf, 2002.

Boer, Charles, trans. *The Homeric Hymns.* Dallas: Spring Publications, 1987.

Boer, Charles, trans. *Ovid's Metamorphoses.* Dallas: Spring Publications, 1989.

Bowers, John. *Chickamauga and Chattanooga: The Battles That Doomed the Confederacy.* New York: Avon, 1995.

Brockelmann, Carl. *History of the Islamic Peoples.* London: Routledge & Kegan Paul, 1949.

Brown, Norman O. "The Apocalypse of Islam," in *Facing Apocalypse,* ed. V. Andrews, R. Bosnak, and K. W. Goodwin. Dallas: Spring Publications, 1987.

Brown, Peter Harry, and Daniel G. Abel. *Outgunned: Up Against the NRA.* New York: Free Press, 2003.

Brownmiller, Susan. *Against Our Will: Men, Women and Rape.* New York: Bantam, 1986.

Burkert, Walter. *Greek Religion,* trans. John Raffan. Cambridge, MA: Harvard University Press, 1985.

————. *Homo Necans: The Anthropology of Ancient Greek Sacrificial Ritual and Myth,* trans. Peter Bing. Berkeley: University of California Press, 1983.

Burnet, John. *Early Greek Philosophy.* London: Adam & Charles Black, 1948.

Caputo, Philip. *A Rumor of War.* New York: Henry Holt, 1996.

Chang, Iris. *The Rape of Nanking: The Forgotten Holocaust of World War II.* New York: Penguin, 1998.

Chapiro, José. *Erasmus and Our Struggle for Peace.* Boston: Beacon, 1950.

von Clausewitz, Carl. *On War,* ed. and trans. Michael Howard and Peter Paret. Princeton, NJ: Princeton University Press, 1984.

Cleary, Thomas. *The Japanese Art of War.* Boston and London: Shambhala, 1991.

Cohen, Eliot A., and John Gooch. *Military Misfortunes: The Anatomy of Failure in War.* New York: Free Press, 1990.

Creasy, Sir Edward. *The Fifteen Decisive Battles of the World: From Marathon to Waterloo.* London: Richard Bentley, 1871.

Cunliffe, Barry. *The Ancient Celts.* New York: Oxford University Press, 1997.

Davis, William C. *The Battlefields of the Civil War.* Norman: University of Oklahoma Press, 1996.

Dawkins, Richard. *The Selfish Gene.* Oxford: Oxford University Press, 1989.

Dawood, N. J., trans. *The Koran.* 3rd rev. ed. Middlesex, England: Penguin, 1968.

De Landa, Manuel. *War in the Age of Intelligent Machines.* New York: Zone, 1998.

Dean, Eric T., Jr. *Shook Over Hell: Post-Traumatic Stress, Vietnam, and the Civil War.* Cambridge, MA: Harvard University Press, 1999.

DeMause, Lloyd. *History of Childhood.* New York: P. Bedrick Books, 1988.

Dennett, Daniel C. "The Bright Stuff." *New York Times,* Op-Ed, July 12, 2003, p. A23.

Dumézil, Georges. *Archaic Roman Religion* (2 vols.), trans. Philip Krapp. Chicago: University of Chicago Press, 1970.

Durand, Gilbert. "Psyche's View," in *Spring 1981.* Dallas: Spring Publications, 1981.

Ehrenreich, Barbara. *Blood Rites: Origins and History of the Passions of War.* New York: Henry Holt, 1997.

Eksteins, Modris. *Rites of Spring: The Great War and the Birth of the Modern Age.* New York: Doubleday, 1990.

Evans-Pritchard, E. E. *Nuer Religion.* Oxford: Clarendon, 1956.

Evelyn-White, Hugh, trans. "To Ares," in *Hesiod, the Homeric Hymns, and Homerica.* London and Cambridge, MA: Loeb Classical Library, 1936.

Fairbairn, A. M. "Tendencies of European Thought in the Age of the Reformation," in *The Cambridge Modern History,* vol. 2. Cambridge, England: Cambridge University Press, 1903.

Farnell, Lewis Richard. *The Cults of the Greek States.* vol. 5. New Rochelle, NY: Caratzas Bros., 1977.

Ferguson, Brian R. In *Natural History,* July–August 2003.

Ferguson, Frances. In *Encyclopedia of Aesthetics,* vol. 4, ed. Michael Kelly, pp. 326–31. New York and Oxford: Oxford University Press, 1998.

Fornari, Franco. *The Psychoanalysis of War,* trans. Alenka Pfeifer. New York: Anchor, 1974.

Foucault, Michel. *Power: Essential Works of Foucault, 1954–1984,* vol. 3, ed. James D. Faubion. New York: New Press, 2000.

Freedman, Jonathan L. *Media Violence and Its Effect on Aggression: Assessing the Scientific Evidence.* Toronto: University of Toronto Press, 2002.

Freud, Sigmund. "Thoughts for the Times on War and Death" (1915), in *Collected Papers IV.* London: Hogarth, 1949.

———. "Why War?" (1932), in *Collected Papers V.* London: Hogarth, 1950.

Friedrich, Paul. *The Meaning of Aphrodite.* Chicago and London: University of Chicago Press, 1978.

Fussell, Paul. *The Great War and Modern Memory.* New York: Oxford University Press, 1977.

Gadamer, Hans-Georg. *Philosophical Hermeneutics,* trans. and ed. David E. Linge. Berkeley and Los Angeles: University of California Press, 1977.

Gaffney, Patrick D. "Fundamentalist Preaching and Islamic Militancy in Upper Egypt," in *Spokesmen for the Despised: Fundamentalist Leaders of the Middle East,* ed. R. Scott Appleby. Chicago: University of Chicago Press, 1997.

Gilje, Paul A. *Rioting in America.* Bloomington: Indiana University Press, 1999.

Girard, René. *Violence and the Sacred,* trans. Patrick Gregory. Baltimore, MD: The Johns Hopkins University Press, 1979.

Gray, J. Glenn. *The Warriors: Reflections on Men in Battle.* New York: Harper & Row, 1970.

Griffin, Susan. *A Chorus of Stones: The Private Life of War.* New York: Doubleday, 1992.

Grimal, Pierre. *Love in Ancient Rome,* trans. Arthur Train Jr. Norman: University of Oklahoma Press, 1986.

Guénon, René. *The Reign of Quantity & the Signs of the Times.* trans. Lord Northbourne. London: Luzac & Company, 1953.

Hall, Nor. *Irons in the Fire.* Barrytown, NY: Station Hill, 2002.

Handel, Michael I. *Masters of War: Classical Strategic Thought*. London: Frank Chase, 2001.

Hanson, Victor Davis. *Carnage and Culture: Landmark Battles in the Rise of Western Power*. New York: Doubleday, 2001.

Harnly, Caroline. *Agent Orange and Vietnam: An Annotated Bibliography*. Metuchen, NJ: Scarecrow Press, 1988.

Harris, John. *The Gallant Six Hundred: A Tragedy of Obsessions*. New York: Mason & Lipscomb, 1974.

Hedges, Chris. *War Is a Force That Gives Us Meaning*. New York: Public Affairs, 2002.

Heraclitus. *Fragments: The Collected Wisdom of Heraclitus,* trans. Brooks Haxton. New York: Viking, 2001.

Hernandez, Miguel. *Selected Poems*. Buffalo, NY: White Pine Press, 1989.

Hersh, James. "From *Ethnos* to *Polis*: The Furies and Apollo," in *Spring 1985*. Dallas: Spring Publications, 1985.

Hillman, James. *The Dream and the Underworld*. New York: Harper & Row, 1979.

———. "Horses and Heroes," in *Dream Animals*, ed. James Hillman and Margot McLean. San Francisco: Chronicle Books, 1997.

Hobbes, Thomas. *Leviathan, or the Matter, Forme & Power of a Commonwealth, Ecclesiasticall and Civill,* ed. A. R. Waller. Cambridge, England: Cambridge University Press, 1904.

Hochschild, Adam. *King Leopold's Ghost: A Story of Greed, Terror, and Heroism in Colonial Africa*. New York: Mariner, 1999.

Homer. *The Odyssey of Homer,* trans. Richard Lattimore. New York: Harper & Row, 1968.

Howard, Michael. *The Invention of Peace: Reflections on War and International Order*. New Haven: Yale University Press, 2000.

Hultkrantz, Åke. *Soul and Native Americans*. Woodstock, CT: Spring Publications, 1997.

Husserl, Edmund. *Ideas,* trans. W. R. Boyce Gibson. London: George Allen & Unwin, 1952.

James, William. *The Varieties of Religious Experience*. London: Longmans, Green, 1902.

———. *The Will to Believe and other essays in popular philosophy* and *Human Immortality* (two books bound as one). New York: Dover, 1956.

Jung, C. G. *The Collected Works*, vol. 13. Princeton, NJ: Princeton University Press, 1967.

Kagan, Donald. *On the Origins of War and the Preservation of Peace*. New York: Doubleday, 1995.

Kant, Immanuel. "Idea for a Universal History with a Cosmopolitan Intent," Thesis 4, 1784, in *Perpetual Peace and Other Essays on Politics, History, and Morals*, trans. Ted Humphrey. Indianapolis: Hackett, 1983.

———. *Perpetual Peace and Other Essays on Politics, History, and Morals*, trans. Ted Humphrey. Indianapolis: Hackett, 1985.

Kaplan, Robert D. *Warrior Politics: Why Leadership Demands a Pagan Ethos*. New York: Vintage, 2002.

Keegan, John. *The Face of Battle*. New York: Penguin, 1978.

———. *The First World War*. New York: Alfred A. Knopf, 1999.

Keegan, John, and Richard Holmes. *Soldiers: A History of Men in Battle*. New York: Elisabeth Sifton, 1986.

Kerényi, Carl. *The Gods of the Greeks*, ed. Joseph Campbell, trans. Norman Cameron. London: Thames & Hudson, 1951.

Kittel, G., ed. "Apokalypto," in *Theological Dictionary of the New Testament*, vol. 3. Grand Rapids, MI: Eerdmans, 1965.

Kristof, Nicholas D. "Believe It, or Not." *New York Times*, Op-Ed, August 15, 2003, p. A29.

Kugelmann, Robert. "Hammering Metaphor from Metal: A Psychology of Stress," in *Spring 1982*, pp. 253–61. Dallas: Spring Publications, 1982.

Kulka, Richard A., et al. *Trauma and the Vietnam War Generation*. New York: Brunner/Mazel, 1990.

Kurs, Katherine. "Snapshots from Our National Poll," in *Spirituality & Health*, Spring 2001, p. 28.

Laffin, John. *Rhetoric and Reality: The Arab Mind Considered*. New York: Taplinger, 1975.

LeBlanc, Steven, with Katherine E. Register. *Constant Battles: The Myth of the Peaceful Noble Savage*. New York: St. Martin's Press, 2003.

Levinas, Emmanuel. *Noms Propres*. Montpellier, France: Fata Morgana, 1976.

———. *Totality and Infinity*. Pittsburgh: Duquesne University Press, 1979.

Lifton, Robert J., and Richard Falk. *Indefensible Weapons: The Political and Psychological Case Against Nuclearism*. New York: Basic, 1982.

Lifton, Robert J., and Nicholas Humphrey, eds. *In a Dark Time*. Cambridge, MA: Harvard University Press, 1984.

Lincoln, Bruce. *Holy Terrors: Thinking about Religion after September 11*. Chicago: University of Chicago Press, 2003.

Lind, Millard C. *Yahweh Is a Warrior: The Theology of Warfare in Ancient Israel*. Scottdale, PA, and Kitchener, Ont.: Herald Press, 1980.

Linderman, Gerald F. *The World Within War: America's Combat Experience in World War II*. New York: Free Press, 1997.

Lingis, Alphonso. *Abuses*. Berkeley and Los Angeles: University of California Press, 1995.

Lippmann, Walter. *American Inquisitors*. New Brunswick, NJ: Transaction, (1928) 1993.

———. *A Preface to Morals*. New York: Time Inc., 1964.

Lohse, Bernhard. *Martin Luther*, trans. Martin C. Schultz. Philadelphia: Fortress, 1986.

Longinus. "On the Sublime," in *Classical Literary Criticism,* ed. Penelope Murray. New York: Penguin, 2000.

Lopez-Pedraza, Rafael. *Hermes and His Children*. Zurich, Switzerland: Spring Publications, 1977.

Loyd, Anthony. *My War Gone By, I Miss It So*. New York: Penguin, 2001.

Luttwak, Edward N. "A Battle of Words over Military Intelligence." *New York Times,* November 22, 2003, p. A19.

Lynn-Jones, Sean M., and Steven E. Miller, eds. *Global Dangers: Changing Dimensions of International Security.* Cambridge, MA: MIT Press, 1995.

Maass, Peter. *Love Thy Neighbor: A Story of War.* New York: Alfred A. Knopf, 1996.

Machiavelli, Niccolò. *Il Principe* (The Prince), ed. L. Arthur Burd. Oxford: Clarendon, 1968.

Marshall, S. L. A. *Men Against Fire: The Problem of Battle Command in Future Wars.* New York: William Morrow, 1947.

———. *The River and the Gauntlet.* New York: Morrow, 1953.

McAlister, Melani. Review of *Armageddon* (by Tim LaHaye and J. B. Jenkins). *The Nation,* September 22, 2003, p. 33.

McCloy, Shelby T. *Gibbon's Antagonism to Christianity* (1933). New York: Burt Franklin, n.d.

McEvilley, Thomas. "Turned Upside Down and Torn Apart," in *Sticky Sublime,* ed. B. Beckley. New York: Allworth, 2001.

Merivale, Patricia. *Pan the Goat-God: His Myth in Modern Times.* Cambridge, MA: Harvard University Press, 1969.

Middlebrook, Martin. *First Day on the Somme—1 July 1916.* New York: Norton, 1972.

Mumford, Lewis. *The Myth of the Machine.* New York: Harcourt, Brace and World, 1967.

National Vietnam Veterans Readjustment Study. *Trauma and the Vietnam War Generation.* New York: Brunner/Mazel, 1990.

Nef, John U. *War and Human Progress: An Essay on the Rise of Industrial Civilization.* New York: Norton, 1968.

Nelson, Keith L., and Spencer C. Olin Jr. *Why War? Ideology, Theory, and History.* Berkeley: University of California Press, 1980.

New York Times. Hiroshima Plus 20, introduction by John W. Finney. New York: Delacorte, 1985.

Nicolson, Harold. *The Age of Reason (1700–1789).* London: Constable and Co., 1961.

Nicolson, Marjorie Hope. "Sublime in External Nature," in *Dictionary of the History of Ideas,* vol. 4. New York: Scribner's, 1973.

Niebuhr, H. Richard. *The Meaning of Revelation* (1941). New York: Macmillan, 1960.

Osborn, William M. *The Wild Frontier: Atrocities during the American-Indian War from Jamestown Colony to Wounded Knee.* New York: Random House, 2000.

Painter, George D. *Proust: The Later Years,* vol. 2, p. 223. Boston: Little, Brown, 1965.

Patai, Raphael. *The Arab Mind.* New York: Scribner's, 1973.

Patton, George S., Jr. *War as I Knew It.* Cambridge, MA: The Riverside Press, 1947.

Patton, George S. *The Secret of Victory.* 1926.

Pelikan, Oswald, and Lehman, eds. *Luther's Works,* vol. 46, p. 95. Philadelphia: Fortress, 1957.

Perrin, Noel. *Giving Up the Gun: Japan's Reversion to the Sword, 1543–1879.* Boston: David R. Godine, 1999.

Province, C. M. *The Unknown Patton.* New York: Hippocrene, 1983.

Pyle, Ernie. *Ernie Pyle in England.* New York: Robert M. McBride, 1941.

Qiao Liang and Wang Xiangsui. *Unrestricted Warfare.* [N.p.] PLA Literature and Arts Publishing House, 1999.

Roe, Frank Gilbert. *The North American Buffalo.* Toronto: University of Toronto Press, 1972.

Ropp, Theodore. "War and Militarism," in *Dictionary of the History of Ideas,* vol. 4. New York: Scribner's, 1973.

Roscher, W. H. *Ausführliches Lexikon der griechischen und römischen Mythologie,* Band VII. Hildesheim: Georg Olms, 1965.

Roth, Philip. *The Human Stain.* New York: Houghton Mifflin, 2000.

Rumscheidt, H. M. *Revelation and Theology: The Barth-Harnack Correspondence.* Cambridge, MA: Cambridge University Press, 1972, p. 32.

Russell, Bertrand. *The Analysis of Mind.* London: George Allen & Unwin, 1924.

Russell, Dick. *The Man Who Knew Too Much*. New York: Carroll & Graf, 1992.

Said, Edward W. *Orientalism*. New York: Vintage, 1979.

Sandburg, Carl. *The Complete Poems of Carl Sandburg*. New York: Harcourt Brace Jovanovich, 1970.

———. *Cornhuskers*. New York: Holt, Rinehart & Winston, 1946.

Sandlin, Lee. "Losing the War." *Chicago Reader*, March 14, 1997.

Santoli, Al. *To Bear Any Burden—The Vietnam War and Its Aftermath in the Words of Americans and Southeast Asians*. Bloomington: Indiana University Press, 1999.

Schwartz, Regina M. *The Curse of Cain: The Violent Legacy of Monotheism*. Chicago: University of Chicago Press, 1997.

Scott, E. F. *The Book of Revelation*, 88f, New York: Scribner's, 1940.

Semerano, Giovanni. *The Origins of European Culture* (English translation of the introduction to the second volume of *Etymological Dictionaries*). Firenze: Olschki, 1996.

Semmes, Harry H. *Portrait of Patton*. New York: Appleton-Century-Crofts, 1955.

Sereny, Gitta. *Into That Darkness*. New York: Vintage, 1983.

Seznec, Jean. *The Survival of the Pagan Gods*, trans. Barbara F. Sessions. Princeton, NJ: Princeton University Press, 1972.

Shakespeare, William. *Complete Works*. London: Oxford University Press, 1952.

Shay, Jonathan. *Achilles in Vietnam: Combat Trauma and the Undoing of Character*. New York: Atheneum, 1994.

Silber, Irwin, ed. *Songs of the Civil War*. New York: Dover, 1995.

Smith, John Holland. *The Death of Classical Paganism*. Southampton, England: Camelot, 1976.

Smith, John L. 118th PA Infantry, letter to his mother, April 15, 1865. Courtesy Appomattox Courthouse National Historic Park.

Sontag, Susan. "Looking at War." *The New Yorker*, December 9, 2002, p. 98.

———. *Regarding the Pain of Others*. London: Hamish Hamilton, 2003.

Stafford, Emma. *Worshipping Virtues: Personification and the Divine in Ancient Greece.* London: Duckworth, 2000.

Stark, Rodney. *One True God: Historical Consequences of Monotheism.* Princeton, NJ: Princeton University Press, 2001.

Stein, Murray. "Hephaistos: a Pattern of Introversion," in *Spring 1973.* New York: Spring Publications, 1973.

Sun Tzu. *The Art of War,* trans. Thomas Cleary. Boston: Shambhala, 1988.

Taylor, A. J. P. *How Wars Begin.* New York: Atheneum, 1979.

Terkel, Studs. *My American Century.* London: New Press, 1998.

Thass-Thienemann, Theodore. *The Interpretation of Language,* vol. 1. New York: Jason Aronson, 1973.

Thompson, Mark. "The Boykin Affair." *Time,* November 3, 2003, p. 31.

de Tocqueville, Alexis. *Democracy in America,* edited and abridged by Richard D. Heffner. New York: New American Library, 2001.

Tolstoy, Leo. *War and Peace,* trans. Constance Garnett. London: Heinemann, 1971.

Trotsky, Leon. *Military Writings.* New York: Pathfinder, 2001.

Tuchman, Barbara W. *The March of Folly: From Troy to Vietnam.* New York: Ballantine, 1985.

Turner, Nigel. "Revelation," in *Peake's Commentary on the Bible,* ed. M. Black and H. H. Rowley. London: Nelson, 1962.

Twain, Mark. "The Mysterious Stranger," in *The Portable Mark Twain,* ed. Bernard DeVoto. New York: Viking, 1946.

———. *The War Prayer.* New York: St. Crispin Press, Harper & Row, (1923) 1951, unpaged.

Vernant, Jean-Pierre. *Mortals and Immortals: Collected Essays,* ed. Froma I. Zeitlin. Princeton, NJ: Princeton University Press, 1991.

Villanueva, Jari A. "24 Notes That Tap Deep Emotions." http://www.westpoint.org/taps/taps.html.

Waltz, Kenneth N. *Man, the State and War.* New York: Columbia University Press, 1959.

Walzer, Michael. *Just and Unjust Wars: A Moral Argument with Historical Illustrations.* New York: Basic Books, 1992.

Weigley, Russell F. *The American Way of War: A History of United States Military Strategy and Policy.* Bloomington: Indiana University Press, 1977.

Whitehead, Alfred North. *Modes of Thought.* New York: Capricorn, 1958.

Whiting, Charles. *Patton.* New York: Ballantine, 1970.

Wiener, Jon. "Fire at Will." *The Nation,* November 4, 2002, pp. 28–32.

Wiley, Bell Irvin. *The Life of Billy Yank: The Common Soldier of the Union.* Baton Rouge: Louisiana State University Press, 1993.

Willetts, R. F. *Cretan Cults and Festivals.* London: Routledge & Kegan Paul, 1962.

Wind, Edgar. *Pagan Mysteries in the Renaissance.* Harmondsworth, England: Peregrine Books, 1967.

Wintle, Justin, ed. *The Dictionary of War Quotations.* New York: Free Press, 1989.

Witkop, Philipp, ed. *German Students' War Letters.* trans. A. F. Wedd. Philadelphia: Pine Street, 2002.

Wright, Evan. "The Killer Elite." *Rolling Stone* #927, July 24, 2003.

Zeldin, Theodore. *An Intimate History of Humanity.* New York: HarperCollins, 1994.

Ziegler, Alfred. *Archetypal Medicine,* 2nd. ed. Putnam, CT: Spring Publications, 2000.

Zinn, Howard. *Terrorism and War,* ed. Anthony Arnove. Toronto: Seven Stories, 2002.

Index

FOR THE BEST IN PAPERBACKS, LOOK FOR THE

In every corner of the world, on every subject under the sun, Penguin represents quality and variety—the very best in publishing today.

For complete information about books available from Penguin—including Penguin Classics, Penguin Compass, and Puffins—and how to order them, write to us at the appropriate address below. Please note that for copyright reasons the selection of books varies from country to country.

In the United States: Please write to *Penguin Group (USA), P.O. Box 12289 Dept. B, Newark, New Jersey 07101-5289* or call 1-800-788-6262.

In the United Kingdom: Please write to *Dept. EP, Penguin Books Ltd, Bath Road, Harmondsworth, West Drayton, Middlesex UB7 0DA.*

In Canada: Please write to *Penguin Books Canada Ltd, 10 Alcorn Avenue, Suite 300, Toronto, Ontario M4V 3B2.*

In Australia: Please write to *Penguin Books Australia Ltd, P.O. Box 257, Ringwood, Victoria 3134.*

In New Zealand: Please write to *Penguin Books (NZ) Ltd, Private Bag 102902, North Shore Mail Centre, Auckland 10.*

In India: Please write to *Penguin Books India Pvt Ltd, 11 Panchsheel Shopping Centre, Panchsheel Park, New Delhi 110 017.*

In the Netherlands: Please write to *Penguin Books Netherlands bv, Postbus 3507, NL-1001 AH Amsterdam.*

In Germany: Please write to *Penguin Books Deutschland GmbH, Metzlerstrasse 26, 60594 Frankfurt am Main.*

In Spain: Please write to *Penguin Books S. A., Bravo Murillo 19, 1° B, 28015 Madrid.*

In Italy: Please write to *Penguin Italia s.r.l., Via Benedetto Croce 2, 20094 Corsico, Milano.*

In France: Please write to *Penguin France, Le Carré Wilson, 62 rue Benjamin Baillaud, 31500 Toulouse.*

In Japan: Please write to *Penguin Books Japan Ltd, Kaneko Building, 2-3-25 Koraku, Bunkyo-Ku, Tokyo 112.*

In South Africa: Please write to *Penguin Books South Africa (Pty) Ltd, Private Bag X14, Parkview, 2122 Johannesburg.*